Germany from Partition to Reunification

Aerial views of Frankfurt am Main, 1945 and in the 1970s

Germany from Partition to Reunification

A Revised Edition of

The Two Germanies since 1945

Henry Ashby Turner, Jr.

Yale University Press

New Haven and London

7o-O\a -38⁴

"Inventory" by Günter Eich (trans. David Young) is reprinted here courtesy of Oberlin College: *Valuable Nail*, Field Translation Series 5, trans. Stuart Friebart, David Walker, and David Young (Oberlin, OH: Oberlin College, 1981), pp. 41–42.

"The Solution" by Bertolt Brecht is reprinted here courtesy of Routledge, Chapman and Hall, Inc.: *Bertolt Brecht Poems*, ed. John Willett and Ralph Manheim (London: Methuen, 1976), p. 440.

Photo credits: German Information Center, New York: ii, iii, 4, 5, 17, 26, 78, 79, 88, 91, 92, 96, 107, 112, 119, 140, 143, 151, 154, 177, 183, 185, 194, 216, 237, 249. Arbeitsgemeinschaft 13. August e.V., Berlin, 90, 91. Bildarchiv Preussischer Kulturbesitz, 94. Landesbildstelle Berlin, 235. Patrick Piel/Gamma Liaison, 236.

Set in Melior type by Keystone Typesetting, Inc., Orwigsburg, Penn.
Printed in the United States of America by Vail-Ballou Press, Binghamton, N.Y.

Library of Congress Cataloging-in-Publication Data

Turner, Henry Ashby, Jr.
  Germany from partition to reunification / Henry Ashby Turner, Jr.
    p.   cm.   .
  Rev. ed. of: The two Germanies since 1945. 1987.
  Includes bibliographical references and index.
  ISBN 0-300-05345-2 (alk. paper). —
ISBN 0-300-05347-9 (pbk. : alk. paper)
    1. Germany—History—1945–   .   2. Germany—History—Unification, 1990.   I. Turner, Henry Ashby. Two Germanies since 1945. II. Title.
DD257.T87   1992
943.087—dc20   92-15192
                                        CIP

The paper in this book meets the guidelines for permanence and durability of the Committee on Production Guidelines for Book Longevity of the Council on Library Resources.

10 9 8 7 6 5 4 3 2

Contents

Preface
to the Revised Edition

The first edition of this book, entitled *The Two Germanies since 1945*, was published in 1987. Since then, momentous events have swept away one of the German states and united the country under the constitution of the other. This revised edition has been expanded to cover those events. Like the first edition, it is intended as an introduction to the subject for readers without access to German-language publications. It makes no claim to definitude and rests not on research in primary source materials but rather on a reading of the publications of scholars who have dealt with various aspects of the history of the Germans since the end of the Second World War. The sections on the events of 1989–1990 are based on published source materials.

I am indebted to Mary Sarotte for her pioneering research on the events of the autumn of 1989 in the German Democratic Republic.

New Haven, December 1991

Abbreviations

CDU Christlich Demokratische Union (Christian Democratic Union)

CSU Christlich-Soziale Union (Christian Social Union)

DBD Demokratische Bauernpartei Deutschlands (Democratic Farmers' Party)

DKP Deutsche Kommunistische Partei (German Communist Party)

DSU Deutsche Soziale Union (German Social Union)

EDC European Defense Community

FDP Freie Demokratische Partei (Free Democratic Party)

FRG Federal Republic of Germany (West Germany)

GDR German Democratic Republic (East Germany)

KPD Kommunistische Partei Deutschlands (Communist Party of Germany)

LPD Liberal-Demokratische Partei Deutschlands (Liberal Democratic Party of Germany)

NATO   North Atlantic Treaty Organization

NDPD   National-Demokratische Partei Deutschlands (National Democratic Party of Germany, GDR)

NPD   Nationaldemokratische Partei Deutschlands (National Democratic Party of Germany, FRG)

PDS   Partei des Demokratischen Sozialismus (Party of Democratic Socialism, formerly SED)

SDP   Sozialdemokratische Partei (Social Democratic Party, GDR)

SED   Sozialistische Einheitspartei Deutschlands (Socialist Unity Party of Germany)

SPD   Sozialdemokratische Partei Deutschlands (Social Democratic Party of Germany, FRG)

VEB   Volkseigene Betriebe (People's plants)

1
Defeat,
Cold War,
and Division

The Wreckage of the Past

Early in May 1945, the German Reich came to an end. It had existed for seventy-four years, long enough for most Germans to regard their country's unification as an irreversible achievement. Yet as the developments that began unfolding in the spring of 1945 were soon to demonstrate, such was not the case.

The Reich had come into being in 1871, ending centuries of German political fragmentation. Five years earlier, the Kingdom of Prussia, under the leadership of Prime Minister Otto von Bismarck, had defeated Austria, its chief rival for preeminence in the German part of Europe. Then, after Prussia's victory over France in 1870, Bismarck succeeded in bringing the smaller German states into a new polity, the Deutsches Reich or German Empire. As a federal monarchy under an emperor from the Prussian ruling house of Hohenzollern, the Empire immediately became one of the great powers of Europe. Led by Bismarck, who served as its chancellor until 1890, the new Germany displayed great vitality. Its formidable military establishment won it respect and fear, while its rapid industrialization quickly thrust it to the economic forefront. By the end of the century, the Reich was making its influence felt around the globe. The resulting frictions with other powers contributed importantly to the outbreak in 1914 of the First World War, in which Germany fought at the side of the decaying Austro-Hungarian and Turkish empires against a coalition that included Britain, France, Russia, Japan, and eventually the United States.

In 1918, in the wake of defeat following more than four years of bloody conflict in World War I, Germany underwent a revolution that transformed the government of the Reich into a parliamentary democracy that became known as the Weimar Republic. After a stormy fourteen years the republic collapsed and was succeeded in 1933 by the so-called Third Reich of National Socialist dictator Adolf Hitler. His Nazi regime imposed a totalitarian tyranny and adopted racist policies that relegated Germany's Jews to the status of resident aliens subject to many forms of harassment. But the regime also surmounted the worldwide depression that defied all remedies in other major industrial countries. Within only a few years the Third Reich had restored virtually full employment and achieved a level of prosperity envied elsewhere. As a result, the dictator won popularity at home and widespread recognition abroad. Hitler intended, however, to use the productive capacities of Germany not to improve the lot of its people but rather to prepare for a war of ruthless and far-reaching conquest. His goal was an empire of continental proportions in which the Germans, by right of alleged racial superiority, would subjugate— or eliminate—lesser peoples.

Following a series of diplomatic triumphs that undid many provisions of the Versailles peace settlement imposed upon Germany by the victors in 1919, Hitler launched what was to become the Second World War by attacking Poland in September 1939. During the ensuing five and a half years Germany, which was joined in 1940 by Fascist Italy, fought against a growing coalition of powers. At first, German military might seemed unstoppable. Poland, France, the Low Countries, Denmark, and

Norway quickly succumbed to Hitler's *Blitzkrieg*, or "lightning war." By the summer of 1940, the Third Reich, allied with the Soviet Union, dominated the European continent and posed a grave threat to the survival of its sole remaining foe, Britain. But in the summer of 1941 Hitler unleashed his armies on the Soviet Union and plunged the Reich into a ruinous war of attrition in that vast country. In December 1941 he declared war on the United States after Japan had attacked American outposts in the Pacific.

Eventually the tide of war turned against the Third Reich. At the end of 1942 the Russians halted the German advance, and the Red Army began pushing the invaders back. The Western Allies expelled the German forces from North Africa and in 1943 pushed northward through Italy, sweeping away Mussolini's Fascist regime. In the summer of 1944 Allied expeditionary forces breached the German defenses on the French coast and began battling their way eastward toward the Reich. In the spring of 1945 the European conflict finally came to an end. With Hitler dead by suicide and the country overrun by invaders, the German army leaders agreed to Allied demands for unconditional surrender. Their signing of the capitulation documents transferred sovereign authority from the German Reich to the victorious occupying powers. Germany had ceased to exist as a state and become a geographical region, ruled by foreigners.

The victors found themselves in possession of a devastated and disrupted country. Whereas the Reich had escaped physical damage in the First World War, which was fought almost exclusively on foreign soil, the second great conflict brought home to Germans the horrors of modern, industrialized war. In the course of Allied bombing raids, millions of tons of high explosives rained down on German factories and cities. During the final stages of the war, large parts of the country became bloody battlefields. The full extent of the human costs can never be calculated with precision, but the toll was heavy. Estimates of the German war dead—military and civilian—run as high as 6.5 million; millions of others suffered disabilities.

Battle wreckage at the Brandenburg Gate in the center of
Berlin, 1945

People struggling to board an overcrowded train, 1945

Barefoot women carrying possessions through the ruins of
a German city, 1945

The war left the German economy maimed, with thousands of mines, factories, warehouses, and other places of business heavily damaged by bombing raids. The economic infrastructure would eventually prove less seriously impaired than seemed the case at the end of the war, when a paralyzed transportation system obstructed distribution of vital goods and raw materials, including the coal that served as the main source of industrial energy. Still, in 1945 the prospect of economic recovery seemed remote, as industrial production sank to a fifth of the prewar level by the end of the year. So did the rebuilding of Germany's bomb-devastated cities. An estimated quarter of the country's housing lay destroyed or damaged beyond use, and in many cities the toll exceeded 50 percent. The resulting acute shortage of housing left millions without adequate dwellings. A disrupted and understaffed health-care system struggled to cope with an incidence of disease that frequently reached epidemic proportions.

The most pressing problem of all, however, resulted from a dire food crisis that reduced the average diet of Germans to levels dangerously close to the malnutrition level. Foodstuffs had become increasingly scarce as fighting surged into the agricultural regions of eastern Germany and Eastern Europe on which the Reich heavily relied for supplies of grain. The exodus of 10–12 million German refugees from these eastern regions compounded the problems of food and housing. Whereas in 1939 the territories that would comprise postwar Germany— East and West—had a population of under 59 million, by 1946 over 64 million lived there, despite the heavy wartime losses and the absence of millions of former soldiers held abroad as prisoners of war.

The war left Germany ravaged in more than merely material ways. In twelve years of tyrannical dictatorship the Nazi regime had ruthlessly crushed the country's democratic organizations and driven their leaders into exile or subjected them to imprisonment that often ended in broken health or death. On political grounds or to assure "racial purity," the Nazis systematically purged the bureaucracy, the universities, the arts, the press, and the professions. Deprived of livelihoods and in peril of persecution, some of Germany's most talented people fled abroad, where the resolute and fortunate among them made new careers, greatly enriching the cultural and intellectual life of their new homelands, particularly the United States. Most of these involuntary emigrés looked back with revulsion at the country that had scorned them and resolved never to return. The Third Reich thus inflicted an enormous intellectual and cultural loss upon Germany. At the end of the war, the country's once proud universities and scientific institutes sat idle and dis-credited after twelve years of collaboration and repression, stripped of much of the talent that had won them worldwide prominence before 1933. The media, which the Nazis had turned into conveyors of propaganda, collapsed along with the regime. In May 1945 the country was without a single function-ing newspaper, magazine, publishing house, or radio station of its own. German art and literature, prostituted to the Nazi re-gime, stood discredited. Once a major contributor to Western civilization, Germany seemed mute and culturally sterile after its relapse into barbarism.

Morally, the country appeared bankrupt in 1945. The Nazi regime had not only inflicted a repressive dictatorship on Ger-many itself but had also deliberately unleashed a brutal war of conquest that resulted in the deaths of some 40 million people across Europe. In the vast territories they conquered, the Nazis imposed an oppressive domination that awakened hatred of all things German. At the head of their many crimes stood the most massive campaign of premeditated genocide in history. By means of calculated mass-murder, the Nazis systematically slaughtered between five and six million innocent men, women, and children whose only offense was their Jewish ancestry. Others, such as gypsies, Russian prisoners of war, and mentally retarded Germans, were classified as subhumans unfit to share the earth with a Germanic master race and were executed or worked to death as slave labor. When the full magnitude of these crimes came to light in the spring of 1945, the very word *German*—already stigmatized by military aggression—became anathema for many people.

Once the Germans learned the extent of the crimes committed in the name of their nation, they had to struggle with a heavy burden of shame in addition to coping with defeat, foreign occupation, and hardship. Few sought to defend the Third Reich. Its leaders had already discredited themselves in the eyes of most by refusing to surrender long after defeat became obvious, thereby condemning millions to senseless death or disablement and much of the country to devastation. Some nevertheless harbored ambiguous feelings about the collapse of a regime that had restored prosperity and made Germany, before the war, once again proud and powerful. But even die-hard Nazis found it difficult to defend a regime that had so obviously ended in a national disaster. Few welcomed the imposition of foreign rule, but no popular indignation arose when the victors tried and convicted surviving leaders of the Nazi regime for war crimes and put some to death. For many Germans, their national heritage seemed bankrupt. For them, 1945 became the "year zero." Shamed or daunted by their country's immediate past and struggling with the ruins bequeathed them by the Third Reich, most sought to erase what had happened from their minds in hopes of starting anew. Something approaching a national amnesia gripped the country.

Differences among the Victors

The victorious Allies, like the Germans, assumed that the issues of the war would, as after previous conflicts, find resolution in a peace treaty. But no immediate steps in that direction followed the capitulation of Germany. In the spring of 1945 the Second World War seemed far from over in the Pacific. The Japanese Empire still defiantly occupied much of China, large parts of Southeast Asia, and many islands of the Pacific. Unaware that detonation of the first atomic bombs over two Japanese cities would put an end to the Pacific war by August, the Americans remained preoccupied by the prospect of a long and costly conflict. For their part, the British and Russians became distracted by the tasks of repairing the extensive damage to their own countries and reasserting their influence over what they saw as strategically vital areas abroad. The French, whose Third Republic had collapsed in 1940 after the country's crushing military defeat, struggled to revive their national institutions and cope with the problems of a crumbling colonial empire.

As a consequence of these distractions, the occupation of Germany quickly hardened along the lines of provisional arrangements arrived at in 1944 by a middle-level wartime inter-Allied planning body. This European Advisory Commission had the task of planning for temporary occupation of a Germany reduced to its pre-expansion borders of 1937. Using the boundaries of former German administrative districts, the advisory commission divided the country into American, British, and Russian occupation zones. The Soviet Union was assigned the eastern part of the country, Great Britain the northwest, the United States the south, plus an enclave around the northern city of Bremen and its port, Bremerhaven, to permit access by sea for American troops and supplies. Berlin was to be occupied jointly by the victors, with each accorded a sector of the city. An Allied Control Council situated in the former capital city was to act on behalf of the victors to exercise joint authority over Germany during the occupation period, which was expected to be brief. The council was to reach its decisions on a basis of unanimity, which meant that each of the occupying powers would have the right of veto.

Before the occupation began, these plans underwent several modifications. At the Yalta conference of February 1945, American president Franklin Roosevelt and British prime minister Winston Churchill secured Soviet leader Josef Stalin's approval for creation of a French occupation zone in southwestern Germany and a French sector in Berlin by agreeing to assign France some of the areas originally earmarked for occupation by Great Britain and the United States. As the Russians advanced into the Reich, they acted unilaterally to assign large parts of their occupation zone to the USSR and Poland, not as occupied territory but rather as lands to be "administered" by those governments. In the case of Poland, where the Soviets installed a regime subservient to them, this assignment of territory amounted to compensation for the USSR's annexation of eastern Poland.

The Western powers had earlier agreed in principle to some sort of eventual territorial compensation in the east at Germany's expense, but the Russians presented their wartime allies with a major fait accompli by immediately carrying out this massive transfer on their own. Most of the severed German territory was handed over to Polish authorities, but the USSR seized the northern part of East Prussia, including the city of Königsberg, a center of German commerce and culture since the Middle Ages. Since the Soviets and Poles expelled virtually all Germans from the areas thus placed under their administration, their actions amounted to a de facto severance from Germany of all territories to the east of a line that ran along the Oder and western Neisse rivers, including large areas that had been inhabited predominantly by Germans for centuries. In this manner, nearly a quarter of the Reich's pre-1938 territory, where some nine and a half million Germans had lived, ceased to be part of the country. At the time, the Americans and British officially took the position that these measures, like the creation of occupation zones, were merely provisional. The demarcation lines drawn on the map of Germany in 1945 would, however, soon harden into the durable political geography of post–World War II Europe.

The provisional arrangements for occupied Germany underwent further refinements at the American-British-Soviet summit conference held at Potsdam, just outside Berlin, in the summer of 1945. There the Western powers acquiesced in the territorial arrangements effected by the USSR in the east but secured the latter's endorsement of the principle that final boundaries must await a peace conference. All the victors agreed that Germany

SWEDEN

NORTH SEA

DENMARK

BALTIC SEA

U.S.S.R.

Königsberg o

TO U.S.S.R.

Danzig o

TO POLAND

o Hamburg

Bremen

TO POLAND

PART OF U.S. ZONE

NETHERLANDS

BRITISH ZONE

SOVIET ZONE

Berlin

POLAND

Warsaw o

BELGIUM

(LUX.)

o Cologne

Bonn o

Kassel o

o Frankfurt

FRENCH

o Leipzig

Dresden o

Breslau o

Prague o

CZECHOSLOVAKIA

SAAR

o Nürnberg

U.S. ZONE

o Stuttgart

ZONE

FRANCE

Munich o

Vienna o

SWITZERLAND

AUSTRIA

ITALY

BERLIN

FRENCH SECTOR

SOVIET SECTOR

BRITISH SECTOR

U.S. SECTOR

0   50   100
MILES

0   5
MILES

—·—·—·—· boundaries of 1937

· · · · · · · · · · · postwar demarcations

should be subjected to denazification, demilitarization, democratization, decentralization, and decartelization. They further agreed that the four-power Allied Control Council should administer Germany as one economic entity. The council was, however, not accorded full control over the country, since the victors assigned executive authority in each of the four occupation zones to the American, British, French, and Russian commandants, who were responsible solely to their own governments. The Potsdam conferees also agreed that the Germans' living standard must remain lower than that of their European neighbors.

The Potsdam agreements provided that reparations were to be extracted in the form of machines and other industrial equipment rather than in monetary payments, which after World War I had contributed to the economic instability that undermined Germany's first attempt at democracy. Each occupying power received authorization to seize and remove factories and other productive facilities in its zone. Since the greatest concentrations of heavy industry lay in the Western zones of occupation, a portion of reparations from those zones was to be turned over to the Soviets, whose zone was heavily agricultural. In return, the Russians agreed to ship foodstuffs and raw materials to the Western zones, which lacked sufficient agriculture to feed their populations. As for political life in Germany, the victors decided to permit the revival of democratic parties and trade unions and to establish German organs of self-administration, staffed by non-Nazis, beginning at the local level. All these arrangements were designated as merely temporary, and the Potsdam conferees assigned the task of preparing for a peace conference to their foreign ministers.

No peace conference ever met. As soon as the occupying powers turned to the task of governing Germany, insurmountable differences developed among them. From the very outset, France, which had not participated in the Yalta and Potsdam conferences, resisted implementation of some of the key agreements. Having suffered three invasions and two defeats at the hands of Germany within seventy years, the French were determined to see their neighbor to the east decisively diminished in size and power. They therefore demanded that the Rhineland, the German-inhabited territory to the west of the Rhine, be separated from the rest of the country and made an independent state. They also wanted the Ruhr valley, the industrial heartland of Germany, placed under international control and the coal-rich Saar basin permanently transferred from Germany to France. When the Americans and British balked at these demands, the French exercised their veto in the Allied Control Council to block proposed measures aimed at restoring a unified German economy in line with the Potsdam agreements.

Whereas implementation of the Potsdam agreements initially became stalled because of French vetos, differences soon developed as well between the Americans and British on the one hand and the Soviets on the other. The Russians, like the French, called for an internationalization of the Ruhr on terms unacceptable to the British, in whose zone the coal-rich industrial region lay, and to the Americans. The Soviets' most bitter disagreements with the Americans and the British arose, however, over the issue of reparations. The Russians, whose country had suffered enormous devastation in years of fierce fighting, felt justified in seizing as much German industrial equipment as they could. They therefore dismantled and shipped to the Soviet Union from their occupation zone entire factories as well as sizable quantities of motor vehicles, railroad rolling stock, and even rails. The amount of productive capacity removed in this fashion has been estimated at as high as a quarter of the total in their zone. The Russians also insisted upon receiving the full share of such goods promised them from the Western zones at Potsdam.

The Western powers soon balked at these arrangements on reparations. Every reduction of industrial productivity in their zones through removal of factories and machines to the USSR had the effect of shifting the cost of feeding the German population to their own taxpayers. Such was the case because the parts of Germany occupied by the Americans and British were incapable of producing enough food to sustain their populations. If those zones were to have any hope of feeding themselves, they would have to pay for imported foodstuffs by exporting industrial products. Compliance with the reparations agreements of Potsdam would not only rule out such self-sufficiency but would also, in effect, force the Western allies to subsidize with food shipments at their own expense reparations extracted from their zones by the USSR. The problem was further exacerbated by the failure of the Soviet occupation authorities to make good on their government's commitment at Potsdam to supply the Western zones with foodstuffs as compensation for part of the German industrial equipment shipped from those zones to the Soviet Union. In addition, the Russians increasingly supplemented the reparations they shipped to the USSR in the form of previously existing machines and other industrial equipment by seizing a portion of the current production of factories in their own zone, many of which they took over and operated themselves.

When all efforts to resolve the reparations problem failed, the American commandant, General Lucius D. Clay, ordered an end to the dismantling of industries in his zone in May 1946 and halted reparations shipments to the Russians. The British and French soon followed his example. Under heavy political pressure at home to reduce costly shipments of food to a dangerously undernourished German population, the American and British governments began to foster industrial recovery in order to enable the Germans to pay for the imported food on which they depended. For their part, the Soviets angrily accused the Western powers of violating the Potsdam agreements and used their veto in the Allied Control Council to block joint actions. The resulting chill in relations among the victors marked the onset in Germany of what became known as the Cold War, which also gained force as the Soviets imposed Communist-dominated puppet regimes on the countries of Eastern Europe in violation of wartime promises to permit the establishment, in areas liberated from Nazism, of independent governments based on free elections.

With the victors deadlocked on how to deal with the country as a whole, the foundations of postwar German life were laid by the occupying powers separately in their respective zones. The Soviets made the most thoroughgoing changes. In line with their Communist ideology, they socialized much of industry and effected a radical agrarian reform that distributed large amounts of land among small farmers. That land reform eliminated the huge rural estates that had served for centuries as the economic foundation of Prussia's agrarian gentry, the Junkers, who had played such a disproportionate and often unfortunate role in Germany's history. The Western powers, on the other hand, instituted only modest economic and social reforms. At the insistence of the Americans, who believed that German big business had played a vital role in the rise and depredations of Nazism, measures to break up large trusts and conglomerates were set in motion. The British Labour government had initially favored socializing at least such basic industries as coal and steel. The war-battered British found themselves, however, too dependent upon economic aid from the United States to defy American opposition to imposing such a fundamental change on the Germans without their consent. The Western powers left such matters to be decided at some future date by a reconstituted, democratically elected German government. Unable to provide the extensive personnel needed to manage the day-to-day affairs of a complex and populous country, all the occupying powers early on turned such matters over to German organs of civil administration set up under their supervision at the local level.

The Soviets put the policy of denazification into effect rapidly by summarily excluding all former members of the Nazi Party from positions of responsiblity in their zone. The Western powers employed more elaborate and time-consuming methods in an effort to distinguish between those who had participated actively in the Nazi regime and mere nominal adherents of the party. But they, too, disqualified and penalized sizable numbers of persons with tarnished pasts. After the International Military Tribunal had reached its verdicts on the surviving leaders of the Third Reich at Nuremberg, the occupying powers conducted further trials of less well known Germans accused of war crimes and crimes against humanity. Nevertheless, in the confusing conditions of the postwar years, with large quantities of records destroyed or missing, many guilty persons escaped punishment. As a consequence of those developments and the pressing need for talented people, some tainted individuals eventually managed to secure positions in the new postwar institutions of all the occupation zones.

The Revival of German Politics

German political life began reviving in the spring and summer of 1945. The USSR was the first occupying power to permit the formation of political parties in its zone, beginning with the Communist Party (Kommunistische Partei Deutschlands or KPD) in June. At the head of the KPD stood two long-time party functionaries who had spent the war years in Moscow, Wilhelm Pieck and Walter Ulbricht. Soon thereafter the Soviets allowed the reconstitution of the Social Democratic Party (Sozialdemokratische Partei Deutschlands or SPD), whose chief spokesman in Berlin was Otto Grotewohl. The Soviets also licensed a wholly new grouping, the Christian Democratic Union (Christlich Demokratische Union or CDU). Its leaders, formerly active in the fragmented moderate parties of the Weimar Republic, including the Catholic Center Party, sought to rally the followers of those parties on the basis of a nondenominational commitment to Christian ethics and democratic institutions. A fourth significant party licensed by the Soviets was the Liberal Democratic Party (Liberal-Demokratische Partei or LPD), which laid claim to the liberal heritage in German politics. The same spectrum of parties soon gained permission to operate in the Western zones as well, although there the liberals called themselves the Free Democratic Party (Freie Demokratische Partei or FDP). The Bavarian affiliate of the CDU constituted itself as a separate party on a regional basis, the Christian Social Union (Christlich Soziale Union or CSU). In addition, a number of minor parties were licensed in the Western zones.

In the Soviet zone this constellation of competing parties quickly gave way to arrangements designed to ensure results of a kind desired by the occupying power. In keeping with the "popular front" tactic applied by the Soviets throughout the parts of Europe under their control at the end of the war, they pressed for cooperation among liberals, social democrats, and communists. By making permission for political activity in their zone conditional upon all the parties' joining together in an "anti-fascist democratic bloc," they in effect forced the other parties into a kind of permanent coalition with the KPD. All decisions of this bloc required unanimity, which gave the KPD veto power. Since the bloc determined the ground rules for political activity in the Soviet zone, it placed tight limits on the other parties' independence and effectively excluded an anti-Communist alliance.

Initially, the Communist Party denied any intent to impose a Soviet-style regime and promised to work to create a parliamentary democracy. From the outset, however, the KPD suffered in the eyes of many Germans from its close ties to the Soviets. The plunder and rape indulged in by Red Army soldiers at the end of the war worked to the disadvantage of the KPD. So did the often harsh occupation regime with its sweeping expropriation measures, in which the Soviets assigned key administrative roles to German Communists. Just how serious a handicap the link to the Soviets represented was suggested by the first postwar national election in Austria, parts of which had also experienced Russian invasion and occupation. In the balloting of November 1945 there, the Austrian Communist Party received only slightly more than 5 percent of the votes. Alarmed at signs that the KPD similarly lacked popularity, the German Communists pressed for a merger with the larger Social Democratic Party.

There was considerable sentiment for such a merger in both parties. The SPD and the KPD both traced their origins to the same socialist movement, which had formed a united party for forty-two years before dividing in 1917 on wartime issues. The resultant split in the socialist political movement was widely regarded as one of the factors that had facilitated Hitler's rise to power. Reunification thus seemed to many one of the best safeguards against a repetition of the calamitous period between 1933 and 1945. Much of the leadership of the SPD remained, however, mistrustful because of the KPD's subservience to Stalin's totalitarian regime in the USSR and the German Communist leaders' reliance on Leninist authoritarian methods in internal party matters. Because of this mistrust, Social Democratic spokesmen in the Western zones, led by a survivor of Hitler's concentration camps, Kurt Schumacher, rejected a merger with the KPD.

Under mounting pressure from Soviet occupation authorities that in some instances assumed coercive proportions, the SPD in the Russian zone, led by Otto Grotewohl, agreed in April 1946 to join with the KPD in forming a Socialist Unity Party (Sozialistische Einheitspartei Deutschlands or SED). As this merger took place on an initial basis of parity, with former members of the old parties equally represented in the policy-making bodies of the SED, the Communists, as the smaller of the two groups, immediately gained in influence. In the "anti-fascist democratic bloc," the SED now completely overshadowed the non-Marxist parties of the Soviet zone. Initially, the new party assumed an ideological position much closer to the SPD than to the KPD, espousing Marxist principles but omitting any mention of Leninism. Its leaders avoided endorsements of the Soviet system and pledged to follow a distinctively German road to socialism.

In the first local elections in the Soviet zone in September 1946, which saw the SED competing for votes with the CDU and the LPD, the new party attained majorities. That apparent show

Communists Wilhelm Pieck (left) and Walter Ulbricht (right) with Social Democrat Otto Grotewohl (center) at the formal founding of the Socialist Unity Party (SED), 1946

of strength resulted in part, however, from the absence of the non-Marxist parties on the ballot in many places because of Soviet delays in certifying their local organizations. A month later, in October 1946, with the other parties more fully represented on the ballots, the SED fell short of majorities in Soviet zone provincial elections. Spokesmen for the CDU and the LPD complained that the Russians favored the SED in allocating paper for newspapers, posters, and brochures as well as in providing access to radio broadcasts. These charges seemed borne out in October 1946 by the first postwar election of a city-wide assembly for Berlin, where four-power rule enabled the other parties to compete on a more even basis with the SED. The outcome was a striking victory for those Social Democrats who rejected the merger with the Communists. The SPD tallied almost two and a half times as many votes as the SED and achieved close to an absolute majority. Stung by that defeat, the SED avoided further contested elections.

The reconstruction of German political institutions proceeded apace in all parts of the country. The occupying powers soon approved the formation of regional organs of self-administration called *Länder*, the term for the constituent states in the federal systems of the Empire and the Weimar Republic. By 1947 the states thus established in the Western zones were headed by minister-presidents chosen by freely elected parliamentary assemblies. Institutional developments followed a similar pattern in the Soviet zone except that the political processes remained considerably less than free because of the Soviet-imposed coalition of the non-Marxist parties with the SED.

When repeated meetings of the foreign ministers of the wartime alliance failed to resolve the differences that blocked movement toward a final peace settlement, the Americans proposed at least the economic amalgamation of the occupation zones so as to foster recovery and free the victors of the burden of feeding the vanquished. At first, only the British, whose zone, like the Americans', required massive food subsidies, responded positively. The result was the formation, at the beginning of 1947, of what came to be known as Bizonia, an economic unit comprising the American and British zones that operated through a set of administrative offices situated in the city of Frankfurt am Main. Bizonia's administrative activities were coordinated by an Executive Council composed of representatives of the democratically elected state administrations. The policies of the Executive Council, in turn, were subject to review and challenge by an Economic Council consisting of 52 members named by the state parliamentary assemblies. The political parties were represented in proportion to their strength in those assemblies. In early 1948 the size of the Economic Council was doubled to 104 members, and it became a quasi-parliament. At the same time a second chamber, the Council of States, came into being, providing the regional administrations with a voice in the shaping of economic legislation. In many respects, Bizonia soon became a proto-government, and its institutional structure provided the model which, with modifications, would eventually serve as the outline for a new West German republic.

In other ways, too, Bizonia anticipated later patterns. Two political parties quickly established themselves as the major alternatives: the SPD and the CDU/CSU. Commanding the largest blocs of seats in the regional parliaments and therefore in the Economic Council of Bizonia, they advocated quite different economic orientations. The Social Democrats held to their party's long-standing commitment to the socialization of basic industries and extensive state control over other aspects of economic life. The Christian Democrats, after initially inclining to a "Christian socialism," swung to espousal of a basically free-enterprise orientation. In March 1948, when the Economic Council chose its first elected Administrative Council, or proto-cabinet, the CDU/CSU joined with the laissez-faire FDP and smaller parties to wrest control of Bizonia's office for economic policy from the SPD. Upon nomination of the CDU/CSU, Ludwig Erhard, an obscure economist without party affiliation, was chosen as chief economic architect, thus beginning a remarkable political career. An advocate of free enterprise, Erhard launched Bizonia upon an economic course that would, like its institutional structure, set the pattern for the future West German government.

Not all Germans in the American and British zones welcomed the emergence of Bizonia. Some influential political figures saw the establishment of such a partial polity as a threat to their country's unity. This gave rise to initiatives designed to bring about cooperation on the part of German office-holders in all four zones of occupation in hopes of surmounting the deadlock that kept the occupying powers from reestablishing institutions for the country as a whole. The boldest initiative came with an invitation issued in the spring of 1947 by the minister-president of Bavaria to his counterparts throughout the country, summoning them to a conference in Munich to consider ways to hold Germany together.

Although the minister-presidents of the states in all the zones assembled in Munich on the appointed day in May 1947, the conference disappointed the hopes placed in it. The spokesmen from the Soviet zone insisted that the agenda must include immediate consideration of German reunification. By contrast, the minister-presidents from the Western zones wanted to avoid thorny political issues that would arouse the occupying powers and call attention to their differences. The Western minister-presidents preferred to limit discussion, at least initially, to economic measures aimed at coping with the pressing problems of feeding the population and reestablishing the flow of goods among the zones. Another obstacle developed when Social Democratic minister-presidents from the Western zones refused to sit down with counterparts who belonged to the SED so long as the SPD was not permitted to operate freely in the Soviet zone. Unwilling to give way on that point and frustrated in their attempts to press consideration of Germany's political future to the fore, the minister-presidents of the Soviet zone departed before the conference formally convened. Although those from the Western zones went on with the meeting, it achieved nothing aside from conclusively revealing that not even the most highly placed German spokesmen were capable of uniting to exert influence on their country's political destiny.

Germany as Focus of the Cold War

A turning point in Germany's postwar development occurred in February 1948 when Britain and the United States decided they could no longer postpone decisions on the future of Germany. Two months earlier, at the end of 1947, the fourth meeting of the council of foreign ministers of the occupying powers had failed to make any progress toward a peace settlement. With no prospect of four-power agreement in sight, the Americans and British concluded that the parts of Germany they occupied could not be allowed to remain in limbo any longer. Economic conditions there continued to deteriorate at a rate that imposed increasing financial burdens on their countries and awakened fears of renewed political extremism. Britain and the United States therefore invited France and the Benelux countries (Belgium, the Netherlands, and Luxemburg) to send representatives to a six-nation conference in London on the future of Germany.

The London Conference, one of the most important of the postwar years, took place in two sessions, February 23 to March 5 and April 30 to June 2, 1948. To deal with the economic problems posed for much of Europe by a still-prostrate Germany, the participating governments decided to authorize extension to the Western occupation zones of the American-sponsored Marshall Plan for economic recovery. Under the terms of the plan, the American government had in 1947 offered massive financial aid to European countries that had suffered wartime damage. The battlelines of the incipient Cold War hardened when the Russians refused to allow the Communist-dominated regimes they had imposed on Eastern Europe to participate in the Marshall Plan. Extension of American aid to the Western zones of Germany now unavoidably shifted the economic frontline of the Cold War to the boundaries between those zones and the portion of Germany occupied by the Soviet Union.

The six-nation London Conference of 1948 also served to focus the political Cold War on Germany by calling for formation of a West German government. French opposition to such a move gave way when the Americans and British accepted the Saarland's de facto detachment from Germany and the close association of that major coal basin with France and, in addition, agreed to place the coal and steel industries of the Ruhr region under supervision of the Western occupying powers.

A major step toward consolidation of the Western zones came through currency reform. By the spring of 1948 the German *Reichsmark* had lost much of its value as a result of the combined effects of far-reaching price controls inherited from the

Third Reich and a swollen money supply left from the war years. Few goods aside from the tightly rationed necessities of life came onto the open market, as producers balked at selling at controlled prices for devalued currency. A burgeoning black market developed, with transactions taking place on the basis of barter or cigarettes, which became a kind of substitute currency. With the purchasing power of money greatly diminished, the incentive to work declined for many wage earners. Introduction of a new monetary system thus became the inescapable prerequisite for an economic revival that would stabilize social conditions and remove the financial burdens occupation had imposed on the victors. When the Russians proved unwilling to surrender control over currency in their zone to a central monetary authority, the Western powers introduced new money in their zones in June 1948. Holders of the old marks were initially permitted to exchange only a limited amount for the new currency, the *Deutsche Mark* or DM, which would become one of the most successful currencies of the postwar era. When the new currency quickly gained acceptance, steps were taken to relax price controls and allow market forces to set the value of goods.

Russian responses to these Western moves took drastic forms. In March the Soviet representative walked out of the Allied Control Council in Berlin, protesting that the London Conference violated the Potsdam Agreement by undertaking decisions on Germany without the participation of the USSR. Then in June the Russians objected strenuously to introduction of the new currency for the Western zones, charging that the Potsdam Agreement required unanimous approval for any such significant measure. Although the Western powers pointed out that the Soviets' exit from the Control Council made unanimous approval on currency matters impossible, the Russians reacted harshly. They imposed a blockade on West Berlin, which was surrounded by territory occupied by the Red Army and lay more than a hundred miles distant from the nearest Western-occupied territory. They sealed off all the railways, highways, and canals upon which the Western sectors relied for delivery of food and fuel as well as for the transport of raw materials into and finished products out of what remained Germany's largest industrial city. They also cut off the delivery of power from generating plants in their zone, upon which the Western sectors depended for most of their electricity. While civilians were permitted to move back and forth between the Western and Soviet sectors of the old capital, transport of goods between the two parts of the city was subjected to close controls and sharply curtailed.

It quickly became evident that the Soviets intended more than merely to block the introduction of the new Western currency into Berlin. As the commandant of their occupation zone soon announced to his Western counterparts, the USSR wanted the steps toward formation of a government for western Germany halted. Until that happened, West Berlin would be held hostage. If the Russians could not realize that goal, they seemed determined at least to drive the Western powers out of Berlin and incorporate the whole city into their zone of occupation, thereby greatly strengthening their hold over part of Germany. In their communications with the Western powers, the Soviets accordingly began to claim that the American, British, and French sectors of the former German capital lay in their zone, and the Soviet commandant began to designate himself as military governor of all of Berlin. As they tightened their noose around the isolated Western sectors of the city, the Russians seemed to hold the overwhelming advantage, for virtually no one believed the more than two million people of West Berlin could long survive such a blockade.

For a brief period after the Russians' imposition of the Berlin blockade the danger of a new war seemed acute. For in addition to prohibiting civilian travel and transport to West Berlin, the Russians refused to permit military units of the Western occupying powers to pass through the Soviet zone to provision their garrisons stationed in Berlin. As the Western powers discovered to their chagrin, they had neglected to reach written agreements with the Russians guaranteeing them use of the rail, highway, and canal links between West Berlin and their occupation zones. Some Western officials favored challenging the Russians militarily by sending a supply column accompanied by tanks along one of the *Autobahnen* (divided highways) that linked western Germany with the former capital city. Had that advice prevailed, a test of will with the potential for triggering a third world war would have ensued. What was to prove the first of several grave crises over Berlin threatened to turn the Cold War into a shooting conflict among great powers.

The Russians had, however, miscalculated. They had overlooked the possibility that West Berlin could be supplied from the air. In written agreements reached during the early stages of the occupation they had granted the three Western powers access rights to their sectors of the city through three air corridors over the surrounding Soviet zone of Germany. Before trying to break the blockade on the ground, the Western allies decided to attempt to supply West Berlin by air. To most observers, this seemed an impossible task. Few could conceive of using airplanes to meet all the needs of more than two million people for food, fuel, clothing, and all other necessities except water. Especially daunting was the task of supplying throughout the winter months a large urban complex wholly dependent upon heavy, bulky deliveries of coal for heating and electricity.

Despite what seemed overwhelmingly unfavorable odds, the Berlin airlift, which came to be known as "Operation Vittles," succeeded. Remobilizing hundreds of planes used in World War II, the Western powers organized and put into operation an unprecedentedly massive display of the possibilities of air transport. At the height of the airlift, one plane reached West Berlin every thirty seconds. Reconditioned bombers dropped cargoes such as coal from the air onto fields cleared for that purpose and returned for reloading to their bases without even landing. Millions of pounds of supplies of all sorts reached the city by air each day. The enormity of the operation required precise planning and exact coordination. To the amazement of the world, it worked. Throughout the severe winter of 1948–49 the airlift met the needs of a West Berlin whose population made

An American plane lands in Berlin during the Berlin airlift of 1948–49

its contribution by making do with a rudimentary diet, minimal heat, and sharply curtailed hours of electricity during an especially cold winter. A high human cost was paid—thirty-one Americans, forty Britons, and five Germans lost their lives in air accidents. But by the spring of 1949 the failure of the attempt to coerce the Western powers by starving and freezing West Berlin into submission had become manifest. On May 12, 1949, the Soviets lifted the blockade, opening access to West Berlin once again via highways, railways, and canals.

The Russians' attempt to prevent the political consolidation of western Germany by blockading Berlin ended by accelerating that development. Instead of halting the movement in that direction begun at the six-nation London Conference, the blockade—along with the Communist coup d'état in Czechoslovakia in early 1948—convinced the Western leaders that they must take swift and decisive measures to strengthen the part of Germany outside the Soviet orbit. The close cooperation which the blockade necessitated among the Western occupying powers in Berlin also served to surmount the remaining differences between the Americans and the British on the one hand and the French on the other. In April 1949 the French began merging their occupation zone into Bizonia to create Trizonia, a quasi-polity encompassing all of postwar Germany except the Soviet zone, Berlin, and the Saarland, the latter of which retained a separate status in close association with France. The experience of the blockade had dispelled the last lingering misgivings among the leaders of France about the advisability of creating a West German government. Henceforth, the three former Western wartime Allies—Britain, France, and the United States—would closely coordinate their policies on Germany. For all three, the Soviet Union had come to replace the Germans as the chief threat to their security and prime peril to the peace.

The Berlin blockade and the successful airlift also lessened German hesitations about proceeding toward creation of a government for the Western occupation zones. Many thoughtful German political leaders had initially viewed the step taken in that direction at the London Conference in early 1948 as an unacceptable threat to the political unity of their country. Still hoping that the victorious powers would manage to resolve their differences and sit down at a peace conference that would deal with Germany as a whole, they preferred to see the country remain under temporary occupation arrangements. That anomalous situation, they argued, would eventually force the victors to put Germany back together under one government, whereas the creation of a government for only part of the country would reduce the incentive for a peace settlement encompassing Germany as a whole.

Those who held such views swiftly diminished in number under the frightening impact of the obvious Soviet determination to subjugate West Berlin during the blockade. Throughout that ordeal, the Russians and the German Communists subjected the hard-pressed West Berliners to sustained psychological warfare. In radio broadcasts and the press of East Berlin they relentlessly proclaimed that all Berlin came under their authority and predicted the imminent abandonment of the city by the Western occupying powers. The Russians also harassed the democratically elected city-wide administration, which sought to conduct its business and the sessions of its assembly in the city hall located in the Soviet sector.

In the autumn of 1948 it became impossible for the non-Communist majority in the Berlin city-wide assembly elected two years earlier to attend that body's sessions in the Soviet sector. As SED-controlled policemen looked on passively, Communist-led mobs repeatedly invaded the city hall, interrupted the assembly's sessions, and physically menaced its non-Communist members. Led by Social Democrat Ernst Reuter, who had been elected mayor a year earlier by the assembly but denied that post by Soviet veto, the majority moved the city administration to the Western part of Berlin in September. There Reuter, at last installed as mayor, rallied the population to hold out during the blockade in the face of privation and intimidation by the Russians. A free election in the Western sectors of the city in December 1948 produced a turnout of 86.3 percent and an overwhelming victory for the non-Communist parties. A month earlier the Soviets had effectively divided Berlin by recognizing an SED-dominated puppet municipal regime in their sector of the city.

In the eyes of most Germans in the West, the airlift to Berlin came to seem a struggle to protect their freedoms, and the Western occupying powers became their protectors. For their part, the Americans, British, and French found themselves working side by side with Germans to keep the necessities of life flowing to the millions of West Berliners whose fortitude and endurance gave rise to admiration and esteem among their former foes. Especially impressive was the rejection by the great majority of West Berliners of food and other supplies offered them by the regime in East Berlin. By the time the Russians lifted the blockade in the spring of 1949, the animosities of the war years had with remarkable rapidity begun to give way among Americans, British, French, and Germans to a recognition of common interests, shared values, and mutual respect.

When the Berlin blockade ended, normal traffic to Berlin resumed and international tensions diminished sharply, but the situation of Germany remained drastically altered. Although the Russians reopened the transit routes to Berlin, they continued to insist that the Western powers had violated the Potsdam agreements. They therefore refused to return to the Allied Control Council in Berlin, so that the four-power occupation authority foreseen at Potsdam could not function. After the creation of Trizonia, Germany (leaving aside the special cases of Berlin and the Saarland) in effect consisted of two distinct political and economic regions. Trizonia, by far the larger and more populous region with about 49 million inhabitants, encompassed territory roughly the size of England, Scotland, and Wales or Pennsylvania and New York. The Soviet zone, with about 17 million inhabitants, was less than half as large or about the size of the state of Ohio. Each had its own administrative system, its own laws and judiciary, its own economic system and currency, its own measure of civil and political liberties. Movement of people and goods between the two parts remained possible. But the breakdown in the spring of 1949 of the last postwar conference of Allied foreign ministers without any progress toward a peace conference served to underline the fact that in the four years since the end of military conflict Germany had become a divided country.

In its immediate origins, that division was the product of deep, often irreconcilable differences among the victors who assumed de facto sovereignty over Germany in 1945. In many instances, each side's case had incontestable validity. The Soviets had strong claims to reparations from a Germany which had invaded and devastated much of their country. The Western powers, on the other hand, saw no reason why they should in

effect finance reparations to the Soviet Union by pumping resources into their occupation zones at the expense of their own
citizens to feed and provision Germans while the Russians extracted goods and resources from the other side of the country.
Because of understandable fears about a revival of the German
industrial power that had made possible repeated invasions of
their countries, first the French, then the Soviets, obstructed
American and British efforts to restore German economic unity
so as to increase industrial productivity, revive internal trade,
and promote the exports needed to enable the Germans in the
populous but agriculturally limited western and southern regions of the country to feed themselves without aid from the
taxpayers of Britain and the United States.

The wartime arrangements for what was then expected to be a
brief period of occupation contributed to the split among the
victors, since those arrangements required unanimity for Allied
decisions. The Americans and British repeatedly found themselves faced with a choice between accepting French and Soviet
vetoes or stepping outside the four-power framework to deal
with the pressing needs of the German population and the demands of their home governments for relief from the cost of
feeding a defeated population. They chose the latter course and
were eventually joined by the French. This enabled the USSR to
claim that the Western powers had violated the Potsdam and
wartime agreements and were therefore responsible for the division of Germany. The alternative hardly represented a viable
option, however, in view of the financial consequences for the
Western powers and the specter of renewed political radicalism
among a German population condemned to protracted depriva-
tion. Moreover, the overwhelming majority of the German population in the Western zones soon rallied behind the decision to
consolidate and revive at least part of Germany in order to
ensure that it would not disappear behind the iron curtain, as
had the other part.

Despite repeated consideration in Allied circles during the
war of a division of Germany into several states, none of the

victors afterward consistently followed policies designed to produce that outcome. The only clear and incontestable responsibility for the country's division lay with the regime that had functioned in the name of the German people in Berlin from 1933 until 1945. By launching its war of calculated aggression against a large part of the world, the Third Reich called into being an unlikely coalition of powers which, as victors after its fall, proved unable to agree on the future of Germany and so ended by partitioning the country.

2
The Birth of
Two New
Governments

The Federal Republic

While the stirring events of the Berlin blockade and airlift held the attention of much of the world, the future political shape of Germany was being determined in less dramatic fashion. Beginning in the West, then in the East as well, adjustments to postwar circumstances produced two new German governments. At the time, both seemed mere improvisations, but they were to prove surprisingly durable.

The proposal by the six-nation London Conference of spring 1948 for creation of a government encompassing the Western occupation zones was relayed to the minister-presidents of the states in those zones at the beginning of July by the American, British, and French military commandants. The three Western governments called upon the West Germans to convene a constituent assembly that would draft a constitution for a new government and submit it to the population for ratification. This new government would operate, they specified, within the confines of an occupation statute that would closely circumscribe its authority and reserve sovereign powers to the occupying countries.

This proposal initially encountered considerable hesitation in German political circles. Many political leaders in Western Germany viewed with dismay the drastic limitations which the draft occupation statute would impose on the authority of a new German government. It seemed to them that they were being asked to set up a mere regional administrative apparatus for the convenience of the occupiers. That apparatus would not, critics argued, give the West Germans significantly more independence than they already had, whereas acceptance of it could cast doubt on their commitment to the goal of a unified government for the entire country. There was widespread reluctance to write a new constitution for only part of the country, as the occupying powers proposed, lest that make eventual reunification more difficult and place the onus for Germany's division on the authors of such a constitution.

Misgivings about the possible consequences of forming a government in the West soon gave way, however, to fears of Soviet expansionism arising from the Berlin blockade and to hopes for better terms than those initially proposed by the occupying powers. In intense negotiations among political leaders in the Western zones during the summer of 1948 a consensus developed which favored acceptance of the proposal if some modifications could be achieved. Supporters of that view argued that formation of a West German government would amount to no more of a hindrance to restoration of national unity than the creation of Bizonia. The best hope for a united and free Germany lay, they insisted, in establishing a new government for at least part of the country so as to bring about political stability on a democratic foundation and ensure rapid economic recovery. Such a government would, they predicted, act as a magnet for the rest of Germany.

Swayed by these arguments and by fear of abandonment to Communist encroachment if the proposal of the Western powers was rejected, the minister-presidents of the states in the American, British, and French zones agreed to move toward formation of the sort of federal government specified by the occupation authorities. In delicate negotiations with those authorities they gained a number of concessions. To lessen the danger of obstructing reunification they successfully insisted that the new government be explicitly designated as a provisional arrangement that would cease to exist as soon as the country as a whole could freely determine its political institutions. In order to emphasize this, they gained the consent of the Western occupying powers for substitution of a Basic Law (Grundgesetz) for the constitution originally foreseen by the London Conference. They also sought, and eventually obtained, elimination of the occupying powers' plan for ratification by plebiscite. Instead, they substituted ratification by at least two-thirds of the state parliaments, a less dramatic procedure which they hoped would underline the provisional nature of the Basic Law.

In line with the desire of the minister-presidents to play down the formation of the new government, the task of designing a Basic Law was assigned to a body called a Parliamentary Council rather than a constituent assembly. Its sixty-five members convened at the beginning of September 1948 after being chosen by the parliaments of the eleven states which then comprised the American, British, and French zones. Since the occupying powers ruled out participation of representatives from Berlin, lest that call into question its four-power status, five observers from the Western sectors of the old capital attended without votes.

In terms of party affiliation, twenty-seven members of the Parliamentary Council belonged to the SPD and twenty-seven to the CDU/CSU, five to the FDP, and the rest to splinter parties, including two Communists. Although many of the members of the council had participated in the strident politics of the Weimar Republic, they demonstrated that they had learned important lessons from the failure of their country's ill-fated first experiment with democracy. Whereas the parliaments of Weimar had often been characterized by unyielding doctrinaire stands and confrontations, the Parliamentary Council displayed a far-reaching commitment to sober practicality and a general willingness to compromise. That willingness to settle for less than the optimal also enabled the members of the Parliamentary Council to find formulas that avoided opposition on the part of the Western powers, with whose spokesmen many points had to be negotiated.

The principal differences within the council arose over the degree of authority to be apportioned to the federal institutions on the one hand and to the states on the other. The SPD and the FDP generally favored stronger central powers than did the CDU or its Bavarian affiliate, the CSU, the latter of which took an extreme position in defense of states' rights. On most points, however, compromise solutions won broad support among the members of the council. On a few issues, such as the degree of fiscal centralization in the new polity, the Western powers' observers at the sessions of the council objected to positions taken by the majority of the delegates. But there, too, mutually acceptable compromises were worked out. By early May 1949 the council had completed its assignment and approved a Basic Law for a Federal Republic of Germany by a vote of 53 to 12, with both of the largest parties, the CDU and the SPD, solidly in favor. After assent by the Western occupying powers, the Basic Law was then ratified by all of the state parliaments except that of Bavaria, where states' rights advocates mustered a negative majority. The Bavarian parliament nevertheless voted to recognize the binding nature of the Basic Law and so entered willingly into the Federal Republic, which officially came into being on May 23, 1949.

Initially, the Federal Republic was far from a sovereign polity. Acceptance of the Basic Law implicitly carried with it acceptance as well of the Occupation Statute drawn up by the Americans, British, and French. That document circumscribed the authority of the new West German state less tightly than had the earlier draft. The occupying powers nevertheless retained ultimate control over foreign relations and foreign trade, over the level of industrial production and reparations as well as over all matters bearing on demilitarization, decartelization, and scientific research of potential military significance. Only with the permission of the occupying powers could the Federal Republic legislate or otherwise take action in those areas. The occupying powers retained the right to veto within twenty-one days any piece of West German legislation which in their judgment was unconstitutional or in conflict with occupation policies. Alterations in the Basic Law required their unanimous consent. They reserved to themselves control over all military matters and the right to resume their full authority as occupying powers in the event of an emergency that endangered the new West German constitutional order. Otherwise, their remaining authority was to be transferred, upon ratification of the Basic Law, from their respective military commandants to three civilian high commissioners.

The new Federal Republic comprised the states of the American, British and French occupation zones. Only six of these had previously existed as political entities: Baden, Bavaria, Hesse, Schleswig-Holstein, and the city-states of Bremen and Hamburg. The remaining five, Lower Saxony, North Rhine-Westphalia, Rhineland-Palatinate, Württemberg-Baden, and Württemberg-Hohenzollern, were creations of the occupying powers. Yet with the exception of the last two, which would, together with Baden, merge in 1951 into a single state of Baden-Württemberg, the new states rapidly established themselves as functioning polities and won widespread acceptance among their populations. When the Saarland joined the Federal Republic in 1957 as the result of a plebiscite, the number of states became ten. Although marked by discrepancies in territory and population, none so greatly exceeded the others in size as had Prussia during both the Empire and the Weimar Republic. A more balanced federal system thus came into being.

Although Berlin was included in the article of the Basic Law which enumerated the states where its validity would apply, that city's status proved complicated. The Western powers were intent upon preserving the four-power occupation of the former capital that provided the legal foundation for their presence in its Western sectors. They therefore refused to allow full incorporation of West Berlin into the Federal Republic. For all practical purposes, however, the Western sectors of the former capital would function like a state of the Federal Republic, whose currency was used there. To preserve West Berlin's special status, important legislation enacted in the Federal Republic would routinely be adopted by its democratically elected government. Measures that raised sensitive issues with the Russians, such as the military draft and the Western powers' recognition of West German sovereignty, would not be applied to West Berlin. In both the Bundestag and Bundesrat the city would be represented by nonvoting delegates chosen by its government. West Berlin would also receive extensive financial aid from the Federal Republic by way of compensation for the economic handicaps resulting from its isolated location. In part to emphasize that removal of the government from Berlin should be viewed as only a temporary expedient, the Parliamentary Council chose as the provisional capital of the Federal Republic the small Rhenish university city of Bonn, where the council had held its sessions in a building formerly used as a teachers' college.

Although the new republic was to exercise authority over only part of Germany, the Basic Law claimed for it the right to represent all Germans until such time as those denied freedom of choice should regain their political rights. When that day came, the Basic Law would give way to "a constitution adopted by a free decision of the German people." To express its claim to the democratic tradition of Germany, the new Republic adopted for its flag the black, red, and gold horizontal stripes that had served as the banner of the unsuccessful revolutionaries of 1848 and as the official colors of the Weimar Republic.

The first section of the Basic Law consists of an enumeration of the civil and political rights of all citizens. As a result of the loss of virtually all individual rights under Nazi rule, a long and detailed list was included. The freedoms enumerated were, however, in some instances not unconditional. Because of the experiences of the Weimar Republic, when extremist movements of left and right exploited the broad liberties granted by Germany's first democractic constitution to work for its overthrow, the Basic Law provides for withdrawal of political rights from those who seek to use them to undermine the democratic foundations of the Federal Republic. Political movements that seek the destruction of democracy can be banned. The provision for freedom of speech is, moreover, so phrased as to exclude its misuse against individuals or groups of people, as in advocacy of anti-Semitism. Because of deadlocks among the parties in the Parliamentary Council, the Basic Law does not contain the sort of provisions which in the Weimar constitution had prescribed relationships between workers and employers. With regard to the economic order, the Basic Law thus remained an "open" document, leaving determination of those matters to democratically enacted legislation. In contrast to the Weimar constitution, however, women gained a guarantee of rights equal to those of men.

In a revival of the states' rights tradition that had prevailed prior to the highly centralized Third Reich, the new West German state was cast as a federal polity. The Basic Law explicitly reserves some areas of legislative competence for the federal government. The most important of these are foreign and military affairs, citizenship and immigration, monetary policy, and the copyright, patent, postal, rail, air traffic, telegraph, and telephone systems. Another broad range of responsibilities may be assumed by the federal government if it deems uniformity necessary, but if it does not lay claim to those matters, they fall to the states. These include civil, criminal, and labor law, public health and welfare, prevention of the abuse of economic power, as well as highway construction and maintenance.

All other public affairs are reserved to the states, except insofar as they have effects that extend beyond a single state. For example, education, including the university level, falls to the states, but if laws affecting education have ramifications for the country as a whole, federal authority may be invoked. Where conflicts develop, the Basic Law specifies that as a general rule federal law takes precedent. As in the Empire and Weimar Republic, the federal government enjoys extensive legislative authority as compared to that of the United States, but execution of most federal laws rests with the states, so that the federal bureaucracy is of limited size. An intricate and carefully designed taxation system divides revenues between the federal government and the states. The states must be democratic republics and uphold the principles set forth in the Basic Law, which also obligates them to provide representative bodies for their citizens at the local level.

The key democratic institution established by the Basic Law is the federal parliament or Bundestag. It enjoys the greatest measure of political power within the governmental system. Approval by a majority of its deputies is required for passage of legislation. Amendments to the Basic Law can be carried only if a two-thirds margin can be attained. The deputies are chosen in elections open to all citizens eighteen years of age and older (until 1971 the minimum age was twenty-one). Bundestag elections must be held at least every four years and may occur after less time has elapsed if sufficient backing cannot be found for a cabinet.

The method of electing parliamentary deputies is governed not by the Basic Law but by a special electoral statute, certain details of which have been revised from time to time. That statute, whose basic outlines have remained the same, was designed to avoid the misfortunes of the Weimar Republic, whose elections had been conducted under a purely proportional system of representation that allocated parliamentary seats on the basis of the share of the votes cast, in large regional electoral districts, for parties rather than individual candidates. In the judgment of West German leaders, that system had contributed to the downfall of the first republic by depersonalizing parliamentary representation and by encouraging the proliferation of splinter parties, thereby weakening the moderate parties on which governmental stability depended. By a compromise arrangement, the electoral law of the Federal Republic combines a basically proportional system of representation with elements of a constituency system similar to those of Great Britain and the United States, in which voters choose among individual candidates in relatively small electoral districts.

This system has come to be known as "personalized proportionality." In an election each voter has two ballots, one for a candidate in the local constituency and one for a list of candidates presented by the party of the voter's choice within the state of the voter's residence. This permits voters to split their ballots, casting one for the constituency candidate of one party, the second for the state list of another. Every local constituency is represented in the Bundestag by the candidate who tallies the most first ballots. The deputies elected in this fashion are then supplemented by an equal number of candidates drawn from the party lists in the states in such fashion as to have the overall political composition of the Bundestag reflect the preferences registered by voters with their second ballots. To discourage a proliferation of splinter parties, the voting law denies representation to any party that fails either to win at least three constituency seats or obtain a minimum of 5 percent of the total second ballots cast throughout the Federal Republic. Similar voting laws govern balloting and the distribution of seats for the state parliaments.

At the head of the state in the Federal Republic stands the president. In the Weimar Republic a crucial part in the destruction of democracy was played by the presidency, a popularly elected office with a seven-year term which commanded extensive authority. Accordingly, the founders of the Federal Republic strove to remove the presidency as much as possible from partisan politics and strictly limit the powers of the office. Rather than being elected by popular vote, the federal president is chosen indirectly, by a Federal Assembly which comes into being only when the need to select a new president arises. Half of this assembly consists of the members of the Bundestag, the other half of delegates chosen by the parliaments of the states. On the first two ballots an absolute majority is required to elect a president, but if that cannot be achieved, a plurality suffices thereafter.

The president performs a variety of functions but has little power. He promulgates all treaties and federal laws but lacks a veto. All his decrees and orders must be countersigned by the head of government, the chancellor. He does, however, exercise the authority to pardon those convicted under the laws of the Federal Republic. For the most part, the president serves, in much the same fashion as do the crowned heads of the democratic, constitutional monarchies of Europe, to relieve the head of government of such time-consuming formal responsibilities as greeting foreign guests and representing the Federal Republic abroad or at commemorations and other ceremonial occasions at home. The president also serves as a symbolic figure of political unity above partisan strife. All the incumbents in the office have, regardless of their own political backgrounds, striven to remain aloof from party politics, just as the framers of the Basic Law intended. Some have used the office effectively as a rostrum from which to educate citizens about the institutions of their democracy and to remind them of the moral values that undergird it.

One of the most important functions of the president is nomination of the chancellor. To succeed, that nomination must be in line with the distribution of political strength among the parties in the Bundestag, which exercises final authority over selection of a chancellor and can override the president's nomination. In the initial rounds of parliamentary balloting an absolute majority is required, but if that proves impossible, the Basic Law permits a chancellor to be elected by a plurality of the deputies. If all attempts to find majority parliamentary support for a candidate fail, the president may, with the concurrence of the incumbent chancellor, dissolve the chamber and schedule new elections. But only under those circumstances does the president command that important power to influence the political process. Once elected, the chancellor nominates a cabinet made up of the heads of the federal ministries; they are then installed by the federal president, who removes them from office, if the need arises, at the request of the chancellor. As leader of the government, the chancellor "determines, and assumes responsibility for, general policy."

Since shifting parliamentary alignments had weakened the chancellorship during the Weimar Republic and reduced the average term of office to less than a year, the authors of the Basic Law included a provision designed to strengthen the chancellor against the Bundestag. It rules out felling a chancellor, as in the Weimar Republic and most other parliamentary democracies, through a vote of no-confidence in which a majority of the deputies express their opposition. In the Federal Republic, such a vote of no-confidence can bring down a chancellor only if it is coupled with a majority vote of Bundestag deputies in favor of a substitute candidate for the chancellorship. This provision for a "constructive vote of no-confidence" resulted in no chancellor's being turned out of office by parliamentary opposition until the Federal Republic was in its thirty-third year, whereas that was a common occurrence in the Weimar Republic. As a consequence, the chancellorship has become, just as the architects of the Basic Law hoped, a powerful office and a stabilizing factor.

The Basic Law accords representation to the states through a federal council or Bundesrat. It functions in many respects as an upper legislative chamber somewhat similar to the British House of Lords or the American Senate. But it is more properly the voice of the state governments. The Basic Law entitles each state to three seats, while those with more than two million inhabitants receive four and those with more than six million five. This arrangement gives the smaller states a greater voice than they would be entitled to simply on the basis of population. The delegates are members of the state governments, appointed by them. The minister-president of one of the states presides. Unlike Bundestag deputies, Bundesrat delegates may not determine their votes independently but must cast them as blocs, upon instruction from their state governments.

The Basic Law gives the Bundesrat more power than the

corresponding body had in the Weimar Republic. On federal legislation affecting the rights of the states the Bundesrat commands an absolute veto. In all other legislative spheres a majority of the Bundesrat can block enactment of bills approved by the Bundestag with what is known as a "suspensive veto." A majority in the Bundestag can, however, override that veto. If the veto is carried by two-thirds of the Bundesrat, only a similar margin in the Bundestag can overturn it. The Basic Law's provision for resolution of legislative differences between the Bundesrat and Bundestag by means of a joint committee has minimized resort to the veto, however. Two-thirds approval by the Bundesrat, as by the Bundestag, is required for constitutional amendments. In times of closely balanced political situations, the Bundesrat serves to make shifts in public opinion quickly felt. When parties in opposition in the Bundestag achieve successes in state elections sufficient to give them control of governments at that level, their influence at the federal level increases through their selection of new Bundesrat delegations bound to vote as their governments instruct. If a majority of the votes in the Bundesrat comes under the control of the opposition, it can obstruct the government's fiscal and legislative program by use of the suspensive veto. If the opposition commands two-thirds of the Bundesrat, it can, through a veto of that margin, force a cabinet unable to muster a similar margin in the Bundestag to modify its program to secure passage. As its designers intended, the Bundesrat has proved a key institution in West German federalism.

The final major institution in the structure of the Federal Republic is its Constitutional Court. The Basic Law made provision for such a judiciary body but left its design to subsequent legislation, which was not completed until 1951. Like the American Supreme Court, the Constitutional Court enjoys far-reaching independence from both the executive and legislative branches of government, a point emphasized by placing the court in the city of Karlsruhe, geographically removed from Bonn. Half of its sixteen justices are chosen by the Bundestag,

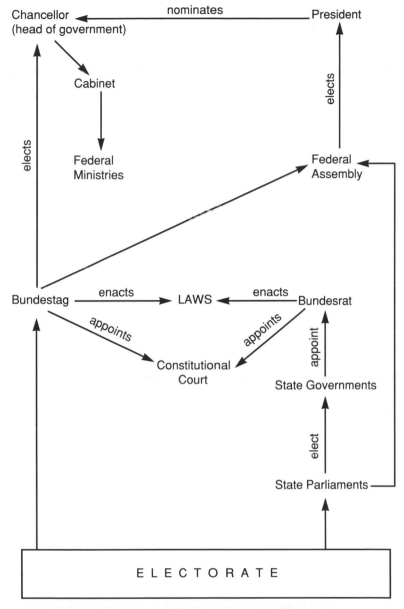

Principal Political Institutions of the Federal Republic of Germany

half by the Bundesrat. They serve for terms of twelve years and may not be reelected. Prior to the point of mandatory retirement, the justices can be removed only by the federal president after a specific request from the court itself. They sit as two separate chambers, each with specific spheres of responsiblity, to review appeals from lower courts. Their jurisdiction encompasses such matters as disagreements among the states or between states and the federal government, the compatibility of state with federal laws, infringements of the basic rights of citizens, violations of electoral laws, and misuse of political rights.

The Constitutional Court has introduced into German law the Anglo-American principle of judicial review. The constitutionality of federal laws and measures taken by the government is subject to challenge before the court, and its findings are binding on the authorities. Although the justices have limited opportunities to shape the law under the German system of codified law, as opposed to the heavy Anglo-American reliance on precedent and case law, the Constitutional Court has played an important role in shaping the Federal Republic. Its justices, unlike those of the high courts of the Empire and the Weimar Republic, have been drawn heavily from the ranks of lawyers previously active in political life rather than from those of legal technicians. They have showed themselves both sensitive to public opinion and vigilant in their protection of the republic's democratic institutions, making the court a respected arbiter of disputes and guardian of the Basic Law.

For a document regarded by its framers as a mere provisional expedient, the Basic Law has proven a remarkable success. By strengthening the executive, it has provided for stable political leadership. Through a variety of safeguards it has protected the democratic institutions it established. By a combination of clear delimitation and flexibility it has enabled the complex federal system to function with a minimum of friction. More than any other German constitutional document of modern times, it quickly won the respect and allegiance of the population.

The German Democratic Republic

While the Parliamentary Council was designing the Basic Law in Bonn, very different developments in the Soviet zone shaped the birth of a second new German state. Of crucial significance for those developments was the increasing demand by the USSR for conformity on the part of the regimes within its power sphere, which in part resulted from the bitter dispute between Soviet dictator Stalin and the renegade Yugoslav leader Josip Tito during 1947 and 1948.

During the period of the Stalin-Tito clash, the SED underwent transformation into an authoritarian party dominated by functionaries subservient to Moscow. This meant an end to the last vestiges of pluralism within its ranks. Instead, a Soviet-style "democratic centralism" prevailed, in which all authority flowed downward from the top leadership. Within that leadership the principle of equal representation for Social Democrats and Communists in all party organs was abandoned. Many former SPD members and even some from the KPD were deemed insufficiently reliable and purged from the SED; others were arrested and accused of being foreign agents. By early 1949 Communists predominated in the key organs of the party, which was now capped by a Soviet-style Politburo. Nominally elected by the Central Committee, a body of several hundred which bore responsibility for carrying out decisions of the infrequent party congresses, the Politburo was actually a small, self-selecting inner circle. It quickly became the locus of power, and all important decisions flowed downward from it rather than, as in theory, upward from the party's membership.

Along with these organizational changes came an important ideological shift on the part of the SED. Its founders' pledges to seek a distinctively German path to socialism were soon forgotten. Instead, the goal became emulation of the USSR and construction of a "people's democracy" similar to those of the regimes set up with Soviet backing in Eastern Europe. In schools and universities throughout the Russian zone, indoctrination in Marxism-Leninism became a compulsory part of the curriculum. So stifling did this ideological pressure become that many faculty members fled to the West. In 1948 a large part of the student body and faculty of the University of Berlin, once the flagship of German higher education but now located in the Soviet sector of the old capital, seceded because of ideological repression and founded the Free University of Berlin in the Western part of the city.

Repressive methods of rule were soon applied throughout the Russian zone by the SED-dominated civil administration. Those holding or aspiring to positions in the bureaucracy, the judiciary, or the school system had to pass ideological scrutiny. An elaborate political police apparatus kept the population under close surveillance. Dissent or even disagreement with policies of the occupation regime was discouraged by denying offenders advancement in their careers, dismissing them from their jobs, or imprisoning them. A tight system of censorship restricted access to print or the airwaves.

These police-state measures further diminished the SED's standing with the population in the Soviet zone. With all signs suggesting the likelihood of a severe setback in the event of new, competitive elections, the SED contrived a substitute for a representative parliament. At the end of 1947 it convened in the Soviet sector of Berlin a so-called People's Congress for Unity and a Just Peace. Most of the more than two thousand delegates were from the Soviet zone, but a few did attend from the Western zones, even though the democratic parties there refused to participate. Rather than being elected by the populace, delegates were chosen by a variety of organizations, most of which were under the control of the SED or, in the West, sympathetic to the KPD. Claiming to represent all of Germany, the People's Congress called for speedy reunification of the country. In October 1948 a committee of the Congress set forth the draft of a constitution for a German Democratic Republic. Originally this draft

The Two Germanies

was proposed for an all-German government, but it eventually served as the basis for an East German constitution.

Once the impending formation of a West German government became clear in the spring of 1949, selection of delegates for a new People's Congress was scheduled in the East. In line with the SED's insistence that it sought reunification, some delegates from the Western zones were again to be chosen by various organizations other than the democratic parties. In departure from previous practice, those from the Soviet zone were to be elected by the populace as a whole. But to ensure an outcome favorable to the SED, those elections would not be free and competitive. Instead of choosing among parties and candidates, voters were permitted only a Soviet-style election, modified slightly to accommodate the German multi-party political pattern. On election day in May 1949 voters in each electoral district therefore faced only the choice of endorsing or rejecting so-called unity lists of candidates.

In these unity lists, SED candidates occupied only a minority position, but that was deceptive. By the spring of 1949 the Christian Democratic and Liberal Democratic parties had been thoroughly intimidated by the Soviet authorities and the SED-dominated civil administration. Some of their leaders had been imprisoned and others had fled to the Western zones. Those who remained at the head of these nominally independent parties managed to do so only by avoiding the displeasure of the SED, since their parties had become little more than its satellites. In order to mobilize voters unattracted by the CDU or LDP, the unity lists also included two new parties cultivated by the SED. These were the Democratic Farmers' Party (Demokratische Bauernpartei Deutschlands or DBD) and the National Democratic Party (National-Demokratische Partei Deutschlands or NDPD). The DBD appealed to a rural population traditionally hostile to Communism, while the NDPD directed its attention to former Nazis, army officers, and others tainted by involvement with the Third Reich. The addition of these two new parties ensured, among other things, further fragmentation of the non-Communist portion of the political spectrum. Since all the satellite parties received substantial subsidies from the SED, they quickly became financially dependent upon it.

In addition to these parties, the unity lists soon came to include candidates named by a variety of organizations such as a league of trade unions, a league of women, a youth league, and a cultural league. All these "mass organizations" were, in reality, also satellites of the SED. Despite that party's apparent minority position on the unity lists, it was thus assured firm control over the new People's Congress chosen in May 1949. Nevertheless, although the ballots were designed to discourage opposition, the SED-dominated Soviet zone civil administration which tabulated the results claimed only that 61.6 percent of the voters had endorsed the unity lists. Opposition sentiment was apparently still too widespread and evident to make plausible the Soviet-style victory margins of more than 99 percent for unity lists that would later become routine.

The new People's Congress "elected" in this manner and augmented with carefully chosen delegates from the Western zones protested vigorously against the preparations for formation of a West German government. It assigned full responsibility for the impending division of the country to the politicians in the West and the Western powers. At the same time, the People's Congress took measures of its own for formation of a separate East German government. In May 1949, a week after proclamation of the Basic Law in Bonn, a People's Council appointed by the People's Congress and consisting of 330 of its delegates from the Soviet zone approved the draft constitution which had been under preparation for some time. Then, on October 7, 1949, following installation of the first cabinet of the Federal Republic, the People's Congress unanimously approved the formation of a German Democratic Republic (Deutsche Demokratische Republik or DDR; in English GDR).

Initially, the intent behind the formation of the new GDR was shrouded in ambiguity. On the one hand, its founders soon proclaimed it, in keeping with Communist doctrine, as "the first worker's and peasants' state on German soil" and depicted it as the product of irresistible historical forces. Their pledges to defend it against all threats suggested a permanent commitment. On the other hand, they described the new state on some occasions as a merely provisional arrangement that could provide the basis for a government encompassing all of Germany if the West German state were abandoned. Adopting, as had the new government in Bonn, the black-red-gold flag that had symbolized national unity at the time of the ill-fated revolution of 1848, the founders of the GDR portrayed themselves as steadfast champions of German reunification and denounced the leaders of the Federal Republic as separatists. There were grounds for skepticism about their commitment to reunification, however. For, barring a nation-wide Communist takeover, the SED would from all indications shrink to the status of a minor party in a free and reunited Germany.

In practice, the GDR quickly became the government of the Soviet occupation zone. Following adoption of the constitution and conversion of the People's Council into a provisional People's Chamber, or parliament, the Soviet military commandant announced that the USSR was transferring the civil affairs of its zone and, nominally at least, foreign affairs as well, to the new government. On October 11, the provisional People's Chamber met jointly with a Chamber of the States made up of representatives of the state governments of the Soviet zone to elect longtime Communist functionary Wilhelm Pieck the first president of the GDR. The next day the provisional People's Chamber chose former Social Democrat Otto Grotewohl of the SED as the first minister-president at the head of a cabinet including ministers from the non-Marxist parties. Some five months after the formation of the Federal Republic, a second German government had established itself in the Russian sector of the four-power city of Berlin.

In line with the Communist pledges to pursue a separate German path to socialism rather than imposing the Soviet system, the constitution of the GDR guaranteed citizens a wide range of fundamental rights. These included freedom of assembly, freedom of the press, and freedom of speech, as well as religious freedom, confidentiality of postal communications, and the right to strike. The right to emigrate was expressly and unconditionally confirmed. The constitution even included guarantees of private property and inheritance rights. Only natural resources were to be socialized immediately. Compensation for dispossessed owners was assured in the event of any subsequent socialization measures.

In formal respects, the governmental institutions provided for by the constitution of the GDR generally paralleled those of the Federal Republic. The chief focus of authority was to be the parliament, the People's Chamber, elected for a term of four years under a system of proportional representation by means of a secret ballot. All citizens over eighteen years of age were entitled to vote. As in the Federal Republic, participation in the political system was restricted to parties that endorsed democracy. The People's Chamber received far more extensive powers than those assigned to the Bundestag in the West, since it could by itself adopt legislation on a broad range of matters. A degree of federalism characterized the constitution of the GDR, too, but it was much weaker than in the West. Its organ was to be a Chamber of States similar in composition to the Bundesrat but with fewer powers. Its consent was not required for legislation, but it was empowered to veto laws enacted by the People's Chamber, with the latter enjoying, like the Bundestag in the West, authority to override such vetos.

The government of the German Democratic Republic, headed by a minister-president, was to be elected by the deputies of the People's Chamber and had to command a parliamentary majority to remain in office. As did the Basic Law, the constitution of the GDR required a constructive vote of no-confidence for removal of a government by the People's Chamber. As in the Federal Republic, the president of the GDR was accorded a largely ceremonial role following election for a term of four years by a joint session of the People's Chamber and the Chamber of States.

The constitution adopted for the German Democratic Republic in October 1949 would have made possible a democratic, parliamentary government quite compatible with that of the Federal Republic. But as events were soon to demonstrate, the decisive political force in the new GDR—the SED—had very different intentions as well as the means to put them into effect.

3

The Ulbricht Era in East Germany

The Communist Regime and Its Leader

Throughout the first twenty-two years of the German Democratic Republic, its policies were dominated by veteran Communist functionary Walter Ulbricht. Never an absolute dictator, he skillfully maintained his primacy within the leadership of the East German state during its formative period and left an indelible imprint upon it.

Born in 1893, the son of an impecunious tailor in Saxon central Germany, Ulbricht grew up in a socialist environment, completed an apprenticeship as a cabinetmaker, and joined the SPD at the age of nineteen. Following service in the army in the First World War, he joined the Communist Party shortly after its formation at the end of 1918. Unswerving in his belief in a simplistic Marxist view of the world and unfailingly subservient to the Soviet Union, Ulbricht rose in the KPD's ranks as a full-time functionary and sat as one of the party's deputies in the Reichstag of the Weimar Republic from 1928 until 1933. After exile in the Soviet Union during the Third Reich, he returned to

Berlin under Russian auspices in the spring of 1945 to oversee reestablishment of the party in Germany.

Ulbricht's success did not result from popularity. Never a colorful or personable figure, he was an inept orator who wrote and spoke in stilted party jargon. He excelled, however, at what many perceived as the dull work involved in overseeing personnel matters and bureaucratic procedures within the party. Following Stalin's example, he exploited that role to build a network of loyal followers by manipulating party patronage so as to reward those who backed him with desirable posts. His management of the central party bureaucracy enabled him to exercise influence over policy decisions by determining which matters were brought to the leadership's attention. His close ties to the Russian occupation authorities placed him in a position to impose his will at crucial junctures by calling upon them for backing. A secretive, mistrustful person, Ulbricht imbued the Socialist Unity Party and the regime it established in East Germany with a conspiratorial elitism similar to that of the Communist Party of the USSR.

When the SED was formed, Ulbricht quickly became the decisive figure in the new party, so that his reign over East Germany began well before the formation of the GDR. Upon establishment of the governmental apparatus in 1949 he assumed only an obscure post as one of several deputies to the minister-president. The modesty of that official post was, however, deceptive. As in the USSR, the government of the GDR was thoroughly subordinated to the ruling party, and Ulbricht's position atop the SED as its general secretary made him the key figure in the new regime. During the GDR's first decade Ulbricht's leadership position remained precarious. In order to retain the support of a majority in the party's decisive body, the Politburo, he repeatedly had to deal with rivals and sometimes had to moderate his course during those years. Only later did he come to wield virtually unchallenged authority.

From the outset, the new East German regime paid little heed to the constitution adopted in 1949. That document specified election of the parliament, the People's Chamber, by proportional representation, a system which distributes seats among parties according to the percentage of the vote they tally. That provision was, however, systematically violated as a consequence of the compulsory coalition which the Soviets had imposed on all political parties in their zone after the war. When the GDR was formed, that coalition became known as the National Front. It encompassed not only the four political parties permitted to operate in the Soviet zone but also the so-called mass organizations subservient to the SED. Through control over composition of the unity lists of candidates on the ballots laid before the voters, this SED-dominated National Front in effect determined the outcome of elections in advance. Voters could choose only between approving the lists in entirety or rejecting them.

Under this system, the word *election* lost all meaning in the sense of voters' exercising a choice. Instead, elections in the GDR became, as in the Soviet Union, occasions when the regime elicited a ritualistic show of affirmation on the part of the population, with great stress placed upon achieving a maximum turnout at the polls. Participation was often less than voluntary, as many voters were marched in groups from their place of work to the polling places. There, public marking of ballots was encouraged and resort to the constitutionally guaranteed right to a secret ballot discouraged. Use of the secrecy of a voting booth soon became a rare exception that branded the individual as a deviant, a status that entailed heavy disadvantages in a society where all-powerful officials determined many aspects of the citizenry's life, such as who would get which jobs and who would be allotted an apartment or quarters at a vacation resort.

Beginning with the first balloting in 1950, parliamentary elections in the GDR invariably produced predictable outcomes. With monotonous regularity the regime proclaimed that turnouts of more than 98 percent of the eligible voters had by margins in excess of 99 percent endorsed the unity lists prepared by the National Front. The distribution of seats in the People's Chamber remained essentially unaffected by the elections. The SED received only a modest minority of the seats. But when combined with those assigned to the mass organizations it dominated, the SED's seats ensured it a firm majority. After 1963 the composition of the People's Chamber froze according to a set formula. The SED occupied 127 seats, the four other parties, the CDU, the LDP, the NDPD, and the DBD, 52 each. The remaining 165 were assigned to the mass organizations. The same techniques produced similar results in local and regional elections.

Aside from this novel electoral system, the formalities of constitutional, parliamentary government were initially observed in the GDR. All legislation was duly enacted by votes in the People's Chamber, which after each election regularly went through the motions of reinstalling Otto Grotewohl as minister-president at the head of nominal coalition cabinets that included ministers from the non-Communist parties. From the outset, however, the Soviet system of "democratic centralism" prevailed behind the scenes. All important policy decisions were made by the SED's Politburo and then effected by the parliament and government. No dissent was tolerated. The parliament met for only a few days each year, not to debate and test the strength of varying viewpoints but rather to transform Politburo policies into law by unanimous vote.

By 1954 the formalities of parliamentary rule were relaxed so as to allow the cabinet, now called the Council of Ministers, to enact laws by decree without approval by the People's Chamber when it was not in session. In the same year the authority of the Council of Ministers was, between its increasingly infrequent full meetings, assigned to an inner circle of ministers, designated as the Presidium and not provided for by the constitution. Two years earlier, in 1952, the federal component was eliminated when the People's Chamber enacted a law replacing the five states of the GDR with fourteen district administrative units thoroughly subordinated to the central government. It was a measure of the regime's indifference to constitutionality that the

Chamber of States remained nominally in existence until 1958, although the states themselves had disappeared six years earlier.

The regime showed scant respect for the rights guaranteed to citizens of the GDR by its constitution of 1949. Although the constitution assured freedom of expression and ruled out censorship, dissenting opinion was suppressed by a variety of methods. The government-controlled radio stations served as propaganda organs of the regime. Theaters and movie houses, all of which depended upon the regime for financial support, were brought into conformity as well. The regime's control over all publishing houses enabled it to determine which books would be printed and which would not be. Newspapers and magazines posed more complicated problems, but they, too, were brought into line. Those which failed to comply found it impossible to obtain adequate allotments of paper from the state monopoly that controlled its distribution. Organizations critical of the regime or out of step with its policies were denied the use of halls for meetings. Whereas the constitution contained extensive guarantees of religious freedom, in practice the regime harassed the churches in countless ways, banning the customary religious instruction from primary schools and imprisoning clergymen who criticized official policies. At the same time, the regime provoked such criticism by seeking to indoctrinate children with atheism at school and through the sole officially approved youth organization, the SED-controlled Free German Youth.

Although the constitution assured citizens equal rights, practice departed sharply from that principle. Children whose parents were classified by the regime as other than workers and farmers were discriminated against by the admissions policies of the state-run universities and other institutions of higher education. In other respects, too, citizens of "bourgeois" background encountered difficulties. Those who sought to flee to the West made themselves vulnerable to prosecution in the GDR, despite the constitutionally guaranteed right of emigration. The regime charged them with "flight from the Republic," a crime for which lengthy imprisonment could be imposed.

The increasingly repressive methods of the SED regime had a stifling effect on cultural life and artistic creativity. At the end of the war many talented intellectuals, writers, and artists had settled in Berlin, the former cultural capital of the country, and applied their energies there and in the surrounding Russian zone. With great idealism they hoped to help create a new and more humane Germany, freed from the reactionary influences that had played such a baneful role in their country's past. Initially the Soviet occupation authorities displayed liberality in cultural matters, tolerating a wide variety of plays, books, and other forms of expression. But with the onset of the Cold War at the time of the Berlin blockade, the Soviets and the SED imposed tight controls on cultural life in the East. Books and plays by Western authors ceased to be sold or staged there; translations of Russian literature flooded the bookstores while Soviet plays received lavish and protracted productions. Organizations of writers, artists, and musicians established after the war, ostensibly to foster their creative efforts, became repressive organs of thought control under a regime-directed League of Culture. Censure—or worse, expulsion—from those organizations curtailed or eliminated the access of offending individuals to galleries, concert halls, or publishing houses, thus making it difficult or impossible for them to find audiences for their work or to make a living through it.

The SED regime did not content itself with punishing deviants in the cultural sphere. Increasingly it emulated the Soviet practice of telling creative people not only what they must not do but also what they must do with regard to both the content and the form of their work. In architecture the heavy, ornate "wedding-cake" style developed in Stalin's USSR became obligatory, and the regime launched construction of a showpiece in East Berlin in the form of a huge housing and shopping project on a major boulevard renamed Stalinallee. Artists and writers were instructed to produce works of "socialist realism." This entailed abandonment of timeless human themes, introspection, and experimental forms in favor of depicting contemporary experiences of the working class in an idealized, optimistic light and in uncomplicated language and simple literary forms. Such works were intended to hold up to millions of readers positive socialist heroes, each totally loyal to the leadership of the SED and the Soviet Union, who would serve as models for emulation. Only through such works, the regime proclaimed, could artists and writers become productive members of a progressive society bent on creating "a new human being."

These strictures, which in practice entailed conformity to shifts in the current party line, made it increasingly difficult for creative persons to continue their work with intellectual honesty. Some gave up and fled to the West. Others conformed readily and were handsomely rewarded by the regime. Still others paid lip service to the regime's demands, producing some works that appeased its ideological watchmen but continuing to pursue in private genuinely creative endeavors in hopes of finding audiences for them in better times. Many incurred the disfavor of the regime for works that failed to measure up to its expectations. Among those who ran into difficulties was the foremost literary figure of the GDR, the poet and playwright Bertolt Brecht, who had with great fanfare chosen to settle in East Berlin (equipped with an Austrian passport and a West German publisher) after his wartime exile in the United States.

Little danger of any organized political opposition existed. Two of the non-Communist parties, the NDPD and the DBD, were from the outset creations and tools of the SED. Although initially independent, the remaining two, the CDU and LDP, quickly fell into the hands of compliant spokesmen. Well before formal creation of the GDR, those of their leaders who displayed independent-mindedness in the Soviet zone found that they risked imprisonment, so that many chose to flee to the West. The formation of the East German state was followed by the arrest or flight of additional leaders of those parties, including some who held ministerial posts in state governments as a result of Soviet-imposed compulsory coalitions. Talk of free elections or criticism of authoritarian methods of rule called forth accusations of conspiracy with an unspecified "enemy" which for some resulted in long prison terms. Those persons who subsequently took over leading positions in the CDU and LDP had to be willing to accept an acquiescent role and to ingratiate themselves with the SED and the regime it dominated. In return, they were well paid for undemanding, secure party jobs.

Increasingly, individual resistance to official policies became criminalized. Those who dissented found themselves accused of participation in counter-revolutionary, imperialistic plots on the part of an allegedly aggressive Federal Republic bent on revenge and renewed war. Since the GDR claimed to be "the first workers' and farmers' state on German soil," any criticism of its policies or methods became subject to denunciation as an attack on those social groups, which comprised a majority of the population. While well-known persons so accused sometimes received show trials staged for propaganda effect, most victims of political repression in the GDR were tried in secret and quietly spirited away to serve lengthy prison sentences without the publication of any specific grounds for their conviction. The arbitrary and coercive system of Stalinist terror that had so long ravaged Soviet society had been transplanted to East Germany in the name of democracy.

The SED, like the Communist Party of the Soviet Union, became itself a prime target of these Stalinist methods. At the time of the new party's formation, Social Democrats had comprised the larger part of its rank-and-file membership, but they soon made themselves suspect in the eyes of the SED's dominant Communist leadership. Their scruples were offended by breaches of constitutionality and police-state methods, and they saw no reason why they should not maintain contact with Social Democrats in West Germany. The latter were, however, anathema in the eyes of the SED leadership, which made *Sozial-demokratismus*, or democratic socialist attitudes, a deviation meriting expulsion. An estimated 200,000 former SPD members were purged from the SED in the years 1948–50 on such grounds. More than 5,000 landed in GDR prisons or Soviet labor camps, and at least 400 died while incarcerated. During 1951 membership in the SED, by both former Communists and former Social Democrats, underwent further reduction when members had to turn in their old party documents and apply for new ones, which were issued only to those who passed close scrutiny for loyalty. Whereas overall membership in the SED had stood at about 2 million in 1948, it had dropped to around 1.2 million by 1952 as a result of these measures.

Through such purges and through restrictive admission policies, the SED ceased to bear the characteristics of a mass party, open to anyone who wished to join, which it had initially inherited from the SPD. Under the direction of Ulbricht and his adherents it became, like the Communist Party of the Soviet Union, an organization reserved for those judged suitable for admission to its ranks after having petitioned for membership and successfully completed a probationary period. After admission, for which membership in the party youth organization would become a prerequisite for younger generations, members would henceforth enjoy good standing only by maintaining a prescribed level of party activity. Those admitted to full membership, about 12 percent of the adult population, could no longer withdraw voluntarily without special reasons. An inner circle of members, the so-called cadre, held the key jobs in the party and the upper levels of the government. A broader circle comprising those known as "activists" assumed more exacting obligations than did ordinary members. The distribution of rewards conformed to this hierarchical pattern.

Only a few years after formation of the SED, little remained of the open, democratic, united working-class party for which so many Social Democrats in East Germany had hoped at the time of the merger with the Communists in 1946. Those who survived the purges found themselves subjugated to an authoritarian Stalinist *Apparat*, a party machine designed to convey orders from top to bottom, ensure conformity, and impose punishment when compliance did not follow. For their part, the members of the SED cadre had become a privileged elite whose dominant status and material rewards depended upon preservation of the regime.

A younger generation of Communists accustomed only to the authoritarianism of the Third Reich and the GDR soon augmented the ranks of those who had experienced democracy during the Weimar Republic. Drawn from underprivileged backgrounds, exposed to higher education in many cases by doctrinaire workers' and peasants' faculties set up by the regime at universities, and shielded from exposure to outside influences by rigid censorship, this second generation of GDR officials was very much the creation of the SED. Its members received advancement as much according to obedience as to ability. With rare exceptions, they unquestioningly accepted policies dictated by the top leadership. As a result, the GDR became a society administered by a small army of subservient functionaries executing decisions reached by remote, self-appointed power-holders.

The SED leadership displayed little commitment to the pledge, set forth in the constitution of the GDR, to move toward the reunification of Germany. To be sure, the regime repeatedly proposed steps it characterized as prerequisites for reunification in extensively publicized open communications directed at Bonn. Its proposals always contained provisos, however, which ensured that they would go unaccepted by the West Germans. The most fundamental of these provisos, repeated over and over again, called for an all-German conference that would draw up plans for reuniting the two parts of the country. While that made good propaganda, these proposals specified that at such a conference the two German governments must have equal voices in determining the country's future, an arrangement that would, in effect, grant the GDR veto power. The same proviso lay at the core of East Berlin's proposals for formation of a confederation of East and West Germany. Granting that sort of parity to the SED regime was wholly unacceptable to Bonn, since the regime in the GDR enjoyed no democratic legitimacy and could in any case speak, even if it somehow became legitimized, for far fewer Germans than could the Federal Republic. Bonn countered by insisting upon free elections throughout both parts of the country in order to reestablish a democratically based political voice with which the German people as a whole could speak out on the terms of reunification and a new nation-wide government. But the regime in East Berlin ignored those appeals rather than face the possibility of competition from other parties in a free and open electoral contest.

Most observers agreed that the monotonous rhetoric of reunification employed by the leaders of the SED served mainly to mask an aversion to ending Germany's division, which had become the basis for their authority over that part of the country where the presence of the Red Army enabled them to rule without regard to the political preferences of the citizenry. In May 1952 the regime in the GDR deepened the division of the country by converting the demarcation line between East and West Germany into a fortified border and limiting passage between the two to a few closely controlled checkpoints. That left Berlin, where four-power occupation remained in effect, as the only place where East Germans could move westward unhindered. West Berliners could still visit East Berlin but were now denied access to the rest of the GDR. Telephone communications between the two parts of the former capital were drastically curtailed by the East German authorities.

Socialization and Industrial Expansion

Although the 1949 constitution of the GDR guaranteed property rights, private ownership of productive assets was from the outset precarious at best. Much property had already been expropriated by German Communist administrators under Soviet auspices during occupation rule. Initially, only the estates of great landowners and the businesses of active Nazis were ordered seized, but "occupation social-ism," as it came to be known, actually resulted in the expropria-tion of many others as well. Nearly half the total farmland in the Soviet zone was seized in the course of the postwar agrarian reform. Some two-thirds of the confiscated land was distributed among small farmers and the rest assigned to collective farms similar to those in the USSR.

Insofar as a socialist revolution occurred in East Germany, it came about at the order of the Soviet occupation authorities, not as a consequence of any popular upheaval. Most industries seized during the occupation became *Volkseigene Betriebe* ("people's plants" or VEB) and were operated initially by the SED-dominated zonal administration and later by the GDR. Spe-cial occupation decrees resulted in the blanket takeover of cer-tain categories of enterprises, such as banks, energy-producing utilities, pharmacies, and motion picture theaters. Some indus-trial plants were seized and exploited for the extraction of rep-arations by the Soviet Union, which only later relinquished them to the GDR, for the most part years after the formation of the East German state.

After creation of the GDR, the SED regime continued the process of socializing the economy, but at a slower pace and usually by indirect means. The constitution of 1949 specified that expropriation must involve compensation for the former owners, but the regime could avoid such payment by bringing about the transfer of property to state ownership without resort to the formal procedure of expropriation. Since owners of pri-vate farms and businesses had to compete for labor and raw materials on unfavorable terms with government-owned enter-prises and had to sell most of their products at prices controlled by the government, they were vulnerable to crippling harass-ment. They were also required to pay heavy taxes, and if they fell into arrears with payments, their property became subject to foreclosure. By 1952, the private sector of the economy had shrunk to the point where over three-quarters of the industrial workers in the GDR were employed by state-owned enterprises.

Also in 1952, despite disclaimers at the time of the postwar land reform of any intent to socialize agriculture, the SED regime began to exert pressure on private farmers to merge their land into collective farms, which then employed only about 15 percent of the rural population. Farmers proved reluctant, however, to surrender title to their land, which many had gained only as a result of the recent agrarian reform.

These and other policies led to a massive exodus from the GDR. Rather than lose their independence through collectivization, many farmers abandoned their farms and fled to the West, leaving uncultivated land behind them. The mounting difficulties encountered by proprietors of independent businesses led many of them to flee as well. Also departing were those East Germans who could not accept the increasingly stringent ideological constraints on intellectual and cultural activities, the harassment of the churches, or the discriminatory policies regarding admission to higher education. During the years 1949–52 over 675,000 persons from the GDR registered in the West as refugees in need of aid. Still others joined relatives there and did not register, so that the full extent of the exodus from the GDR went unrecorded. Those who did register amounted alone to more than 3.5 percent of the GDR's 1949 population. That represented the highest annual population loss in the world during that period. Since the exodus consisted mainly of young, able-bodied people, its economic consequences bulked even greater than the numbers of those leaving would suggest.

This sustained population drain posed a major handicap to the SED regime's attempt to make the economy of the GDR viable. Even without handicaps, that attempt posed a formidable task. The territory of the new East Germany had long been integrated into the larger economy of the Reich. The predominantly light industries located there had mainly manufactured finished goods made from raw and half-finished materials purchased largely in other parts of Germany or abroad. Those manufactured goods had in turn been sold throughout Germany and the world. Establishing a separate economy for the GDR thus entailed extensive investment in heavy industry and in other essential sectors that had previously remained underdeveloped. Since the Soviet Union ruled out acceptance of Marshall Plan aid from the United States and offered little assistance itself, most of the capital for that investment had to be obtained through a bootstrap operation. That is, a considerable part of production was withheld from consumption so that it could be invested in the development of basic industries. These included steel plants and rolling mills, installations for extracting coke from lignite, and factories to manufacture items such as agricultural tractors, which had previously been mainly obtained from other parts of Germany. Another significant part of current production had to be withheld from consumption and exported to earn the foreign currency needed to purchase raw materials and technical equipment unavailable in the GDR.

From the outset, the economy of the GDR reflected the regime's dependence on the Soviet Union. Through 1953, the USSR exacted heavy reparation payments, placing still another drain on current production. During the GDR's first two years, no less than 25 percent of the gain realized by the regime from industrial production had to be earmarked to cover the costs of reparations and maintenance of Russian troops in East Germany. Trade, which had previously flowed predominantly westward, toward the rest of Germany and Europe, shifted eastward. Coal, for example, which the GDR lacked but could have purchased more cheaply from West Germany, was imported from Siberia at a much higher price. Much industrial production was geared to the needs of the Soviets and shipped eastward, often on terms disadvantageous to the GDR. By 1954 nearly three-quarters of its trade was with the Eastern bloc, which marked a profound redirection of the traditional flow of goods and commodities.

The economy was operated, as in the USSR, through centralized planning and administration. The governmental machinery of the GDR, which politically played only the limited role of enacting and enforcing the decisions of the SED, became for the most part one great monopolistic economic enterprise. Through centralized planning, beginning with a two-year plan for 1949–50 and continuing with a five-year plan for 1951–55, the regime allocated investment capital, distributed scarce resources, administered trade, managed plants and mines, and set prices and wages. Since no constraints of a competitive nature restricted the resulting proliferation of administrative personnel, a luxuriant economic bureaucracy soon developed, imposing still further burdens on the productive parts of the economy.

Despite all these obstacles, the regime made remarkable progress toward realizing the first five-year plan's goal of increasing industrial production by 190 percent between 1951 and 1955. Annual output of steel, which in 1936 had amounted to 1.2 million tons in the parts of Germany that became the GDR but which had stood at only about 10 percent of that level in 1946, increased to 2.1 million tons by 1953. Similarly dramatic advances were achieved in other basic industries, such as chemicals and energy generation. At the end of 1952 the regime announced that overall production had reached 108 percent of the 1936 level. That figure lost some of its luster when compared with the level of 143 percent achieved by then in the Federal Republic. But the GDR's attainment was impressive by virtue of its having pulled its economy upward by its own bootstraps, whereas West Germany's economic miracle had been facilitated by American aid under the Marshall Plan.

The price for these accomplishments was a depressed standard of living for most East Germans, for the growth of heavy industry came at the cost of the wage-earning consumer. Despite the overall growth of the economy by 1953, the output of consumer goods had failed to reach prewar levels. Low wages held purchasing power down, and even where money became available for discretionary spending consumers could choose from only a very limited selection of goods. Housing remained an acute problem for many East Germans forced to continue living in crowded, outmoded dwellings by the regime's slowness in allocating resources and manpower to new construction. Economic experts in the GDR itself estimated the purchasing power of workers' wages in 1950 variously between half and three-quarters of the prewar level. The dearth of consumer items was worsened by the inefficiencies of the centralized planning system, which frequently failed to produce what was planned. The system also proved sluggish in adjusting production to shifts in consumer tastes and needs, so that unwanted goods went on being produced while new needs went unmet. The cumbersome government distribution system repeatedly delivered goods where they were not needed or failed to provide them where they were.

Food became a chronic problem. Problems arising from the expansion of collective farming and from the abandonment of land by farmers who fled to the West rather than submit to collectivization resulted in repeated shortages of foodstuffs. Butter, cooking oil, meat, and sugar remained under rationing controls, as available supplies lagged far behind prewar levels. Imported foods, such as citrus fruits and chocolate, were rarely available, and then only at exorbitant prices, because the regime tightly controlled foreign currency to reserve it for purchases abroad essential to the expansion of industrial plant.

All these difficulties loomed larger when compared with the rapid emergence in the West of an affluent, consumer-oriented economy in which workers' purchasing power steadily increased, enabling them to choose from an expanding array of imported foodstuffs, automobiles, electrical appliances, fashionable clothing, and new, modern dwellings. Travel and correspondence between East and West, as well as Western broadcasts, made it difficult for East Germans not to notice the extent to which, for all the triumphs of the regime's five-year plan, their standard of living lagged far behind that of Germans in the Federal Republic.

Since the SED justified its rule on the grounds that it formed the vanguard of the proletariat, it placed great stress upon winning the loyalty of the GDR's workers. The importance and dignity of manual labor were celebrated ceaselessly in the regime's propaganda. Workers who set new production records received awards and lavish publicity. Athletic organizations and recreational outings offered free leisure activities. Group transportation to Berlin and other cities enabled workers to attend plays and operas with subsidized tickets and take part in special educational tours of museums and art galleries. Free lending libraries and inexpensive, subsidized editions of literary classics promoted reading. A comprehensive welfare state relieved workers of concern about the cost of health care. Guaranteed employment banished the specter of joblessness that still haunted some West German workers during the 1950s. The cost of housing was held down by a government system of rental administration. The construction of new housing, although lagging far behind that in the West, enabled at least some workers who enjoyed good standing with the regime to move into modern quarters. Preferential admission of workers' children to higher education further underlined the GDR's social priorities.

Despite all these measures, worker morale remained a problem. The GDR's laggard standard of living and the chronic shortages of consumer goods and foodstuffs left many workers less than grateful to a regime that claimed to be theirs. Fundamental conflicts of interest also plagued relations between workers and the regime. Only by extracting a maximum of labor at the lowest cost in terms of consumer goods could the regime realize its goal of rapid, bootstrap industrialization. But after years of toil under spartan conditions, many workers felt entitled to immediate material rewards for their labor and became impatient with promises of a bounteous socialist future. Attempts to appease workers by appealing to their idealism and by pitting factories against each other in "socialist competitions" designed to raise production proved of only limited effectiveness.

The absence of any organizations that workers could regard as their own increased the alienation of many. In 1948, even before formation of the GDR, Communist administrators had abolished the elected factory councils spontaneously set up after the war to provide a representative voice with which workers could make their grievances known. Given the choice, workers had tended to elect former Social Democrats or colleagues without party affiliation rather than Communists. As a result, the factory councils frequently proved troublesome obstacles to Communist administrators' efforts to accelerate production regardless of the burdens imposed upon those who provided the labor. The constitution of 1949 guaranteed workers the right to participate through trade unions in decisions regarding production, wages, and the conditions of work. But the unified labor union organization established after the war, the Free German Trade Union League, soon fell, like the SED itself, under Communist domination and became a mere organ of the regime rather than a genuine vehicle of the workers themselves.

Starting in 1951 officials of the SED-controlled trade unions began to present workers with Soviet-style plant contracts. By the terms of those contracts, the workers committed themselves "voluntarily" to increase output, often beyond even the level set by the five-year plan. Their pay was determined by production quotas set by the government, that is, by management. The quotas applied to groups of workers rather than individuals, with bonuses going to members of those groups that exceeded their quotas. This system was designed to provide workers with an incentive to spur on laggard colleagues.

So many workers protested vigorously—in some instances with work stoppages—against the rigorous production quotas set by the new plant contracts of 1951 that the regime had to revise many output schedules downward in order to reduce the labor requirements. In 1952 additional resistance from the workers brought still further concessions on quotas. Some quotas dropped below reasonable production expectations, enabling workers to augment their income substantially by routinely collecting the bonuses available for exceeding the prescribed levels of output. Instead of accurately reflecting the potentialities and limitations of production as originally intended by the planners, the quotas were being set by what amounted to informal bargaining between the regime and the workers in whose interest it claimed to rule.

Unwilling to accept the curtailment of rapid industrial growth which such concessions to workers entailed, Ulbricht and his associates embarked upon a hard-line course. At a party conference of the SED in July 1952 they arranged for adoption of a resolution proclaiming that conditions had reached a point that permitted the GDR to begin "the construction of socialism." In Communist terminology this meant more rapid development of basic industries at the expense of consumer-goods production and improvement in the standard of living. The conference also proclaimed that it was time to move ahead with the further collectivization of agriculture and the absorption of independent tradesmen, such as auto mechanics, plumbers, and other artisans, into cooperatives. In the coming phase of development, the conference warned, a heightening of class conflict would be unavoidable.

The Uprising of June 17, 1953

The course charted at the second party conference in July 1952 soon jeopardized the reign of Ulbricht and seems to have cast doubt, at least briefly, upon the viability of the GDR in the eyes of some of its Soviet patrons. Under heavy criticism from the SED for making too many concessions to workers in the past, the official labor union organization pressed for austerity in the operation of government-owned plants and for establishment of work quotas determined by the realities of productive capacity rather than by worker resistance. In practice, this meant a raising of quotas in the new plant contracts for 1953 and a resulting reduction of worker income. To enforce compliance, the regime instituted a number of show trials at which supervisory workers in government-owned plants were found guilty of sabotage for failing to meet the new production goals. In the countryside government officials exerted pressures designed to bring private farmers to turn their land over to collective farms. Some success was achieved, but the regime's harsh measures also accelerated the exodus to the West. By the end of 1952, nearly 15,000 farmers and their families had fled, leaving about 13 percent of the GDR's arable land untended. As a consequence, food shortages developed.

The problems triggered by the regime's adoption of hard-line policies multiplied throughout late 1952 and early 1953. In attempting to cope with shortages of food, the authorities withdrew ration cards from those who earned their living independently, such as craftsmen, shopkeepers, repairmen, and other small businesspeople. To obtain vital foodstuffs such as butter, cooking oils, meat, and sugar they now had to pay the greatly inflated prices that prevailed outside the rationing system. By way of reducing demand for consumer goods and acquiring additional capital for acceleration of industrial investment, the regime raised prices and increased a number of taxes. A new wave of secret police arrests and political show trials, as well as a purge of Jews in the ranks of the SED on the charge of Zionist sympathies with Israel, added to the atmosphere of repression. The response of many was to flee. In the second half of 1952 some 110,000 East Germans registered as refugees in the West, whereas about 72,000 had done so during the first half, before adoption of the regime's new hard line. During the first half of 1953, some 225,000 followed, a figure that would swell to over 330,000—nearly 2 percent of the total population—by the end of the year. This loss of manpower led to a decline in tax revenues that added to the woes of the economy, and the regime fell behind its schedule for industrial growth.

This mounting crisis came to a head in the spring of 1953. At the time of Soviet dictator Stalin's funeral in March, Minister-President Otto Grotewohl sought to obtain aid from the USSR for the GDR's faltering economy, but in vain. Despite cautionary advice from the new leaders of the Kremlin, Ulbricht and his associates decided to toughen their already hard-line course, invoking Stalin's methods as justification. In mid-May the Central Committee of the SED denied any responsibility for the plight of the economy, blaming instead such "class enemies" as Trotskyites, Zionists, Free Masons, traitors, and morally degenerate individuals. By way of remedy, the Central Committee proposed an increase in work quotas on the average of 10 percent, which amounted to a wage cut of the same extent. At the end of May the Council of Ministers adopted the new quotas and scheduled them to take effect at the end of June, when festivities to celebrate Ulbricht's sixtieth birthday were planned.

Upon learning of these actions, the cautious new collective leadership in the Kremlin intervened and forced the SED regime to beat a retreat. Embarking in early June upon what became known as the New Course, the East Berlin regime rescinded many of the harsh measures of the previous year and promised to improve the living standard of the population. Investments in basic industrial projects were scaled back. Additional funds and resources were allocated to production of consumer goods. Foreclosures on farmland and other private property for delinquent taxes were halted. Credit, seeds, and farm machinery were offered as inducements to attract back farmers who had abandoned their land and fled to the West. Similar enticements were held out to owners who had been forced to close private businesses. Ration cards for foodstuffs once more became available to all citizens. Schools were again opened to students who had been expelled because of their families' political or religious views. Many of those imprisoned in the recent crackdowns were accorded amnesty. New and vigorous efforts to establish ties with West Germany and bring about reunification were pledged. In the course of announcing these measures in early June 1953, the regime confessed to having committed many "errors" in the past.

As did not go unnoticed by many workers in the GDR, the increase in work quotas scheduled to take effect at the end of June remained unaffected by the New Course. Any hope that this might have been an oversight seemed dashed on June 16, when the newspaper of the SED-controlled labor union organization published an editorial stating that the quotas must remain in effect. Despite pressure from Moscow for more moderate policies, the East Berlin regime thus stubbornly upheld the one measure which more than any other had aroused the ire of the very workers whose interests it claimed to place above all else. The result was the uprising of June 17, 1953, the first attempt at revolt within the postwar Soviet bloc.

On the morning of June 16, members of the construction crews at work on the Soviet-style buildings going up along the boulevard Stalinallee in East Berlin laid down their tools. Joined by other workers along the way, they marched to the headquarters of the official labor union organization in the center of the city to protest against the regime's failure to rescind the new, higher work quotas. Finding the union headquarters tightly locked up, the procession of workers, which had by then grown to about 10,000, proceeded to the Council of Ministers building. When they discovered that its doors, too, were barred to them, the swelling crowd of workers stood outside and demanded in chants to speak with Ulbricht and Minister-President Otto Grotewohl.

As the situation grew increasingly tense during the early afternoon, the minister for heavy industry emerged from the beleagured government building to announce that the new work quotas had been rescinded. The initially calming effect of that announcement was, however, dispelled when trucks bearing loudspeakers moved through the streets of East Berlin during the afternoon, broadcasting the text of an obscurely worded Politburo resolution that seemed to leave in question whether the quotas had in fact been rescinded. One of these trucks was commandeered by some of the demonstrators, who used its loudspeaker as the crowd dispersed to issue a call for a general strike the next morning. News of that development reached others in East Berlin that evening through a radio news broadcast from the American sector of the city.

On the morning of June 17, many workers in East Berlin declined to take up their tools. Instead, they gathered at their places of employment, elected strike committees, and marched to the government district, where they took over the city hall and surrounded the headquarters of the regime with a mass of humanity. On the way into the city, they tore down the regime's ubiquitous propaganda posters and billboards. Through Western news broadcasts, workers elsewhere in the GDR learned of developments in East Berlin and joined the strike, which quickly spread to over 200 localities throughout the GDR, especially those where industrial workers were numerous.

Encountering no resistance, the demonstrators in East Berlin began to add political demands to the economic ones that had given rise to the strike. Some shouted that Ulbricht and Grotewohl must step down. Others called for free elections. As the day wore on with no resolution in sight, the crowds, swollen by spectators, some from West Berlin, grew increasingly unruly. The headquarters of the political police in East Berlin was ransacked and then burned. Still other buildings were seized and plundered. Fire was set to kiosks where regime-controlled newspapers and magazines were displayed for sale. Prisoners, including some common criminals, were released from jails. Police agents of the regime were mishandled and, in a few cases, killed. Elsewhere in the GDR similar incidents took place.

From the outset, the crowds lacked any coordinated leadership or practical goals. The demonstrators merely vented their anger on whatever representative or symbol of the regime they found at hand. As a consequence, the uprising had already begun to disintegrate when Russian troops and tanks appeared in East Berlin and other cities throughout the GDR during the afternoon of the seventeenth and dispersed the crowds, in some places forcibly. The next day, the SED regime found itself back in control, thanks to its Soviet patrons. According to official GDR statistics, 21 persons had died, but other evidence suggests a considerably higher toll of fatalities. Afterward, severe retribution followed from the side of the GDR, whose courts sentenced at least 18 persons to death and more than 1300 East Germans to prison terms, some for life.

The uprising dealt the Ulbricht regime a staggering moral and political blow. Officially, East Berlin portrayed the events of June 17 as the result of a fascist, imperialist plot on the part of

Stalinallee, the showpiece of Soviet-style architecture in East Berlin, where construction workers began the protests that set off the uprisings of June 17, 1953, against the East German regime

Demonstrators at the Brandenburg Gate in Berlin during the uprising against the East German regime on June 17, 1953

Young Germans throwing pavement stones at one of the Soviet tanks used to suppress the uprising of June 17, 1953

Washington and Bonn to overthrow the GDR and subjugate East German workers to capitalist exploitation. But the absurdity of that explanation was obvious to those in the GDR who had observed the uprising's spontaneous origins and the lack of any coordinated leadership. Also, the official version failed to explain the inactivity of the West during the uprising and the absence of any Western attempt to interfere with the suppression of the demonstrations by Red Army divisions stationed in the GDR. The official version omitted as well any explanation for the lack of resistance to the uprising among the East German workers who purportedly made up the backbone of the regime. Shortly after the event, the foremost Communist literary figure of East Germany, Bertolt Brecht, gave expression to the sentiments of many in a poem he secretly circulated among his acquaintances after publicly endorsing the regime's suppression of the uprising:

> After the uprising of the 17th June
> The Secretary of the Writers' Union
> Had leaflets distributed in the Stalinallee
> Stating that the people
> Had forfeited the confidence of the government
> And could win it back only
> By redoubled efforts. Would it not be easier
> In that case for the government
> To dissolve the people
> And elect another?

Paradoxically, the uprising of June 17, 1953, had the effect of strengthening the position of Walter Ulbricht and ensuring the survival of the GDR. On the eve of the event, there had been signs that the new leadership in Moscow was considering Ulbricht's replacement, since he had been the main source of resistance to Soviet pressure to modify the harsh policies adopted by the SED in 1952. During the uprising Ulbricht had proved indecisive and ineffectual. Afterward, however, the Russians apparently concluded that removal of the central figure in the East German regime would be viewed as a sign of weakness. Ulbricht was therefore allowed to retain his dominant position.

Prior to the uprising, there had also been intimations that at least some of Stalin's successors in the Kremlin were giving consideration to sacrificing the GDR altogether in exchange for the neutralization and disarmament of Germany as a whole. After nearly five years, grounds certainly existed for doubting the viability of the East German regime and its economy. The danger must have seemed real that the GDR might become a burden instead of an asset for the USSR. But the decision to blame the mass upheaval of June 1953 on a Western plot made it difficult, if not impossible, for Moscow to open negotiations with the West over a new status for all of Germany. The purge, shortly after the uprising, of Lavrenti Beria, the member of the collective leadership in the Kremlin widely believed most inclined to abandonment of the GDR, further reduced the threat to its preservation. In the wake of that development, Ulbricht felt sufficiently emboldened to purge some of his leading critics from the Politburo of the SED. The justice minister, a former SPD member who had, just after the uprising, reaffirmed the constitutional right of workers to strike, was removed from office, expelled from the SED, and imprisoned. Just days after he had seemed doomed, Walter Ulbricht had emerged more fully in command than ever.

The New Course Gives Way to Renewed Repression

Although he remained skeptical about the New Course adopted at the prodding of Moscow's new leadership, Ulbricht upheld that policy line after suppression of the uprising. As a result, the GDR felt some of the effects of what came to be known as the post-Stalin thaw in the USSR. The non-Marxist political parties were allowed greater leeway, at least in their internal affairs. The campaign to dissuade people from attending church and enrolling their children for religious instruction was eased. Ideological constraints were somewhat relaxed so that artists and writers felt less pressure to conform to the formulas of "socialist realism." Despite his sometimes irreverent political utterances and his deviant views on drama, Brecht was assigned a theater in East Berlin for his repertory company and given considerable liberty in its direction. Other Communist intellectuals, among them the young social theorist Wolfgang Harich, began to ask whether the institutions and methods the GDR had taken over from the Stalinist USSR were suitable for realization of a society both socialist and democratic. Hopes for a more humane future that had been dashed a half decade earlier were rekindled.

The New Course also made itself felt in the economic sphere, as the regime recognized the unavoidability of at least some material concessions to the inhabitants of the GDR in the wake of the uprising. Accordingly, priorities were altered to give greater attention to consumer goods, which resulted in a slow-down of investment in basic industries. Measures to force private farmers to join collectivized farms were suspended. So were efforts to force small private firms out of business. Many of the goals of the first five-year plan were in effect abandoned, although the regime would claim fulfillment of the plan in 1955.

The Russians, whose commitment to the GDR had been strengthened by the uprising, came to the aid of Ulbricht and his shaken regime. Previously, the Soviets had contributed to the economic problems of East Germany by extracting heavy reparations. Now they agreed to end all reparations by the beginning of 1954. For the first time, they wrote off debts and extended large-scale credit to East Germany, some of it in convertible currencies usable for purchases of needed resources and machines from the West. They also handed over 33 major industrial plants confiscated after the war and operated by the USSR since then to produce, by way of reparations, goods amounting to about 12 percent of the GDR's overall industrial output. Finally, Moscow reduced the payments imposed upon East Germany to cover the cost of the hundreds of thousands of Soviet troops stationed there.

In addition to this material aid, the USSR upgraded the GDR within the Soviet sphere of influence so as to make its international status appear comparable to that of the Federal Republic. Previously, as a part of the Germany which had invaded and devastated the USSR, the GDR had been relegated to a tightly circumscribed secondary status within the emergent Soviet bloc, so that the SED regime was denied the sort of recognition Moscow extended to its other satellites. Now, in the wake of the regime's survival of the 1953 uprising, that began to change. In March 1954 the USSR proclaimed the GDR a sovereign state. In May 1955 East Germany was included as a charter member in the Warsaw Pact, the Eastern alliance that linked the countries of the Soviet bloc under Russian leadership and subordinated their armed forces to Moscow. A National People's Army, a professional military force whose nucleus was provided by already armed People's Police units, officially came into being in March 1956. The GDR had become an integral part of the Eastern bloc's military system. Since 1950 East Germany had been integrated as well into that bloc's economic system through its trading organization, the Council for Mutual Economic Aid or Comecon. The adoption in 1959 of a new flag that differed from that of the Federal Republic through the superimposition of an emblem consisting of a hammer and draftsman's compass on the black, red, and gold stripes added symbolic emphasis to the regime's efforts to promote a sense of separate identity among the population.

The New Course did not last long in the economic sphere. Less than a year after the uprising, the regime began to shift its economic priorities once again toward rapid industrialization at the expense of wage-earning consumers. A second five-year plan, covering 1956–60, closely resembled the first plan in its overall thrust. Independent farmers once more came under pressure to turn over their land to agricultural collectives. Plumbers, mechanics, and other craftsmen found it increasingly difficult to maintain their independence, so that many joined the artisan cooperatives sponsored by the regime. Private businessmen encountered similar difficulties, with the result that increasing numbers abandoned their businesses while others entered into joint ventures with government enterprises that put an end to their independence.

The regime also soon resumed its attacks on the churches. Beginning in 1954, membership in the official young people's organization became contingent upon participation in a secular "youth consecration" ceremony that amounted to a negation of religious values. The Protestant church, to which the vast majority of religious East Germans belonged, objected to the atheistic content of this ceremony, which the regime sought to make obligatory for all, and withheld religious confirmation from youths who participated. When the regime retaliated by denying admission to higher education to those who received religious confirmation, the church had to back down, however. In 1955 the educational authorities sought to diminish the influence of religion by banning Christian student groups from the universities. The SED regime also objected to the organizational links between the Protestant churches in the two Germanies, which served as a reminder of the country's past unity. The religious authorities resisted pressures to sever that link until 1969, when they finally gave in on that point and constituted the Eastern church as a separate body. But the quiet struggle of will between churchmen and the atheistic regime would continue throughout the duration of the GDR.

Ulbricht's stock soared in Moscow when the GDR proved impervious to the wave of rebelliousness that shook much of the Soviet bloc during 1956 and culminated in the bloody, unsuccessful Hungarian revolution that autumn. Thus strengthened, he settled scores with critics in the leadership of the SED who objected to his doctrinaire imposition of Soviet patterns on the GDR. Branding them as an "anti-party group," he succeeded in stripping those critics of their government and party offices and relegated them to insignificant positions. His dominance received formal expression in 1960 when he became chairman of a newly created National Defense Council. Later that year, following the death of President Wilhelm Pieck, he assumed chairmanship of a newly created State Council elected by, and responsible to, the People's Chamber. Through constitutional amendment, the presidency was abolished and its functions, along with others, were assigned to the State Council, making it the nerve center of the government apparatus that carried out the policies of the SED. After a decade of sometimes precarious dominance, Walter Ulbricht had secured for himself a position of what seemed unassailable paramountcy atop both party and government.

Repression also increased in the cultural and intellectual spheres. The campaign of de-Stalinization launched by Soviet leader Nikita Khrushchev had never appreciably curtailed the police state apparatus of the SED regime, so that the crackdown amounted to only an intensification of standard practices. Still, heavy blows fell upon the intellectual community in the GDR. The social theorist Wolfgang Harich, who had become an admirer of Tito's heterodox Communist regime in Yugoslavia, was arrested in November 1956 and sentenced to ten years' imprisonment the following year for allegedly conspiring to alter the social order of the GDR by threat of force. Numerous less well known persons also went behind bars. For many artists and writers the regime's heightened insistence on conformity to the party line meant the end of hopes raised by the New Course. Some chose to stay on, even if, as in the case of writers, they could hope to make their works known only by smuggling them to the West. Some gave up and migrated westward, so that much promising creative talent was lost. Engineers, physicians, and scientists along with other highly skilled professionals also left as the migration of hundreds of thousands of East Germans to the Federal Republic via the open borders of Berlin continued throughout the latter part of the 1950s.

Despite the repressive methods of the Ulbricht regime, the GDR made notable progress economically. Sustained investment in basic industries began to yield results. Industrial and handicraft production, which had accounted for 43.7 percent of the total in 1950, rose to 53 percent by 1960. Agricultural output, which had stood at 30.8 percent of the whole in 1950, shrank to

18 percent in the expanded economy of 1960. By 1958 the regime was able to end the last remnants of food rationing, but only by depressing demand through higher prices. Consumer goods became less difficult to find, although those available still often failed to please the public. By the latter part of the decade, the 45-hour workweek had become general in state industries, an achievement that paled only slightly in view of the fact that West German industrial workers had, with rare exceptions, already achieved the 40-hour workweek and enjoyed significantly greater purchasing power with which to choose from a larger selection of higher-quality goods. Such knowledge, along with antireligious measures and ideological repression, continued to feed the yearly exodus of thousands upon thousands of GDR residents to the West via the open borders in Berlin. During 1960 nearly 200,000 persons from East Germany officially registered with West German authorities as refugees, while an unknown number of others settled in the West without claiming that status.

Increasingly, the ire of the Ulbricht regime focused on West Berlin. Simply by arriving there on foot or by public transportation from East Berlin, residents of the GDR could gain immediate recognition as West German citizens and fly to the Federal Republic, where a new life awaited them. This exodus imposed a costly drain on the Eastern economy, since most of those who left were young, skilled people. It also imposed limits on how much the regime could require of those who remained but had the ready option of leaving. For many years the regime appears to have seriously hoped to end the flow to the West by realizing its promises to provide a higher standard of living and a more just society than could be found in the Federal Republic. But by the late 1950s that goal seemed as remote as ever. The regime and its patrons in Moscow therefore focused their attention on Berlin in the knowledge that so long as the four-power status of the old German capital kept the border between East and West open, there would be no way to halt the outward flow of humanity that had become so damaging and embarrassing.

In November 1958 Soviet leader Nikita Khrushchev issued an

ultimatum to Britain, France, the United States, and the Federal Republic: Unless the Berlin problem were solved within six months, the USSR would sign a peace treaty with the GDR and turn over to it responsibility for West Berlin, which Khrushchev claimed lay on the territory of the GDR. Surrounded by Soviet and East German troops, West Berlin would become a demilitarized "free city," emptied of occupying powers, and the West Germans would have to negotiate with the GDR (the existence of which Bonn did not recognize) for access to it. Conflict, possibly even war, between the USSR and the Western powers over Berlin seemed imminent. But when the West ignored Khrushchev's ultimatum, it proved a bluff, for the Soviets took no action against West Berlin. Instead, the Berlin crisis flared and subsided repeatedly at the verbal level over the next three years as the Russians issued new threats, each time occasioning concern about a great-power conflict over the former German capital.

The Berlin Wall

Within the GDR developments were taking shape that contributed to the climax of this second postwar Berlin crisis. Beginning in late 1959 the regime launched a massive drive to collectivize the remainder of privately owned farmland. By mid-1960 only a small fraction of those who had been independent farmers only months earlier retained title to their land. At least 15,000 deserted their farms and fled to the West rather than submit to collectivization. Their departure, along with the dislocations occasioned by a wholesale reorganization of much of the GDR's already collectivized agriculture, led to another major food shortage when the 1960 crops fell far short of expectations. That, in combination with another escalation of Khrushchev's threatening rhetoric about West Berlin in the spring and summer of 1961, produced a panicky flight from the GDR of persons fearing that the option to leave would soon disappear. The exodus reached proportions not seen since 1953. By the second week of August, more than

Refugees fleeing East Berlin through an apartment house at the border to West Berlin at the time of the Berlin Wall's construction by the East German regime in August 1961

155,000 residents of the GDR had registered in the West as refugees since the beginning of 1961. That brought the total of those who had fled Communist rule since the end of the war to over three million, or one out of every six persons in the part of Germany occupied by the USSR in 1945.

At that point, in the early morning hours of August 13, 1961, the regime moved to stanch the population hemorrhage by sealing East Berlin off from West Berlin. Under the guns of the People's Police, workmen blocked with barbed wire entanglements the many street crossings between the two parts of the city. GDR guards permitted passage at only a handful of points, turning back all Germans from East and West who lacked the SED regime's permission to cross. The fortifications that would soon grow into the Berlin Wall went up all around West Berlin, more than a hundred miles in length, sealing off access from the East. The few telephone lines in operation between East and West Berlin were severed. Transport between the two parts of the city by subway and elevated trains was closed down with the exception of one transit point, which was tightly policed by the East to prevent unauthorized departures to the West. In contrast to the blockade of 1948–49, no move was made to interfere with the overland transit routes or rail service between West Berlin and the Federal Republic. Military and civilian personnel of the occupying powers continued to pass between East and West Berlin, but only at a few crossing points.

During the weeks and months that followed erection of the wall the rest of the world was witness to numerous frantic escape attempts by East Germans. When buildings in East Berlin bordering on western parts of the city became escape routes, the doors and ground-floor windows were bricked up. Desperate East Germans then began leaping into West Berlin from upper-story windows and roofs, usually into nets held below by West Berlin firemen but sometimes to injury and even death. As a result, the buildings were sealed off entirely and then demolished. Soon the eastern side of the wall was rimmed by a desolate strip of land containing only multiple barbed wire fences, watchdog runs, searchlights, and towers manned by armed guards with instructions to shoot to kill anyone attempting to flee. Similar barriers were erected to bolster the GDR's border with the Federal Republic. Some East Germans managed to surmount these obstacles to reach the West, but others were shot by zealous border guards. Still others escaped through tunnels laboriously and secretively excavated beneath the wall in Berlin.

Escape became progressively more difficult and hazardous as the GDR authorities discovered gaps in their inward-facing fortifications and closed them. Desperate East Germans nevertheless continued to seek ways out. In 1962 West German authorities recorded 5,761 successful escapes, and in 1963 a high point of 6,692 was reached. Thereafter the number declined, reaching the level of a few hundred each year by the 1980s. The SED regime re-

To thwart escape attempts after the closing of the border between East and West Berlin on August 13, 1961, the GDR authorities blocked with barbed wire the first-floor windows of apartment buildings in East Berlin that looked into West Berlin. When that failed to halt the flight, the windows were bricked up. Arbeitsgemeinschaft 13. August e.V.

In August 1961, after GDR authorities bricked up the first-floor windows of East Berlin buildings that looked into West Berlin, some East Berliners escaped through upper-floor windows by jumping into nets held, as here, by West Berlin firemen. The regime responded by sealing up the windows on all floors, but when would-be refugees continued to flee by jumping from the roofs—some to their deaths—the buildings were demolished altogether. Arbeitsgemeinschaft 13. August e.V.

Windows and doors of apartment houses at the border between East and West Berlin, bricked up by the East German regime to prevent their use by refugees as an escape route after construction of the Berlin Wall in August 1961

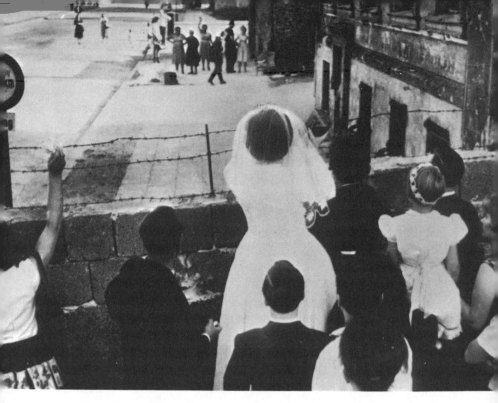

A newly married couple waving to relatives across the Berlin Wall soon after
its construction

leased no statistics on thwarted escapes, but gunfire as well as the
explosion of land mines and other automatic explosive devices
at the Berlin Wall and along the border with West Germany left
little doubt that these were numerous. In all, more than two hundred East German citizens would die at the Berlin Wall and the
fortifications along the GDR's border with the Federal Republic.

Construction of the Berlin Wall revealed that the Soviets had,
at least for the time being, abandoned their designs on West Berlin and decided instead merely to allow the Ulbricht regime to
contain the population of the GDR. In that, the move proved successful. When the Western powers failed to obstruct erection of
the wall, the flood of refugees diminished to a trickle. The price
was hardship for countless innocent persons. Thousands of fam-

ilies found themselves separated by an impassable barrier. Those with relatives on the opposite side could see them only by exchanging waves over the wall and across the no-man's-land on its eastern side that prevented approach by citizens of the GDR, now prisoners of their own government. By way of justifying its measures, the Ulbricht regime announced that construction of an "anti-fascist, protective wall" had proved necessary to halt infiltration by Western agents preparatory to a planned military assault on the GDR by West Germany. Observers noted, however, that the new fortifications were designed to thwart approach primarily from the East rather than from the West and that the Federal Republic had no troops in West Berlin.

The wall between East and West Berlin not only reduced the flood of refugees but also represented a step toward solution of another major problem of the Ulbricht regime. Previously, its capital in East Berlin lay, legally speaking, outside of the territory of the GDR, which comprised what had been the Soviet occupation zone. This anomalous situation existed because of the four-power status of the old German capital under the terms of the occupation agreements. The Russians had continued to respect at least some of those agreements in order to assert their occupation rights in West Berlin, which included providing military guards for a Soviet war memorial and a prison for Nazi war criminals, both in the British sector of the city. They had therefore hitherto restrained the GDR from incorporating East Berlin into its territory, even though in actuality the USSR had long since turned over administration of its sector of the city to the Ulbricht regime. With the construction of the wall, the regime could now, with the permission of the Soviets (who nevertheless continued to exercise their rights in West Berlin), lay claim to authority over its own capital city.

That claim was promptly recognized by the other Communist-ruled countries, but the Americans, British, and French refused to do so. They made a point of asserting their rights throughout the old capital by sending into East Berlin Western occupation personnel who refused to recognize the authority of

American tanks (foreground) confronting Soviet tanks (above) at Checkpoint Charlie in Berlin following the East German regime's erection of the wall separating the two parts of the former German capital in 1961

East German border officials and would deal only with Russians. When the Russians absented themselves at the border, the Western powers acquiesced to the extent of allowing their officials to show their credentials to GDR guards through closed car windows upon entering East Berlin. During the winter of 1961–62 this situation brought the world perilously close to a war between the superpowers when altercations at Checkpoint Charlie, the principal crossing point between the two parts of the city for western vehicles, led to a prolonged confrontation of American and Soviet tanks separated only by a few dozen yards of pavement. In the end, however, a modus vivendi was worked out, and the tension subsided. Henceforth the SED regime governed East Berlin as an integral part of the GDR, despite the

Western powers' continuing assertion that it legally remained under four-power occupation. The Berlin crisis, which originally had arisen with regard to the status of West Berlin, thus ended in at least partial alleviation of the handicap posed for the GDR by the special status of East Berlin.

While the Berlin Wall exacted a heavy toll in human misery and became the scene of numerous escape attempts that ended in death, its construction facilitated stabilization of the GDR. Previously, the regime had been forced, by its need for labor, to tolerate a great deal of complaining and malingering in order to minimize defections to the West. Now it could crack down on dissent without fear of such consequences. Slacking on the job in government-run enterprises became a punishable crime, and prison sentences were imposed upon some convicted of that offense, obviously as an example to others. In factories and other places of work throughout the GDR, the SED orchestrated "discussions" designed to identify malcontents and convince them of the error of their ways. Party activists began a campaign to effect "voluntary" increases in work quotas, which rose on the average of 5 percent within months. Brigades of Free German Youth groups identified television antennas aimed toward Western transmitters and put pressure on their owners to reorient them to receive only the programs of the SED-controlled channels. Ideological constraints on the arts and scholarship were again tightened. The wall also made it possible to strengthen the GDR militarily, for with the escape route through West Berlin sealed off, the regime could for the first time institute conscription for the National People's Army without fear that draftees would flee westward. A law to that effect, obliging all able-bodied young men to perform military service for eighteen months, took effect in January 1962. Beginning in 1964, those unwilling to bear arms for reasons of conscience were allowed to serve in army construction units. No alternative civilian service similar to that in the West was permitted, and those who refused to don a military uniform became subject to prosecution and imprisonment.

The Berlin Wall

The New Economic System and the Second Constitution

The effects of the wall soon became evident in the economic sphere. For the first time, the regime could make labor allocations for the economy without having to reckon with the constant, yet unpredictable, loss of skilled workers and supervisors. No longer would an appreciable part of its investment in education drain away, since the option for young people to leave for jobs in the West after completing their schooling in the East had, except for the most venturesome and determined few, disappeared.

After this stabilization of the labor force, the regime struggled with a succession of experiments in an effort to extract better performance from the economy. In 1962 it announced abandonment of a seven-year plan which had been launched with great fanfare in 1959 with the goal of nearly doubling production in key sectors of industry but which had fallen far behind schedule. In an effort to eliminate the heavy-handed inflexibility of the central planning system, Ulbricht in 1963 proclaimed implementation of a New Economic System (which he renamed the Economic System of Socialism four years later). Far greater discretionary authority than ever before was assigned to individual productive plants, whose performance was now measured in terms of profitability rather than the mere quantity of goods produced. Managers of those plants no longer had to accept whatever materials and equipment the plan assigned to them but could shop for the best available quality and the most favorable terms. Plants in the same sectors of production were encouraged to join together to form "socialist concerns" that would cooperate to increase output. Market mechanisms such as interest rates and prices that at least partially reflected supply and demand were introduced in an effort to provide some self-regulation of the economy. The role of central planning was to be restricted, according to the new system, to establishment of overall goals and allocation of scarce materials. Individual managers whose plants registered profits received bonuses and extra vacations. The New Economic System proved difficult to manage, and the constant adjustments it required kept the administrative organs in turmoil. But it did loosen up the rigid bureaucratic structure of the East German economy somewhat and encourage individual initiative and innovation on the part of managers of state-owned plants.

The New Economic System never functioned as envisioned, but it did work well enough to produce what came to be known as the "other German economic miracle." During the 1960s the industrial economy of the GDR became, in terms of per capita productivity, the strongest in the Eastern bloc. The peak achievements came in the period 1964–67, when the regime claimed a growth rate in national income of 5 percent and in industrial output of 7 percent. Although those figures were regarded in the West as inflated, virtually all observers were impressed at the performance of the GDR's economy. In terms of the standard of living, the GDR outstripped the USSR and its client states in Eastern Europe. Basic foods became available at prices wage-earners could afford, although the centralized distribution system still gave rise to annoying shortages from time to time.

Even though the GDR still lagged behind the Federal Republic in the production of consumer goods, it began to appease the hunger of its citizens for material conveniences. Whereas in the 1950s private automobiles had been virtually unknown, by 1969, when 47 percent of the households in the Federal Republic owned a car, 14 percent in the GDR had acquired a vehicle despite inflated prices and waiting periods of years for delivery. Only 6 percent of East German households had possessed refrigerators in 1960, but by 1969 the figure had risen to 48 percent, as compared to 84 percent in West Germany. Also by 1969, 48 percent of households in the GDR owned washing machines, whereas the figure for the Federal Republic was 61 percent. Two-thirds of East German households, as contrasted to nearly three-quarters in the West, had acquired television sets by that time.

Increased access to television created problems for the SED regime, as it brought with it in most parts of the GDR exposure to broadcasts from West Berlin and the Federal Republic. The attempts of the regime to discourage viewers from watching Western broadcasts soon proved in vain. In addition to giving East Germans an alternative source of information about the world, those broadcasts provided compelling visual reminders of the extent to which the economy of the GDR lagged behind that of the West in the production of affordable consumer goods. That in turn served as a goad to the SED regime to make more and better goods available.

East Germans also became better dressed and enjoyed more leisure time. More clothing than ever before was produced, and both the quality and the range of choice grew. With the workweek reduced to five days in state industries by 1967, people now had more time to enjoy the fruits of their labors. In terms of the hours of work necessary to pay for consumer items, however, citizens of the GDR still had to toil considerably longer for what they acquired than did West Germans, who continued to enjoy a greater choice among better-quality goods. The length of vacations was also increased, but for citizens of the GDR vacation trips abroad still had to be limited to Soviet-bloc countries. The prohibition on travel to Western countries, including West Berlin and the Federal Republic, became a source of chronic discontent.

After a crackdown on dissenters and deviationists following the erection of the Berlin Wall, the regime somewhat relaxed its controls over artists and writers during the 1960s. The Stalinist style of architecture gave way to venturesome experiments with what was known in the West as "the international style." Abstract works of art and experimental theater found greater toleration. Some interesting books and plays came out of an undertaking endorsed by Ulbricht at a writers' gathering in the town of Bitterfeld in 1959. This "Bitterfeld movement" called upon writers to experience the lot of workers by laboring for a time in factories or on collective farms before writing about contemporary life. The movement also sought to encourage workers to take up writing themselves, but little came of that.

For a brief period, talented and serious writers in the GDR found the regime willing to allow them to deal with life there honestly. Symptomatic was the novel *Divided Heaven*, published in 1963 by Christa Wolf. It gave expression to the painful dilemmas that honest, hard-working East Germans faced in deciding whether or not to flee to the West, and also accurately depicted some of the shortcomings in the GDR that had led so many to leave. Wolf's book, along with some others by younger East German writers, quickly won acclaim in both parts of Germany. By late 1965, however, another of the recurrent ideological freezes began to set in. Venturesome writers again encountered difficulties in getting their works published in the GDR or ran afoul of the regime's ideological watchmen when they expressed themselves in heterodox fashion. Much of the best writing produced in East Germany could still be published only in the Federal Republic.

By the latter half of the 1960s Walter Ulbricht dominated the GDR as never before. As first secretary of the SED, chairman of the State Council and of the National Defense Council, he brought together in his hands the key posts in the one-party dictatorship. By using his control of personnel matters in the SED to reward those loyal to him, he ensured the subservience to him of the "nomenklatura," the privileged elite which filled the top party and government jobs.

Ulbricht also began to assert a claim to ideological leadership in the Communist world. In 1967 he formulated a new interpretation of what was known in Marxist-Leninist doctrine as "socialism." Soviet theoreticians had long held that socialism would prove a brief transitional phase between the class-conflict-ridden society of capitalism and the future classless society of communism, in which the state would wither away. Ulbricht challenged that position by contending that socialism—which the GDR claimed to be constructing—amounted to a distinct phase of history in its own right. It could be expected—along with a continuing role for the state—to last for some time, he asserted. His version had the virtue of providing an explanation for the persistence of socioeconomic inequalities and the continuing dominance of the bureaucracy. Not content with speaking out independently on doctrinal matters customarily left to Moscow, he also suggested that the GDR could serve as a model for other Communist-ruled countries, another role previously reserved for the USSR. In boasting that East Germany had achieved a "developed socialist society," Ulbricht seemed to infer that the GDR had surpassed the other countries in the Soviet bloc, including the "motherland of the revolution."

By 1968 Ulbricht felt sufficiently secure to seek institutionalization of his rule through adoption of a new constitution for the GDR. That document reflected the many changes in governmental structure that had taken place since 1949, when the first constitution had been put into effect. The new document aban-

doned the fiction that the GDR was a politically neutral, democratic entity. Instead, it proclaimed the GDR to be "a socialist
state of the German nation." The SED-controlled National Front
received constitutional recognition as the sole organ through
which the political parties and so-called mass organizations
shaped the development of socialist society. The parliament, the
People's Chamber, remained, but the new document contained
nothing that would enable it to function as anything other than
the obedient rubber stamp of the SED it had always been. The
provision in the 1949 constitution for elections by proportional
representation disappeared, so that the unity list system of balloting no longer violated the constitution. The Council of Ministers, the cabinet installed by the People's Chamber, was down-
graded, becoming an organ for the implementation of policy.
The head of the cabinet no longer enjoyed the title minister-
president, becoming merely chairman of the Council of Ministers. At the top of the government the new constitution placed
the Council of State, the body which Ulbricht had chaired since
its founding in 1960. Its chairman and his deputies were to be
installed by vote of the People's Chamber. Policy-making authority resided with it rather than with the Council of Ministers. The
Council of State was to represent the GDR internationally and
nominate the chairman of the Council of Ministers. Between the
infrequent and brief sessions of the People's Chamber, the Council of State was empowered to carry out "all fundamental tasks."

The most striking feature of the 1968 constitution lay in its
elimination or diminution of the generous guarantees of citizens' rights contained in the old constitution. While the new
document echoed the earlier assurances about freedom of
speech, the press, peaceful assembly, and religious practice, it
qualified those freedoms with the proviso that they must be
exercised in harmony with the principles of the new constitution. In practice, that proviso enabled the regime to restrict
freedom in those spheres whenever it chose. The right to emigrate disappeared altogether. So did the right to strike. Work
now became not only a right but also a duty. The regime-con-

trolled trade unions achieved constitutional recognition as the sole permissible organs for representation of workers. In these and other provisions the realities of Walter Ulbricht's GDR found expression in the constitution of 1968. Put to the populace in a referendum, it received, according to official statistics, a surprisingly low affirmative vote by GDR standards: 94.5 percent. In East Berlin the figure was only 90.9 percent.

During the so-called Prague Spring of 1968, when Communist reformers in Czechoslovakia ended censorship and began to dismantle that country's system of closed bureaucratic rule, Ulbricht's regime consistently attacked the reformers across its southern border and cowed sympathizers at home. When, in August 1968, the USSR put an end to the Czech experiment by instigating a Warsaw Pact invasion, East German troops marched across that border and took part in the occupation alongside troops from the Soviet Union and its client states in Eastern Europe. Under Ulbricht's leadership the GDR seemed to have developed into a model "people's democracy," unshakably loyal to the USSR.

Despite the apparently unassailable position that Ulbricht had come to occupy atop the GDR by 1968, he fell from power only three years later. The grounds for his removal were shrouded in the secrecy with which the Communists of East Germany and the Soviet Union cloaked their political affairs, but a number of factors seem to have played a role. At home, Ulbricht's policies gave rise to uneasiness within the leadership of the SED. His increasing allocation of authority to the Council of State, an organ of the government, appears to have aroused apprehension among party officials, for whom that development represented a threat to the political paramountcy of the SED over the state. In the economic sphere Ulbricht's championship of greater autonomy for the technical managers who directed the factories and other units of the economy that actually produced goods seems to have produced similar dissatisfaction in the upper reaches of the SED, which had been accustomed to party control over economic policy. A different sort of concern arose from Ulbricht's growing preoccupation with achieving a dramatic technological breakthrough that would permit the GDR to leapfrog beyond the Federal Republic economically. His pursuit of that goal involved the diversion of a mounting portion of the regime's investment capacity into ambitious research and development projects in new fields such as cybernetics, an undertaking which many in the SED hierarchy regarded as wasteful and unrealistic. Setbacks in other areas of the economy further heightened doubts about the party leader's judgment.

Although difficulties at home may have facilitated Ulbricht's removal, a great deal of evidence indicates that he ultimately fell because he had lost favor with his patrons in Moscow. His claim to originality in the sphere of ideology, as expressed in his theory of a distinctly socialist phase of history, seems to have proved offensive to some in the leadership of the USSR, which had grown accustomed to unchallenged ideological preeminence in the Soviet bloc. Ulbricht's attempts to present the GDR as a model for other Communist-ruled countries appears also to have encountered hostility in the ruling circles of the USSR. Still another factor in Moscow's disenchantment with Ulbricht apparently lay in his ill-concealed misgivings about the implications for the GDR of the thaw in relations between the USSR and the Federal Republic that set in at the end of the 1960s.

When the Soviet axe finally fell in the spring of 1971, the seventy-eight-year-old Ulbricht was permitted a dignified exit. In a speech before the Central Committee of the SED in May 1971 he requested to be relieved of his position as head of the party on grounds of failing health. Stripped of his power although allowed to retain the title of chairman of the Council of State, he died in obscurity in 1973. Only forty-eight days after his demise, following a period of conspicuous hesitancy, did the new regime in the GDR provide a state funeral for the man who, more than any other, had shaped East Germany and preserved it against the many perils that beset it during its early years. In the official announcements, no mention appeared of the presence at the funeral of a Soviet representative.

4
Two Decades of Christian Democratic Leadership in the Federal Republic

The Ascendancy of Konrad Adenauer

In contrast to the manipulated electoral process in the East, voters in the first election for a West German Bundestag could choose among an array of genuinely competing parties. On election day in August 1949, 78.5 percent of the eligible voters took part in the first fully free balloting beyond the regional level since 1932. When the results were tallied, close to a dozen political parties had gained representation in the new Bundestag. Only a few of these were strong enough to become politically significant. The largest bloc of seats, 139, went to the Christian Democratic Union (CDU) and its Bavarian affiliate, the Christian Social Union (CSU). Next in strength came the Social Democratic Party of Germany (SPD) with 131 seats. The Free Democratic Party (FDP) gained 52. Two regional parties, the Bavarian Party and the German Party (which found its principal support in the northern part of the country), captured 17 seats each. The Communists won 15 seats. The remaining 31 were scattered among splinter parties.

The central issue of this crucial election campaign was the economic system already established in Bizonia and then extended to Trizonia, which basically relied on free enterprise. The venerable SPD, the party with the largest membership and the most fully developed organization, criticized that system as a return to a discredited past and called for extensive socialization of the economy. At a time when the shock of the sweeping expropriations carried out in the Soviet zone in the name of socialism was still fresh, this stand proved a handicap to efforts by the Social Democrats to supplement their traditional blue-collar constituency with middle-class support. The young CDU/ CSU, which had abandoned its early receptivity to at least some socialization, identified itself with the existing economic system, which its leadership had largely shaped. The CDU/CSU captured most Catholic voters, who made up roughly half of the electorate, including many wage-earners, but in parts of the country it also fared well with Protestants. With a following that spanned employees and employers, farmers and urban middle-class persons, the CDU/CSU had emerged as a "people's party" that transcended the barriers of class and religion that had traditionally fragmented the German party system. The third-strongest party, the FDP, held to classical liberal, laissez-faire economic principles, defended the rights of the individual in all spheres, and opposed the religious involvement in public education fostered by the CDU/CSU. The FDP's votes came mainly from middle-class Protestants, particularly from businessmen and professionals, for whose support it competed with the CDU/CSU.

The composition of the first cabinet of the Federal Republic proved of decisive importance for its formative years. As quickly became apparent, the SPD's socialistic economic program ruled out a coalition between that party and the FDP. The Social Democratic leadership therefore favored a cabinet based on a so-called grand coalition of SPD and CDU/CSU that would command an overwhelming majority in the Bundestag. A similar coalition had shaped the postwar Austrian republic, and some

Christian Democratic leaders favored such an arrangement in West Germany, too. Within the CDU/CSU, however, those prevailed who favored a narrower majority based on a coalition consisting of the CDU/CSU, the FDP, and the German Party. The SPD thus became the opposition. With the help of the CDU/CSU, the FDP's candidate, Theodor Heuss, who had sat as a liberal democratic deputy in the parliament of the Weimar Republic, was elected the first federal president. On Heuss's nomination, Konrad Adenauer of the CDU then received the absolute majority in the Bundestag necessary for election as chancellor on the first ballot by a margin of one vote—his own.

At the time of his election, the seventy-three-year-old Adenauer was widely expected to serve only as a stop-gap chancellor who would soon give way to a younger successor. Yet he was to execute that office vigorously for fourteen years, two years longer than Hitler had headed his Third Reich and as long as the entire duration of the Weimar Republic. A Rhinelander, Adenauer was a product of the German Catholic political tradition and a veteran of the Catholic Center Party of the pre-Nazi period. He had become lord mayor of his hometown of Cologne during the last years of the Empire and held that post until the Nazis ousted him in 1933. Although he had occupied a seat in the Weimar Republic's Reichsrat (the precursor of the Bundesrat) and had briefly been considered for the chancellorship in 1926, he had remained a provincial politician. His career seemed terminated by the Third Reich, when he retired to his country home. But in 1945 the British, in whose occupation zone Cologne lay, reinstalled him in the city hall, only to dismiss him within months because of insubordination. That dismissal freed Adenauer to play a key role in the formation of the CDU and enabled him to build a political following throughout the Western zones of occupation. He gained further recognition when he chaired, by virtue of his seniority, the Parliamentary Council that drew up the Basic Law. Once installed in the chancellorship, Adenauer assumed firm command and in countless ways influenced the formative stages of the new Western republic. A

Ludwig Erhard, West German economics minister (1949–63) and chancellor (1963–66), with Konrad Adenauer (chancellor, 1949–63)

shrewd but undramatic person, he provided an authoritative yet low-key leadership that corresponded to the needs of a people who had so recently experienced a disastrous regime that ceaselessly indulged in theatrics and sought in every conceivable way to whip up fanaticism. Most West Germans proved ready to rely upon the calm, grandfatherly figure who soon became popularly known as "the old man" (der Alte).

By appointing Ludwig Erhard as his economics minister, Adenauer set the course for the Federal Republic's economic and social development. As chief architect of the economic policies of Bizonia and, later, Trizonia, Erhard had rejected demands for a planned economy and a government takeover of basic industries put forward by the Social Democrats and echoed even by some Christian Democrats during the early postwar years. He insisted that economic planning would inevitably spawn a crushing bureaucracy that would stifle individual initiative and impose, through its cost, a drain on resources better applied to productive purposes. Developments in East Germany, which was following just such a course at the expense of the population's standard of living, lent force to Erhard's analysis. Instead of a government-administered economy, he advocated what came to be known as *soziale Marktwirtschaft*, which can best be translated as welfare-state capitalism. His formula left the means of production in private hands and allowed market mechanisms to set price and wage levels. The prospect of profit, Erhard maintained, provided the best incentive for efficiency and productivity. He recognized, however, that not everyone had an equal opportunity to partake of profit. He therefore advocated governmental intervention through welfare-state measures to assure an equitable distribution of the productivity generated by the pursuit of profit. Otherwise, his formula called for government to limit itself to indirect influence on economic activity through the sort of monetary, taxation, and trade measures common to Western countries.

In line with Erhard's formula, the new government adhered to a policy of liberating private enterprise from most of the restrictions imposed upon it by the Third Reich and the occupation regime. Tax laws and other forms of legislation affecting business were rewritten to encourage investment and risk-taking. In an effort to assure open and fair competition, the Federal Republic departed from the practice of past German governments by attempting to combat cartels and other business combinations designed to limit production and manipulate prices. Direct government participation in the economy was kept to a minimum. Indirectly, government played a major role, however, through promotion of international competition by means of liberalized tariffs and other policies facilitating foreign trade.

Along with these steps to promote free enterprise came measures that soon made the Federal Republic into one of the world's most elaborate and encompassing welfare states. Building upon a tradition that reached back to Bismarck's time, government social insurance coverage was expanded for the elderly, the disabled, and the unemployed. A comprehensive system of government-regulated health insurance provided the ill with medical attention and hospitalization. Government subsidies helped with the cost of providing for children and supplemented the rental payments of those who could not otherwise afford decent housing. Generous public financing of privately built apartment buildings spurred the rapid construction of desperately needed dwellings to replace those destroyed or damaged by the war. To correct inequalities resulting from the war, inflation, and the takeover of eastern German territories by Poland and the Soviet Union, "burden-sharing" legislation enacted in 1952 transferred purchasing power from those who had emerged from the upheavals of the recent past economically unscathed to those who had suffered severe losses because of events beyond their control. In terms of the percentage of gross national product allocated by the government to such welfare-state measures, the Federal Republic ranked at the forefront internationally among the world's democracies, alongside the Scandinavian countries.

The Economic Miracle

The application of Erhard's formula of welfare-state capitalism produced such a rapid and sweeping recovery that it became known as the West German *Wirtschaftswunder* or economic miracle. The foundations had been laid during the interval of Bizonia and Trizonia, when Erhard had begun to shape the Western economy. The removal of most price controls after the monetary reform of 1948 brought a flood of goods onto the market, where long-deprived consumers eagerly sought them. The stability of the new currency, which was controlled by an autonomous central bank (soon to be named the Bundesbank) spurred saving and investment. Large-scale infusions of American aid under the Marshall Plan supplemented domestic capital formation. The flow of refugees from the East provided an abundant reservoir of labor to replace wartime losses. In a new spirit of cooperation, organized labor and management collaborated to reduce the loss of productivity through strikes to a level far below that of other West European countries. Restraint on the part of the trade unions with regard to wages helped to keep the price of German goods highly competitive in international markets. Added stimulation came from the so-called Korean War boom that began in 1950. To the astonishment of virtually everyone, a West Germany whose factories had sat idle only a few years earlier quickly emerged once more as a beehive of productive economic activity. Overall output (*Bruttosozialprodukt*) leapt upward at an average annual rate of 8.2 percent in the years 1950–54 and 7.1 percent in the years 1955–58.

The economic miracle transformed the lives of the Federal Republic's citizens. West Germans again had enough to eat and could afford new clothes, shoes, and household goods. Millions of new housing units replaced those destroyed or damaged in the war and provided living quarters for the newcomers who had swelled the population as refugees from the East. Glittering new urban centers rose from the rubble of war. Labor-saving electrical household appliances became widely available. With a rush, Germany entered the automotive age. Before the war it had lagged behind other major industrial countries in that respect, as passenger cars had remained luxury items reserved for the well-to-do; now they became available to millions, in part as a result of the success of the mass-produced, low-cost Volkswagen. To facilitate auto travel, construction went forward on the system of divided highways begun during the late Weimar Republic and continued with great fanfare by the Third Reich. Between 1949 and 1966 production of passenger cars increased more than twenty-seven-fold, enabling the Federal Republic to produce annually over ten times as many vehicles as had the whole of Germany in 1937. During that same period, industrial production increased six times over, attaining a level well above that of 1937.

This startling increase in productivity resulted in part from the wholesale substitution of new and advanced industrial machinery for older equipment lost through bombing or seized as reparations. Paradoxically, whereas the victorious countries remained saddled with much outmoded industrial plant, the West Germans enjoyed the competitive advantages of standing at the technological forefront. Exports, encouraged by liberal trade policies and priced advantageously because of tight monetary practices that prevented inflation, skyrocketed during the 1950s. By the end of the decade, the Federal Republic ranked second only to the United States in world trade, with a share considerably exceeding that of the much larger interwar Reich. This enabled West Germany not only to pay for the imported food and raw material on which it was dependent but also to accumulate one of the world's largest currency reserves. The size of that reserve eventually occasioned complaints from other countries, which objected to the influx of inexpensive German imports, and in 1961 the Federal Republic revalued its currency upward by 5 percent, thus raising the price of German goods abroad.

Not all citizens of the Federal Republic benefited immediately from the economic miracle. The government's tight-money policies and its refusal to assume a direct role in the economy through large-scale expenditures on public works contributed, during the early years, to a high level of unemployment that was exacerbated by a continuing flow of refugees from the East. The Social Democratic opposition accused the Adenauer government of using joblessness to depress wages by keeping workers reluctant to strike for pay increases because of the risk of losing their jobs to unemployed persons. The government held to the position that large-scale intervention to create jobs would either give rise to ruinous inflation or impose such a heavy tax burden on the economy as to stifle recovery. The best cure for unemployment, Economics Minister Erhard insisted, lay in sound growth that would generate jobs for all. By the late 1950s Erhard was claiming vindication, for the Federal Republic was ap-

The Kurfürstendamm in West Berlin, with the ruins of a church preserved as a reminder of the devastation of war, reflected the prosperity of the West German "economic miracle"

proaching full employment. With demand for labor outstripping supply at home, West Germany began recruiting "guest workers," first from Southern Europe, later from Turkey. But for some West Germans, the rewards of recovery came slowly and late.

Other critics found additional grounds for misgivings about the economic miracle. The need to rebuild a devastated country seemed to some an opportunity to construct a new and more just economic and social order. They hoped to see reduced, if not eliminated, the inequalities which had in the past set Germans against each other and poisoned the political atmosphere. Those who harbored such hopes saw them dashed by the Adenauer government. By relying on free enterprise and abstaining from extensive direct participation in the economy, the government in effect reestablished the traditional relationship between capital and labor. Only a few fundamental reforms were effected in the socioeconomic sphere.

One such reform, "codetermination," involved granting employees a voice in the management of private firms. Far-reaching steps in that direction were vigorously advocated by the German Trade Union League. That organization, which encompassed most organized wage-earners in the Federal Republic, had been formed after the war by a merger of the socialist, Christian, and liberal trade union movements which had competed with each other, sometimes acrimoniously, prior to their suppression by the Nazis. In 1951 the unions brought the Adenauer cabinet to abandon its opposition to codetermination by threatening a mass strike. The resulting Codetermination Law was patterned on arrangements earlier introduced into the steel industry of the Ruhr by the British occupation authorities at the direction of the postwar Labour government. By the terms of the 1951 law, representatives of workers in West German coal and steel companies with more than a thousand employees would henceforth hold a number of seats equivalent to those of stockholders' spokesmen on the supervisory boards which exercised ultimate corporate authority over those firms. An additional seat would be set aside for a supervisory board member acceptable to both sides. In addition, worker representatives would hold one seat on the managing boards that served as the executive bodies of firms in the coal and steel industries.

The adoption of the 1951 law did not resolve the question of codetermination. Strong forces within the German Trade Union League pressed for its extension to all industries but, at the urging of the business community, the Adenauer government balked. In 1952 the government did, by supporting adoption of a Factory Constitution Law, require a measure of codetermination from all joint-stock corporations. By the terms of that law, however, labor was limited to a third of the seats on supervisory boards in industries other than coal and steel, which meant that representatives of stockholders could always outvote them. The

Factory Constitution Law established, in addition, works councils elected by employees of all but the smallest of firms. In consultation with management, these councils were to resolve problems affecting the workplace other than those covered by the basic terms of collective-bargaining contracts. As works councils received no direct voice in management, they were dismissed as a palliative by the frustrated advocates of thoroughgoing codetermination. The councils nevertheless often proved an effective device for reducing friction between management and labor.

While most West Germans were busy with material reconstruction, others worked to revive their country's rich cultural heritage. Almost as soon as the fighting ceased, orchestral concerts and theatrical productions resumed before packed houses in often damaged and unheated buildings. After twelve years of a dictatorship that had proscribed much fine music, art, and literature as racially tainted or politically subversive, a thirst for the forbidden became evident. Jazz was again performed and abstract art displayed. Plays and books by emigré German authors and translations of foreign works were in great demand. Distinguished exiles like the writer Thomas Mann were entreated to visit the homeland that had rejected them a decade earlier. Much of the reading public and many writers of the older generation hoped to reconnect with what they regarded as the noble traditions of German literature interrupted by the years of Nazi barbarism.

On the other hand, a younger generation of writers who had come to maturity under Nazi tyranny and experienced the horrors of what they saw as a senseless war called instead for a radical break with older literary traditions. They believed that these, like most aspects of the German past, had contributed to the country's calamity. In hopes of freeing the German language from what they saw as the corrupting influences of the past, they set out to create a new, fresh, humanistic literature. This involved for most a rejection of lofty themes and preciousness of expression in favor of directness, simplicity, and everyday aspects of individual experience. Typical of efforts in that direction was a poem by Günter Eich, a writer just returned home after six years as a conscripted soldier and prisoner of war:

Inventory

This is my cap,
this is my coat,
here's my shaving gear
in a linen sack.

A can of rations:
my plate, my cup,
I've scratched my name
in the tin.

Scratched it with this
valuable nail
which I hide
from avid eyes.

In the foodsack is
a pair of wool socks
and something else that I
show to no one,

it all serves as a pillow
for my head at night.
The cardboard here lies
between me and the earth.

The lead in my pencil
I love most of all:
in the daytime it writes down
the verses I make at night.

This is my notebook,
this is my tarpaulin,
this is my towel,
this is my thread.

In 1947 Eich joined with other younger writers in forming Group 47, a loose organization for the promotion of a new German literature. By awarding prizes for distinguished writing and by providing a forum at its annual gatherings to which aspiring authors could present their works, Group 47 became a dynamic and lasting force in West German literary life. By the latter part of the 1950s two of its members, Heinrich Böll and Günter Grass, had achieved international acclaim for novels and stories which breached the prevailing collective amnesia about the recent past by giving compelling literary expression to what they and others had experienced under the Nazi regime. Böll's work would in 1972 gain for him the honor of becoming the first German writer since Thomas Mann in 1929 to receive the Nobel Prize for Literature. After a barren period, Germany was again producing writers of world stature.

By the mid-1950s most lingering reservations among West Germans about the formation of the Federal Republic had been swept away. More quickly than anyone had expected, Germans had been accepted back into the international community as a result of the political stability of the new democratic polity and the economic and cultural achievements of its citizens. West Germans found to their relief that they were no longer regarded abroad as pariahs but were once more welcomed as business associates, professional colleagues, and travelers. At home, the economic miracle had speeded consolidation of the new polity. Germany's first experiment with democracy, the Weimar Republic, had struggled throughout its existence with grave handicaps imposed by adverse economic conditions. Democracy became associated for much of that generation with hardship and anxiety. It seemed easy then to blame economic troubles on democratic institutions. In the Federal Republic, by contrast, Germans saw for the first time that democracy could be compatible with prosperity. Whereas during Weimar many had longingly looked back to the authoritarian but economically burgeoning Empire as a lost golden age, the Third Reich, which had restored prosperity but also plunged the country into a disastrous war and economic catastrophe, awakened no such nostalgia among those who found themselves beneficiaries of the economic miracle. For most West Germans the materially plentiful, democratic present came to seem the best of times.

Alignment with the Western Democracies

Next to fostering economic recovery, the greatest challenge that faced the Adenauer government lay in charting the Federal Republic's course in international affairs. The most pressing task lay in finding ways to remove the restrictions imposed by the Occupation Statute. Whereas the chancellor left economic policy largely to his minister of economics, he himself took on the determination of foreign policy. Not until 1955 did he appoint a foreign minister, and even after that he made all major decisions in that sphere. Unlike most postwar German leaders, Adenauer harbored no illusions about a speedy reunification. A highly realistic man, he concluded that once Soviet power had become established in Germany, dislodging it would be no simple task. In his judgment, the Germans in the West had no prospect of effecting Russian withdrawal by themselves. Nor did he envision the Western powers quickly repulsing the expansion of Soviet power brought about by the war. He therefore accepted the country's division as an unavoidable fact of life for an indefinite period of time.

In this acceptance, Adenauer's background played a role. As a Catholic Rhinelander, oriented toward Western Europe and unimpressed by the Prussian tradition, he found it easier to contemplate a lengthy separation from the territories to the east than did those whose backgrounds made reversal of the unification effected by Bismarck seem almost unthinkable. For the coolly calculating Adenauer, the only hope for eventual reunification lay in making the Federal Republic into a bastion of freedom and prosperity that would exercise a magnetic attraction for the Russian-dominated part of the country. Faced with what he perceived as a choice between self-rule for at least some Germans in association with the democracies and an uncertain prospect of reunification on terms set by the Russians, he opted for freedom over unity. This accorded with his personal values, which assigned the highest priority to restoring what he regarded as the moral, social, and political values of Western civilization in at least part of Germany following the country's descent into barbarism. To achieve that, he believed that the Federal Republic must be firmly linked with the Western democracies, even at the price of protracted national division.

The need for what Adenauer characterized as a "policy of strength" in the face of Soviet power also inclined him to a Western orientation. Only a united West, he argued, could marshal the strength necessary to deter the Russians from encroaching upon the young Federal Republic and, someday, prevail upon them to relinquish their hold over part of Germany. In order to survive politically, Adenauer joined with the other German politicians of the day in tirelessly pledging in public his determination to seek reunification. But in practice he set out to make the Federal Republic an integral part of the Western camp, fully aware that such an alignment might well rule out the possiblity of reunification for the foreseeable future by leading the Soviets to tighten their control over the part of Germany they dominated.

Adenauer's acceptance of a lengthy period of division and his policy of tying the Federal Republic to the Western powers met with vehement resistance from his great adversary, Kurt Schumacher, who led the oppositional Social Democrats until his death in 1952. An heroic opponent of Nazism who had emerged from one of the Third Reich's concentration camps in 1945 with severe physical disabilities, Schumacher accorded priority to reunification. As a man who himself hailed from the Prussian East and whose political party had traditionally enjoyed strong backing in the industrial areas of what had become the Soviet zone, Schumacher remained reluctant to accept Germany's divi-

Social Democratic leader Kurt Schumacher (right) with party colleague and lord mayor of West Berlin, Ernst Reuter

sion. As a democrat, he balked at consigning the population of Germany's eastern regions to Communist rule. As a socialist, he was deeply suspicious of the capitalistic United States and its allies in Western Europe. To his mind, the primary task lay in restoring German control over the whole country. Viewing the defeat of the SPD at Hitler's hands as the result, in large measure, of his party's insufficient recognition of the factor of nationalism, he had resolved that the Social Democrats must never again appear to be indifferent to Germany's national interests. This, too, contributed to his resolute insistence on according priority to reunification and his resistance to integration into the Western camp.

Recognizing that Adenauer's policies would heighten the risk of a prolonged division, Schumacher advocated keeping the Federal Republic free of commitments to either side in the Cold War so as to keep open as many options as possible for restoration of German unity. While he believed that Germany belonged to the West in terms of its fundamental values, he rejected Adenauer's policy of tying the Federal Republic to the Western democracies on the grounds that this would deepen the divide between the two parts of the country and erect insuperable obstacles to reunification. Unlike some other critics of the chancellor, Schumacher did not view neutralization as a desirable course for Germany, but he nevertheless favored keeping that option open if it should prove the only price acceptable to the Russians for ending the country's division. He and his party therefore opposed at every step Adenauer's policy of cooperation with the Western powers. Denouncing Adenauer as "the chancellor of the allies," Schumacher warned that his policies would make permanent the division of Germany and place the Federal Republic in servitude to foreigners.

Since Adenauer, rather than Schumacher, commanded the support of a majority in the democratically elected Bundestag, the Federal Republic adopted a strong Western orientation. This became manifest with its entry into the new institutions that linked the democracies of Western Europe. In October 1949 West Germany joined the Organization for European Economic Cooperation, which managed distribution of Marshall Plan aid and sought to lower economic barriers between the Western democracies. In June 1950, under the terms of the Petersberg Agreement of the previous November with the three allied high commissioners, West Germany became a non-voting, associate member of the Council of Europe, which, with its seat at Strasbourg, aimed at the political consolidation of Western Europe. In May 1951 the Federal Republic became a full member of the council. A month earlier, it had joined the European Coal and Steel Community, an organization proposed by French Foreign Minister Robert Schuman to rule out future wars among the states of Western Europe by fostering economic interdependence through a common market and unified tariff system for coal and steel.

At every stage in this process of integration into the West European alliance, the Federal Republic under Adenauer's leadership patiently extracted concessions that enhanced its authority. As became increasingly clear, the chancellor strove to win sovereign rights for the new West German government as rapidly as possible. By the end of 1949 Bonn had gained from the Western occupying powers the right of consular, if not yet ambassadorial, representation abroad. Those powers also agreed to ease a number of economic restrictions imposed by the Occupation Statute, such as those limiting shipbuilding. In March 1951 the Occupation Statute was revised to allow West German legislation to take effect without a waiting period for scrutiny by the allied high commissioners, who nevertheless still retained authority to annul laws. At the same time, Bonn also won full authority over its own currency and expanded rights in the sphere of foreign policy. As a member of the Coal and Steel Community, the authority of which superseded the controls imposed on the Ruhr by the Western countries, the Federal Republic gained a major role in industrial policy not only in that key region of West Germany but also in the rest of Western Europe.

Rearmament and Sovereign Rights

This process of Western integration and expansion of Bonn's authority received added impetus from the war in Korea. Communist military aggression in that divided country awakened fears in Bonn, as in other Western capitals, of a similar conflict in Germany. The West German government viewed with mounting alarm the expansion of the so-called People's Police of East Germany to a level of 55,000 men, fitted out in military uniforms and including units equipped with artillery and tanks. By contrast, under the terms of the Occupation Statute the Federal Republic was permitted no military force at all, and the units posted there by the Western occupying powers lacked the capacity for large-scale combat. In the light of developments in Korea and the mounting tensions of the

Cold War in Europe, the West European governments became increasingly convinced of the need for a military force capable of deterring or repelling an attack from the East. When the Americans, heavily involved in Korea, indicated that they would retain troops in Europe only if the Europeans participated more fully in their own defense, the question took on added urgency.

This situation gave Adenauer a lever with which to pursue his goal of sovereignty for the Federal Republic. For without West German manpower, a Western European defense force could not hope to attain a level of strength sufficient to deter or withstand aggression from the Soviet bloc. With memories of Hitler's conquests still fresh, however, the Western countries were reluctant to authorize creation of a new German army. In October 1950 the French won wide support among the continental democracies for a plan that called for a West European army within the structure of the Council of Europe. Under this plan, which became known as the European Defense Community or EDC, German troops would be integrated into a supranational force along with those of other democracies of Western Europe.

Bonn responded positively to the EDC plan. Adenauer's government insisted, however, that West German soldiers could be assigned to the projected West European army only if the Federal Republic were accorded equal status with the other participating countries. That, Adenauer left no doubt, entailed granting sovereign status to the Federal Republic. Since West German troops would make up the largest component of the planned EDC army and since Bonn could not be compelled to join against its will, its claims could scarcely be ignored.

In protracted and often arduous negotiations over the EDC project, Adenauer patiently extracted concession after concession from his bargaining partners and won their increasing respect in the process. By July 1951 the Western democracies had agreed to declare the state of war with Germany at an end even though no peace treaty was in sight. By May 1952, when the EDC agreement was initialed by the projected participants, the Americans, British, and French had worked out with West Germany the draft for a treaty which would greatly expand the sovereign rights of the Federal Republic and abolish the Occupation Statute. The Western allies reserved the right, however, to resume their occupation authority if an emergency should arise. Otherwise, their troops would remain in Germany not as occupying forces but as part of a mutual defense system. Berlin was not covered by the draft treaty, and the three Western powers retained their full occupation authority there. All four countries pledged themselves to seek the unification and democratization of Germany and stated that its frontiers could be determined only by a freely negotiated final peace settlement. The draft treaty which incorporated these provisions would, its signato ries agreed, come into effect upon ratification of the treaty embodying the EDC.

When in the summer of 1954 the French parliament balked at integration of the army of France into the international force proposed under the EDC, the project died. This jeopardized the draft treaty concerning the authority of the Federal Republic, which had been tied to the EDC. A last-minute solution was provided by the British, whose earlier refusal to join the EDC had helped to undermine it. As a substitute security arrangement, British Foreign Secretary Anthony Eden proposed in the fall of 1954 formation of a West European Union which would link the United Kingdom with the continental democracies in a security system composed of national defense forces, including one from the Federal Republic, as opposed to the supranational force foreseen for the EDC.

Eden's plan provided for a West German defense force of half a million men but placed upon the Federal Republic certain restrictions not required of the others. The West Germans were to be prohibited from producing or possessing certain kinds of armaments, most notably those of a nuclear, bacteriological, or chemical nature. Bonn had further to agree not to use its defense force to seek German reunification or the alteration of existing frontiers by military means. The Federal Republic would become a full member of the North Atlantic Treaty Organization

(NATO), the defense system formed in 1949 to link Canada and the United States with the West European democracies. Unlike the other partners, however, Bonn would be required to subordinate all its forces to NATO, to retain none outside its structure, and to maintain no general staff of its own. Otherwise, West Germany would become an equal partner in the alliance. For their part, the West European countries undertook by the terms of the Eden plan to recognize the Federal Republic as the sole legitimate spokesman of the German people in the international sphere until a peace treaty resolved the issues left from the war, including that of Germany's frontiers.

The Eden plan was swiftly approved by all concerned in the autumn of 1954 by means of what came to be known as the Paris Treaties. Among these was a German Treaty, signed by the Federal Republic and the Western occupying powers, which incorporated the essential terms of the earlier draft treaty dealing with the relations between those powers and Bonn. The West European Union was approved by Britain and the continental democracies. When the Paris Treaties took effect in May 1955, the Federal Republic became a partner in the Union and a member of NATO. The Occupation Statute lapsed, and the West German state gained far-reaching sovereign rights. Having won acceptance by the Western democracies, Bonn promptly established full diplomatic relations with them and exchanged ambassadors. Soon thereafter the Adenauer government joined in negotiations that would lead in 1957 to the Treaties of Rome, which established a European Economic Community (EEC), also known as the Common Market, of which the Federal Republic's robust economy formed a key component.

As these developments made manifest, just a decade after the disappearance of the Reich a new German state had won acceptance as a respected member of the community of democratic countries. The Federal Republic's sovereignty remained subject to certain restrictions, and foreign troops still stood on its soil. But those restrictions did not impinge upon the authority of the new West German government within its boundaries so long as there was no international emergency that would lead the Western powers to reactivate their occupation rights. American, British, and French troops were now stationed in Germany at the request of a democratically elected government, as part of an international defense alliance. Konrad Adenauer had achieved his goal of winning sovereign rights for the new Federal Republic and binding it firmly to the democratic West.

Establishing the West German military, the Bundeswehr, posed one of the most delicate tasks facing the government as a consequence of the recent war of aggression and Germany's long tradition of militarism. In order to exclude unsuitables, including veterans who had compromised themselves during the Third Reich, screening of candidates for posts in the Bundeswehr was turned over to a special board of civilians that included prominent surviving members of the opposition to Nazism. To prevent a predominance of professional military men, a conscription law adopted in 1956 obligated all able-bodied young men to a year's service upon their eighteenth birthday (the term was raised to eighteen months in 1962, then reduced to fifteen months in 1973). Since the Basic Law ruled out compulsory military service, conscientious objectors were permitted to perform corresponding terms of civilian service. From the outset, efforts were made to break with past practices, particularly the traditions of unchallengeable authority and unquestioning obedience. Both officers and enlisted men were taught to regard the Bundeswehr as a defense force composed of civilians in uniform. A special school was established to instruct officers about the place of the military in a democratic society. Civilian control, through the minister of defense, was emphasized, and parliamentary scrutiny facilitated. Within the Bundeswehr, ombudsmen were assigned the task of responding to grievances voiced by servicemen.

Originally, the size of the Bundeswehr had been projected at just short of half a million men, but that goal was temporarily scaled back. The end of the Korean War in 1953 reduced the sense of military urgency, and the labor shortage generated by the economic miracle made it seem inadvisable to remove so many men from the workforce. Nevertheless, by 1961 the Bundeswehr, with some 350,000 men in uniform, had become the second strongest component of NATO command structure forces next to that of the United States. By the 1970s it would approach the half-million level, as originally foreseen. At home, the new defense force soon gained general acceptance despite the controversy that had surrounded the decision to launch it.

Adenauer followed up his option for what he called a "policy of strength" based on integration into the Western alliance with a regularization of relations with the Soviet Union. The Russians had long viewed with apprehension the emergence of a West Germany linked with the Western powers and had on several occasions held out the prospect of a reunified, neutral Germany. In the spring of 1952, in the midst of delicate negotiations over the terms of the Federal Republic's integration into the Western alliance, Stalin proposed such a formula to London, Paris, and Washington, conceding even the Western powers' demand for free, all-German elections. But when the Russians were pressed, it became clear that before such elections they wanted a peace treaty signed that would impose neutrality on a reunified Germany. The Western allies contended, in response, that only a democratically elected all-German government could accord binding status to a peace treaty. Such a government, they argued, must be left free to determine its own foreign policy, as did other sovereign states. As exchanges of views between Moscow and the Western capitals continued through the summer and into the autumn of 1952, the allied statesmen, seconded by the Bonn government, concluded that the Soviet offer was not seriously meant but instead represented an effort to derail the negotiations for inclusion of West Germany in the Western alliance.

When the Treaties of Paris went before the Bundestag for ratification in 1955, Moscow again held out the prospect of a reunified, neutral Germany, but that alternative had by then lost its credibility. After the Paris Treaties went into effect, the Soviet

Union reacted angrily, abrogating its wartime alliance treaties with Britain and France. Behind the scenes, however, the Russians soon began cultivating the Federal Republic, whose economic potency exercised a strong attraction. The resultant negotiations broke into public view in September 1955, when Adenauer journeyed, by invitation, to Moscow for a week of conferences with Stalin's successors. He returned, having achieved the release by the Soviets of some 10,000 German prisoners and having established full diplomatic relations with Moscow. His policy of strength was beginning to work, Adenauer announced upon his return.

In addition to joining the new institutions of the Western alliance and gaining recognition by all the major powers, including the Soviet Union, the Federal Republic further enhanced its standing by shouldering onerous burdens from the German past. Under the terms of the Luxemburg Agreement of 1952 the West German government volunteered to deliver 3 billion marks' worth of goods and services to the state of Israel by way of restitution for Nazi persecution and murder of Jews. Hundreds of millions of additional marks went to compensate individual Jews who had suffered at the hands of the Third Reich. In numerous other ways, too, West Germany extended help to Israel, and in 1965 formal diplomatic relations were established between the two governments. Still other burdens in the form of Germany's prewar foreign debts were assumed by the Federal Republic when it signed the London Debt Agreement of 1953 and began punctual interest and amortization payments on those debts as well as on postwar obligations, in all more than 15 billion marks.

The growing stature of the Federal Republic became apparent when a plebiscite revealed the determination of a sizable majority of the Saarland's population to sever that coal-rich region's postwar ties with neighboring France and join the new West German state. For a decade the German-speaking Saarlanders had lived under an autonomous government set up under sponsorship of the French occupation authorities. Paris made no secret of its desire to see the Saarland permanently separated from Germany and tied to France, which had controlled it during the Napoleonic era and for most of the period between the world wars. Since 1946 a customs union had linked the Saar with the French economy, and when the West German currency was reformed in 1948 France insisted that the Saarland government establish separate money of its own. In 1947 an election for a regional representative assembly, from which the French authorities barred German-oriented parties, produced overwhelming support for separation from a Germany devastated by war and prostrate in defeat and disgrace. Nearly 90 percent of the votes went to parties favoring an independent Saarland in close association with France. The Federal Republic balked, however, at conceding the Saarland to France, and for years the issue caused friction. During the negotiations that produced the Paris Treaties of 1954 the two sides agreed to compromise by making the Saarland an autonomous entity and placing it under the authority of the new West European Union. But when the Saarlanders were asked to endorse that formula by plebiscite in October 1955, more than two-thirds rejected it. Clearly, they now preferred to join the prosperous West Germans. After lengthy negotiations between Paris and Bonn, the Saarland became a state of the Federal Republic in 1957.

With a few exceptions such as the Saarland issue, the policies of the Adenauer government at home and in the international sphere encountered stubborn opposition from the SPD. That party rejected the revival of private enterprise in the economic sphere as a reactionary step that would only perpetuate and deepen class conflict. The Social Democrats opposed as well Adenauer's foreign policy, contending that he had, in his single-minded determination to integrate West Germany into the Western alliance, squandered numerous opportunities for progress toward reunification through negotiations with the USSR. The SPD Bundestag deputies voted against most of the agreements that linked the Federal Republic to the West, and the party joined in a campaign of marches and demonstrations against rearmament.

Most West Germans did not, however, heed warnings by the SPD that Adenauer was leading them down a false path. When 86 percent of the voters went to the polls to elect the second Bundestag in September 1953, the CDU/CSU scored sweeping gains, increasing its seats in the chamber from 139 to 243. Adenauer's party profited not only from the successes of his government but also from revulsion at developments in the GDR, the suppression of the uprising of June 17 in particular. That revulsion swept the Communist Party out of the parliament altogether. The failure of the KPD, as well as several other small parties represented in the first Bundestag, to gain the minimum votes necessary for representation enabled the SPD to increase its 131 seats to 151 despite receiving a smaller share of the vote than in 1949. The FDP, a junior partner in the Adenauer cabinet, lost votes and slipped from 52 to 48 seats. The other partner in the ruling coalition, the German Party, held on to 15 of the 17 seats it had won in 1949. A Refugee Party formed after the 1949 election appealed to the millions of Germans displaced from homes in eastern regions and gained a surprising 27 seats. It was included, along with the CDU/CSU, FDP, and German Party, in the second Adenauer cabinet formed after the 1953 election.

Four years later, in 1957, the election of the third Bundestag, in which 87.8 percent of the eligible voters took part, brought the CDU/CSU its greatest triumph. It became the first political party in German history to gain an absolute majority in a major election. The SPD made smaller gains and increased its seats in the Bundestag to 169. The CDU/CSU, with 270 of the 497 Bundestag seats, could have formed a cabinet by itself. Adenauer chose, however, to include the small German Party, which increased its representation from 15 to 17 seats. The FDP, which had left the coalition in 1956 because of various disputes with the chancellor and his party and had also lost part of its following from defections to the CDU/CSU, fell from 48 to 41 seats. It remained in opposition. The Refugee Party failed altogether to gain representation, in part because of the success of the CDU/CSU in absorbing its followers. Whereas nearly a dozen parties had gained representation in the first Bundestag, a process of political consolidation left only four by 1957. The Constitutional Court, to be sure, had banned two parties as antidemocratic. One of these, the Socialist Reich Party, had been outlawed in 1952 because of its neo-Nazi orientation. In 1956 the ban fell on the Communist Party. Most observers agreed, however, that those parties represented no serious threat to the democratic institutions, as neither had commanded the allegiance of more than a tiny fraction of the public.

The SPD's Godesberg
Program of 1959

The election outcomes of 1953 and 1957, which saw the SPD fall ever farther behind the CDU/CSU, gave rise to a change of course by the Social Democrats. Although the SPD had fared well at the regional level, dominating some state and many municipal governments, a sizable majority of West German voters remained unwilling to entrust control of the Bonn government to it. In the judgment of some of its leaders, the SPD stood in danger of remaining forever an oppositional party, prevented by its own policies from gaining the support of more than a third of the electorate. By 1959, however, reformers had gained the upper hand, and in November of that year they secured approval of a new program at a party congress held in Bad Godesberg, a suburb of Bonn. With the adoption of that Godesberg Program, as it came to be called, the SPD broke with its past as a working-class organization and became, like the CDU/CSU, a "people's party" that sought to appeal to a broad spectrum of voters.

The Godesberg Program marked a sharp departure from the traditions of German Social Democracy. The discrepancy between radical rhetoric and moderate practice that had character-

ized the SPD since the nineteenth century was finally eliminated. Gone was the Marxist theoretical framework and along
with it the assumption that class conflict was unavoidable. The
claim to scientific status for socialism gave way to the statement
that democratic socialism in Europe had sprung from Christian
ethics, humanism, and classical philosophy. In place of the
SPD's traditional economic goals of socializing key industries
and implementing governmental planning, the Godesberg Program announced acceptance of private enterprise as the basis of
the economic order. As long as it did not interfere with social
justice, private property would be entitled to governmental protection. Only where powerful special interests obstructed competition should the government intervene. "As much competition as possible—as much planning as necessary," became the
SPD's operative slogan in the economic sphere. Recognizing that
their party's anticlerical heritage hindered efforts to reach voters
with strong church ties, the reformers wrote into the Godesberg
Program a religious plank that accorded a legitimate and special
social mission to the churches and disavowed the long-standing
contention that socialism represented a replacement for religion. The new program also abandoned opposition to the rearmament so stubbornly resisted by the SPD earlier and committed the party to national defense. The program said little
about foreign policy, but in June 1960 one of the reformers,
Herbert Wehner, announced in a major speech before the
Bundestag the SPD's acceptance of the Federal Republic's integration into the Western alliance.

In preparation for the Bundestag election of September 1961
the reformed leadership of the SPD set out to test the political
viability of its new program. Abandoning its traditional red, the
party campaigned under blue banners. As their chancellorship
candidate the Social Democrats chose one of the reformers,
Willy Brandt, the mayor of West Berlin. Born an illegitimate
child with the name Herbert Frahm in the Baltic port city of
Lübeck, he had devoted much of his youth to democratic socialist activities. While in exile in Norway and Sweden during the

Third Reich, he assumed the name Willy Brandt and retained it when he returned to Berlin after the war as a correspondent for Scandinavian newspapers. There he joined the SPD and rose within its ranks, becoming head of the city government in 1957. In 1961, ruggedly handsome and vigorous at age forty-seven, he imparted verve and dynamism to the SPD. He stood in marked contrast to the colorlessness of Erich Ollenhauer, the stodgy party functionary who had succeeded Kurt Schumacher as leader and gone down to defeat twice as the SPD's candidate for the chancellorship in 1953 and 1957. As challenger to the eighty-five-year-old Adenauer, Brandt could claim to be the candidate of youth and progress. Some Christian Democrats responded by insinuating that Brandt's illegitimate birth disqualified him for high office and by questioning his patriotism on the grounds that he had spent the war years abroad and had briefly worn a Norwegian army uniform to elude the Nazis.

Brandt's campaign benefited from his resoluteness in rallying the morale of West Berlin's shaken citizenry following the GDR's erection in August 1961 of the wall dividing the former capital city. The mayor's inspirational defiance in the face of that shattering development contrasted favorably with Adenauer's tardy and hesitant response. Moreover, the East German regime's success in closing the last remaining point of unobstructed interchange between the two parts of divided Germany cast doubt on the chancellor's predictions that his policy of aligning the Federal Republic with the Western democracies would inevitably result in reunification. For his part, Adenauer contended that the cruelty and disregard for human rights displayed by the Communists in sealing the East Germans off from their relatives and compatriots in the West only confirmed his westward-oriented "policy of strength."

The results of the 1961 election, in which 87.7 percent of the voters took part, did not give Brandt the chancellorship but did boost the strength of the SPD impressively. Whereas the party had held 169 seats in the old chamber, it captured 190 in the new one. The CDU/CSU, by contrast, suffered its first setback, dropping from 270 seats to 242 and losing its absolute majority. The FDP, which campaigned against further welfare-state measures, made its strongest showing ever, raising the number of its seats from 41 to 67. The small German Party, which with a conservative following in northern parts of the republic had participated in the first three Adenauer cabinets, disappeared before the election, most of its leaders having defected to the CDU. That left only three parties in the new Bundestag.

A CDU/CSU-FDP coalition seemed the most likely result. The FDP called, however, for replacement of the eighty-five-year-old Adenauer. He countered by opening talks with the SPD, which raised the possibility of a CDU/CSU-SPD government that might revise the electoral law's requirements so as to exclude the FDP from future parliaments. After nearly two months of maneuvering, the FDP gave way and joined with the CDU/CSU in forming a new cabinet under Adenauer when he held out the prospect of retiring partway through the four-year legislative term.

From Adenauer to Erhard

The election setback of 1961 signaled the twilight of Adenauer's chancellorship. Always a strong-willed man, he had become increasingly overbearing after more than a decade in power. His authoritarian style might have seemed defensible during the first years of the West German government, when its institutions were new and their personnel often inexperienced. But as the government matured, his "chancellor democracy"—the label of critics for his often high-handed methods—encountered increasing resistance. His practice of using the cabinet as a rubber stamp for decisions which he and his inner circle of advisers had already reached became a particular target of criticism and made it increasingly difficult to maintain coalition cabinets.

The chancellor had diminished his own stature in 1959 when he engaged in what seemed to many observers cynical and self-serving political maneuvers demeaning to the institutions of the young republic. With a presidential election due upon the expiration of Theodor Heuss's second term, Adenauer put himself forward as a candidate after unsuccessfully attempting to have Economics Minister Ludwig Erhard stand for the job. Only a short time later, however, he withdrew from consideration after realizing that the office of president offered little prospect of influencing government policy and after discovering that his party intended to name Erhard as his successor in the chancellorship despite his grave reservations about Erhard's political abilities. With Adenauer's backing, the undistinguished CDU minister of agriculture, Heinrich Lübke, was elected president by the Federal Assembly in July 1959. By his behavior, however, Adenauer aroused widespread skepticism about whether he could ever be expected to surrender his hold on the chancellorship voluntarily.

Behind the decline in Adenauer's popularity lay mounting dissatisfaction with what appeared to a growing number of West Germans, especially of the younger generation, as an entrenched, self-satisfied, conservative regime in Bonn. In too many respects, critics charged, the government had rested content with restoring an older order rather than strengthening the democratic organs of the Federal Republic by reforming social institutions whose structures had originated in Germany's authoritarian past. Critics took issue as well with what they saw as the Adenauer government's insensitivity about the crimes of the Nazi regime. Too little had been done, they charged, to track down and prosecute those responsible for the most horrendous atrocities of history, so that many criminals had been left free to enjoy the fruits of the economic miracle. This seeming indifference toward the recent past extended even to the personnel policies of the Adenauer government. Under the terms of a federal law passed in 1951 to regulate the status of former civil officials, many who had served under Hitler became eligible for jobs in the West German government. The judiciary in particular remained heavily staffed with judges who had administered what passed for justice in the Third Reich. Even some cabinet ministers and members of the chancellor's staff had dubious pasts. No one seriously attributed pro-Nazi sympathies to Adenauer, but his readiness to make use of men with tainted careers raised doubts about his standards for others.

A year after Adenauer formed his fourth cabinet in November 1961 on the basis of a CDU/CSU-FDP coalition, his position was shaken by an affair that took its name from West Germany's most popular weekly news magazine, *Der Spiegel*. In October 1962 its publisher and its defense correspondent were arrested along with nine other persons and imprisoned under suspicion of treason. The defense correspondent was seized with the assistance of the police of rightist dictator Francisco Franco in Spain, where he was visiting, and flown to Germany under guard. Federal police agents ransacked private residences and offices of the magazine, confiscating copies of a forthcoming issue. For many observers, the brusque and overbearing fashion in which these actions were carried out called to mind disturbing memories of recent experiences with police-state methods. As justification for its actions the government alleged that an article in *Spiegel* casting doubt on the defense capability of the Bundeswehr derived in part from secret documents improperly removed from Defense Ministry files. Since *Spiegel* had for some time leveled sustained and pointed criticism at Defense Minister Franz Josef Strauss of the Bavarian CSU, however, suspicion immediately arose that ulterior motives had played a part. As a result, a wave of protest swept through the Federal Republic.

At first, both Strauss and Adenauer denied any part in the affair. But under searching interrogation by opposition deputies during the Bundestag's question hour, contradictions between their accounts and those of others involved began to emerge. Further investigations indicated that certainly Strauss and possibly Adenauer had been closely involved in the decisions that led to the arrests, searches, and confiscations. Worse, it soon became apparent that the FDP minister of justice, who was constitutionally responsible for federal indictments and for the federal police, had been left wholly uninformed about those measures. Adenauer sought a way out of the affair by proposing to dismiss or suspend the second-level officials directly implicated. The crisis deepened, however, when the junior partner in the government coalition, the FDP, withdrew its ministers from the cabinet and announced its resolve to remain in opposition until Strauss was replaced. Adenauer, in turn, again began negotiating with the SPD. That once more brought into line the FDP, which agreed to revive the coalition with the CDU/CSU, enabling the chancellor to form his fifth cabinet in December 1962. To appease critics, he replaced the controversial Strauss and expressed his intent to give up the chancellorship within a year.

While the *Spiegel* affair brought discredit upon the Federal Republic in the eyes of many by revealing that some top officials had abused their authority, it also offered considerable encouragement to those concerned about the durability of democracy in West Germany. Most notably, the free press emerged unscathed and strengthened. All charges against the publisher of *Spiegel*, Rudolf Augstein, who spent fourteen weeks behind bars, as well as those against the magazine's defense correspondent, were eventually dismissed as groundless. No convictions resulted from the affair. Moreover, much of the West German press joined in the quest for truth that frustrated efforts on the part of high office-holders to cover up the facts. This was the case not only with newspapers and magazines but also with the public radio and television stations to which regional authorities had entrusted broadcasting after the war. When put to the test posed by the *Spiegel* affair, the broadly representative, non-partisan supervisory boards to which those stations were responsible proved an adequate safeguard against political manipulation of news and commentary. The affair thus demonstrated that the Federal Republic had developed mass media that were protected from governmental manipulation, open to a wide variety of viewpoints, and vigilant in their defense of democratic institutions. University students and faculties had also protested against the misuse of governmental authority. In sharp contrast to the Weimar Republic, when the intellectual community had displayed indifference, if not outright hostility, toward its democratic institutions, the vast majority of West German intellectuals had rallied behind those of the Federal Republic.

Adenauer's remarkable career finally came to an end when he resigned in October 1963 at age eighty-seven after occupying the office of chancellor longer than anyone since Bismarck. He left a record of notable achievement. During his fourteen years in office, the new West German government established its legitimacy at home and gained sovereign rights sooner than anyone had expected. The Federal Republic became an integral part of the Western alliance. Its military, the Bundeswehr, established despite strong popular resistance at home and grave misgivings abroad, developed in such fashion as to represent a mainstay of the NATO security system and yet pose no militaristic threat to West German democracy. Put to the test during the *Spiegel* affair, the republic's institutions proved capable of coping even with misuse of authority by its highest officials. In his final years Adenauer achieved, through cordial personal relations with French president Charles de Gaulle, a reconciliation with Germany's most important continental neighbor to the west. At home, the West German economy continued throughout his chancellorship to recover with astonishing rapidity from the devastations of war and the disruptions of division. Some 12 million refugees had been provided with livelihoods and homes, as mass joblessness rapidly gave way to full employment. In the international economy, the Federal Republic had emerged as one of the leading industrial and trading countries of the world. By the end of Adenauer's chancellorship, however, he appeared to be a leader who, having accomplished his goals, rested content with maintaining the status quo.

In the foreign policy sphere, the status quo was proving increasingly inadequate. In all agreements with other countries even vaguely related to territorial questions, Bonn insisted upon clauses to the effect that the German frontiers of 1937—those prior to the expansion under Hitler—would remain legally unaltered until a peace conference. But as the passage of time and the deepening Cold War made the convening of such a conference seem less and less probable, this position left the Federal Republic vulnerable to charges that it harbored aggressive designs on the former German territories to the east of the Oder-Neisse line, which had long since been incorporated into Poland and the Soviet Union and populated by their nationals. Suspicions on that count posed a formidable barrier between Bonn and the countries of the Soviet bloc.

Another barrier was the Hallstein doctrine, which took its name from Walter Hallstein, one of Adenauer's chief foreign policy aides. First enunciated in 1955, that doctrine sought to prevent international recognition of the German Democratic Republic by refusing to maintain diplomatic relations with countries that established relations with East Berlin. The sole exception was made for the Soviet Union itself when Moscow and Bonn exchanged ambassadors in 1955. Otherwise, the Federal Republic insisted that, as stated in the preamble to the Basic Law, it alone spoke for the German people until such time as a freely elected government for all of the country could be achieved. The Hallstein doctrine thus prevented Bonn from establishing formal diplomatic relations with the governments of Eastern Europe, all of which maintained ties to East Berlin. When non-aligned Yugoslavia recognized the GDR diplomatically in 1957, Bonn had to break off its relations with Belgrade. The Hallstein doctrine thus deprived the Federal Republic of any chance to wield diplomatic influence in Eastern Europe or to foster economic ties there with countries which had traditionally traded extensively with Germany. Critics further charged that the Hallstein doctrine served to consolidate the Eastern bloc and enabled Communist regimes to justify their rule by portraying the Federal Republic as a hostile and aggressive reincarnation of past German regimes.

The Hallstein doctrine worked much as intended, at least for a time. None of the countries of the Western bloc recognized the German Democratic Republic, despite its leaders' efforts to gain acceptance. West Germany's economic potency, in particular its expanding foreign aid, also enabled it to prevent many developing countries of Africa and Asia from extending recognition to East Germany. But the Hallstein doctrine made Bonn vulnerable to extortion, since some countries quickly discovered they could exact economic favors from the Federal Republic by threatening to recognize East Germany. Both in political and in material terms, Adenauer's policy toward Eastern Europe thus became increasingly expensive while achieving no progress toward resolution of the problems created by Germany's postwar division. As a result, the chancellor's ritualistic public reaffirmations of his commitment to reunification came to seem increasingly empty, if not downright cynical.

When Adenauer finally resigned as chancellor in October 1963, the CDU/CSU ignored his reservations about Ludwig Erhard's political abilities and joined with the FDP to make the minister of economic affairs the second chancellor of the Federal Republic. As the phenomenally successful architect of the economic miracle, the rotund, cigar-puffing minister of economics enjoyed widespread popularity. In the international sphere, he and the foreign minister he inherited from Adenauer, Gerhard Schröder of the CDU, attempted to break the stalemate in relations with the countries of Eastern Europe to which Adenauer's policies had led. Without violating the letter of the Hallstein doctrine, they ignored its spirit by expanding trade relations with countries in the Soviet bloc. In the last months of Adenauer's cabinet, Schröder had arranged to exchange trade missions with Poland. In the first months of the new cabinet, Schröder reached similar arrangements with Bulgaria, Hungary, and Rumania. Among other advantages, these exchanges served to strengthen the Federal Republic's claim to represent West Berlin, which was covered in the new trading arrangements. Further progress toward expansion of relations with Eastern Europe remained blocked, however, by the Erhard cabinet's insistence upon the validity, pending a peace conference, of the German frontiers of 1937 and its continuing adherence to the letter of the Hallstein doctrine.

Charles de Gaulle, president of France, 1958–69, visiting Chancellor Konrad Adenauer in Bonn, 1961

In its Western policies, the Erhard cabinet distanced itself somewhat from Adenauer's alignment with the France of President de Gaulle and sought to improve relations with the United States. Because of de Gaulle's opposition to futher integration of Western Europe and to admission of Great Britain to the Common Market and other European institutions, Bonn's close association with France had threatened to become an obstacle to the goal of a united Western Europe that Adenauer himself had earlier so vigorously promoted. As a consequence of de Gaulle's coolness toward the United States, the alignment with France also led to a deterioration in the Federal Republic's relations with Washington. Adenauer's ill-disguised disdain for the youthful and inexperienced President John F. Kennedy also contributed to that deterioration. By cultivating close and cordial relations with Kennedy's successor, Lyndon B. Johnson, and by acceding to American requests for help in financing the American military forces stationed in West Germany, Erhard successfully set out to restore and strengthen the links between Bonn and Washington.

Despite Adenauer's doubts about Erhard's political abilities, he proved a capable vote-getter as his party's candidate for the chancellorship against the SPD's Willy Brandt in the Bundestag election of 1965, in which 86.8 percent of the voters participated. The CDU/CSU remained the largest bloc in the chamber with 245 seats, three more than it had amassed in 1961. The SPD added 12 seats, which brought it to 202, but fell considerably short of its aim of capturing, for the first time, more than 40 percent of the ballots. The junior coalition partner, the FDP, suffered a severe setback, losing 18 seats and retaining only 49. In part because the FDP's critics had accused it of becoming a mere satellite of the CDU/CSU, the smallest of the three major national parties began after the election to assert more forcefully its commitment to classical liberal, laissez-faire economic principles. It continued to insist upon curtailing taxes, governmental involvement in the economy, and growth of the welfare state.

That stand brought the FDP into collision with the chancellor in 1966, when a recession halted the boom of the economic miracle and reduced government revenues to a level that made it impossible to meet welfare-state obligations while conforming to the Basic Law's specification that the federal budget must be balanced. Erhard saw no alternative to increasing taxes, a policy the FDP rejected categorically. The resulting protracted crisis seemed to bear out the skepticism about Erhard's leadership abilities long voiced by Adenauer, who remained head of the CDU until he finally stepped down at age ninety in early 1966. From his semi-retirement the former chancellor contributed to his successor's declining prestige by publicly commenting condescendingly on his performance. At the end of October 1966 the FDP finally broke the stalemate by withdrawing its ministers from the cabinet and depriving Erhard of his majority in the Bundestag. By that time, even the majority of CDU/CSU deputies had become convinced that the chancellor must be replaced. Ironically, Erhard, the architect of the economic miracle, had fallen because of failure to deal adequately with problems arising from a recession.

The Grand Coalition

The departure of Erhard led in November 1966 to the entry, for the first time, of the SPD into a cabinet of the Federal Republic. With the CDU/CSU and FDP at loggerheads, the Social Democrats could choose between a "little coalition" with the FDP, which would hold a narrow majority of three seats in the Bundestag, or a "grand coalition" with the CDU/CSU, which would command more than three-quarters of the chamber. The SPD chose the grand coalition. It conceded the chancellorship to the larger CDU/CSU, which assigned that office to Kurt Georg Kiesinger, the minister-president of Baden-Württemberg. Kiesinger had joined the Nazi Party at age twenty-nine in 1933 after Hitler came to power and had worked during the war in a subaltern position in the propaganda ministry. He had, however, repented and become a staunch defender of the Federal Republic's democratic institutions. The genuineness of his conversion seemed confirmed when SPD leader Willy Brandt, who had impeccable anti-Nazi credentials, agreed to serve in his cabinet as vice-chancellor and foreign minister. The leader of the Bavarian CSU, Franz Josef Strauss, who had been forced out of the cabinet four years earlier after the Spiegel affair, returned as finance minister.

The grand coalition gave the Federal Republic a stable government with which to move toward recovery from the economic recession, but deep differences between the CDU/CSU and SPD ruled out any far-reaching policy initiatives. The coalition did secure passage in 1967 of a law regulating the political parties and providing them with generous funding from the federal

CDU Chancellor Kurt Georg Kiesinger (right) and SPD Foreign Minister Willy Brandt (left), leaders of the Grand Coalition cabinet, 1966–69

treasury as a means of diminishing their financial dependence on contributions from special-interest groups. Mainly at the insistence of the SPD, the cabinet suspended for ten years the statute of limitations with regard to atrocities committed during the Third Reich and facilitated indictment and prosecution of the perpetrators of such crimes. The Kiesinger cabinet also succeeded in resolving the ticklish question of emergency powers. Under the German Treaty of 1954 the Americans, British, and French had reserved to themselves the authority to resume their occupation rights in the event of an emergency situation resulting from an external threat. The West German government began in the early 1960s to assert a claim of its own to emergency authority, but the early drafts of such a constitutional amendment encountered stubborn resistance from critics who believed they too closely paralleled the emergency powers provision which had proved a fatal flaw in the Weimar constitution. In 1968 the cabinet finally arrived at a set of carefully designed constitutional amendments that gained overwhelming endorsement. With their enactment, the former Western occupying powers allowed their residual emergency powers to lapse, so that the Federal Republic's sovereignty expanded significantly.

In the sphere of foreign policy the grand coalition cabinet's major move came with its abandonment of the Hallstein doctrine by establishing diplomatic relations with Rumania and Yugoslavia in 1967 despite their long-standing recognition of the GDR. Kiesinger also responded to letters from the SED leadership in East Berlin and showed interest in further contacts until the GDR's participation in the Soviet-led invasion of Czechoslovakia in the summer of 1968 put a halt to his soundings.

The political stability provided by the grand coalition helped the Federal Republic to weather the increasingly turbulent 1960s. Some of that turbulence resulted from the growing American involvement in the Vietnam War and from the United States' unresolved racial problems at home. Since many West Germans looked to the United States as the ultimate guarantor of their freedom and the inspiration for their own democracy, American failures produced widespread disillusionment and doubt, particularly among younger people, about the wisdom of the Federal Republic's close reliance on the United States. That disillusionment, together with dissatisfaction about the compromises struck by the SPD with the CDU/CSU on domestic issues within the grand coalition, gave rise on the left to what became known as "extraparliamentary opposition." Its advocates scorned what they dismissed as the mere "formal democracy" of the Federal Republic and rejected the established parties. They promoted what they envisaged as a truly democratic alternative outside the existing political system. For many, that increasingly meant the propagation of one Marxist formula or another. For a fanatical few, it meant a resort to kidnapping, incendiarism, and political murder aimed at destroying the fabric of a society they regarded as hopelessly materialistic and corrupt. For the next decade, clandestine bands practicing various forms of terrorism would plague West Germany, claiming the lives of a number of prominent citizens.

Much of the dissatisfaction and unrest of the late 1960s surfaced in student protests at West German universities. Initially, those protests were inspired by the painfully apparent inadequacies of the postwar university system. Under pressure from the Western allies, admission policies had been liberalized, permitting for the first time large numbers of young Germans to attend what had traditionally been universities reserved for a small elite. But while enrollments ballooned, little or nothing was done to adjust faculties or facilities to the new conditions. Lecture halls became overcrowded, libraries and laboratories inadequate. Professorships remained strictly limited in number, and their holders retained the near dictatorial authority over both students and junior faculty traditional in the German system even before the Third Reich. When protests against these increasingly intolerable conditions produced little in the way of response from the state governments responsible for the universities, the protest movement grew and expanded in scope, soon incorporating student demonstrations against Bonn's acquiescence in America's Vietnam involvement. For the first time since the turbulent late years of the Weimar Republic, the streets of West German cities again became the scene of clashes between crowds of demonstrators and police.

While the student protest movement came to be aligned increasingly with the extreme left, another kind of protest developed on the extreme right. It found expression in a new political party, the National Democratic Party (Nationaldemokratische Partei Deutschlands or NPD). Beginning in late 1966, when the effects of the economic recession were being acutely felt and the stalemate within the Erhard cabinet seemed to reveal a failure of authority in Bonn, the NPD managed to secure enough votes to gain representation in several state parliaments. Although the NPD avoided any overt endorsement of Nazi principles, many observers were disturbed by its emphasis on nationalism and its xenophobia, which was directed primarily at the more than a million "guest workers" who had come to West Germany from Southern Europe and Turkey with the blessing of the government to meet the heavy demand for labor generated by the economic miracle. When the economy faltered in the mid-1960s and competition for jobs became tighter, these foreigners made a ready target for nationalistic agitators such as the leaders of the NPD. The Nazi pasts of some NPD leaders also occasioned grave misgivings. Many observers denounced the new party as a neo-Nazi organization and called upon the government to ban it. But instead of invoking against the NPD the Basic Law's prohibition of antidemocratic political activity—as had been done with the neo-Nazi Socialist Reich Party in 1952—the grand coalition cabinet decided to place its trust in the good judgment of the electorate. Similarly, the cabinet took no measures against a new German Communist Party (Deutsche Kommunistische Partei or DKP), formed in 1968, even though the old Communist Party, the KPD, had been banned in 1956.

The presidential and Bundestag elections of 1969 vindicated both the SPD's decision to enter the grand coalition and the cabinet's toleration of extremist parties. The election of a new federal president took place in July, earlier than normal, when the lackluster CDU incumbent, Heinrich Lübke, announced that he would retire several months before completion of his second term so that the presidential election would not be overshadowed by that for the new parliament. His standing had been damaged by his inept response to East German disclosures that he had during the Third Reich worked for a construction firm that built barracks later assigned to slave laborers, including concentration camp inmates. As its presidential candidate, the SPD nominated Justice Minister Gustav Heinemann. A prominent Protestant layman who began his postwar political career as a Christian Democrat, Heinemann had resigned from the first

Adenauer cabinet in 1950 in protest against rearmament and later gravitated to the SPD after attempting unsuccessfully to form a pacifist party. With the help of votes from the FDP in the Federal Assembly, Heinemann narrowly defeated the CDU/CSU presidential candidate, former foreign minister Gerhard Schröder. In the Bundestag election of September 1969, participated in by 86.7 percent of the voters, neither the NPD nor the DKP managed to surmount the 5-percent barrier necessary for representation in the new chamber. The NPD, whose leaders had confidently expected the election to make their party a significant political force, never recovered from this setback. It soon lost its representation in state parliaments as well and ceased to be a serious factor. The CDU/CSU lost three seats but remained the largest bloc in the chamber with 242. The FDP, which had stood in opposition to the grand coalition, suffered a heavy setback, losing 19 of the 49 seats it had obtained in 1965 and only narrowly escaping exclusion under the 5-percent rule. Only the SPD, led by its candidate for the chancellorship, Vice-Chancellor and Foreign Minister Willy Brandt, could lay claim to victory. It gained 22 seats, emerging with a deputation of 224 and, for the first time, with more than 40 percent of the crucial second ballots which so largely shaped the outcome of elections.

Participation in the grand coalition had yielded an impressive harvest of votes for the Social Democrats. Clearly, their responsible role in the Kiesinger cabinet had rendered the Christian Democrats' long-standing contention that the SPD could not be entrusted with power implausible in the eyes of many voters who had not previously supported that party. With a Social Democrat as federal president and the SPD at its all-time high of strength in the parliament, the stage was set in the autumn of 1969 for the Federal Republic's first full-blown change of regime after twenty years of Christian Democratic leadership.

5

The Social-Liberal
Era and the Return to
Conservatism in the
Federal Republic

Willy Brandt's Cabinet and the
New Eastern Policy

Bolstered by their gains in the Bundestag election of 1969, the Social Democrats captured the chancellorship of the Federal Republic for the first time. This marked the end of a period out of power that had begun nearly forty years earlier, in 1930, when the last cabinet of the Weimar Republic headed by a Social Democratic chancellor had fallen.

The SPD succeeded in claiming power only by virtue of a reorientation on the part of the third party represented in the Bundestag, the FDP. The Free Democrats, who regarded themselves as heirs to the German liberal tradition, had chafed, as intermittent junior coalition partners of the CDU/CSU, under the domination of that party before their relegation to the status of a precariously small opposition when the two large parties formed the grand coalition in 1966. The FDP's advocacy of laissez-faire economics and its resistance to expansion of the welfare state had generally placed it at odds with the SPD in the spheres of economic and social policies. Now, however, under the leadership of a new party chairman, Walter Scheel, the Free Democrats agreed to join with the SPD in forming a coalition government in Bonn. The result was thirteen years of what would come to be known as the social-liberal era.

After nearly a month of painstaking coalition negotiations, FDP and SPD Bundestag deputies joined forces to elect SPD chairman Willy Brandt the first Social Democratic chancellor of the Federal Republic in October 1969. Brandt appointed Scheel foreign minister in a cabinet that included two other Free Democrats and eleven Social Democrats in addition to the chancellor. The new cabinet rested from the outset on an extremely precarious parliamentary basis. Nominally, it commanded a majority of six votes in the Bundestag, but not all the FDP had accepted the switch to an alignment with the Social Democrats, who remained anathema to much of the liberal party's right wing. The Bundestag vote that installed the cabinet in office revealed the parliamentary fragility of the coalition, as enough FDP deputies abstained or cast invalid ballots to reduce the margin of Brandt's victory to only two more than the absolute majority necessary for election of a chancellor in the first round of balloting.

Once installed, Brandt proclaimed himself a "domestic-reform chancellor." Whereas the CDU/CSU had long used the slogan "no experiments," the new social-liberal cabinet announced that it would be guided by the principle "no fear of experimentation." Chancellor Brandt pledged his cabinet to a reform of law statutes governing such sensitive social issues as abortion, divorce, and pornography, some of which had gone unrevised since the Empire. He promised as well that the cabinet would press ahead with adaptation of the welfare state to new needs and with expansion of labor's participation in industrial decision-making through codetermination. The differing views of the SPD and the FDP on economic and social policy posed, however, formidable obstacles to realization of the chancellor's domestic program. So did control by the CDU/CSU over a majority in the Bundesrat. As a result, the cabinet took few swift actions on those issues, which gave rise to protracted bureaucratic preparation and hard behind-the-scenes political bargaining.

By contrast, the social-liberal cabinet moved quickly and boldly in the sphere of foreign policy. It pledged continued adherence to the NATO alliance and to the multinational institutions of Western Europe, leaving no doubt that the Federal Republic would remain firmly integrated in the Western bloc. But with regard to policy toward the USSR and the rest of the Soviet bloc, including the GDR, the Brandt government made clear its intention to embark upon a new course. Both the chancellor and the foreign minister believed the time had come for a reduction of East-West tensions in Central Europe. Although unwilling to meet the GDR's demands for full diplomatic recognition, Brandt and Scheel were prepared to accord to the East German regime a degree of acceptance that would permit a far-reaching normalization of relations. The Germans in East and West, Brandt explained in his initial speech as chancellor, must first learn how to live alongside each other and then, eventually, how to live with each other. Progress in that direction, he and his foreign minister predicted, would result in improvement of the day-to-day lot of those Germans locked behind the fortified borders of the GDR who continued to bear the penalty for the Third Reich's criminal war of aggression. The time had come, the leaders of the social-liberal government contended, to place the interests of living people above concern about the abstract notions of nation and *Volk* invoked by those who rejected anything short of complete reunification and thus opposed any recognition whatever of the GDR by the Federal Republic.

The initial overtures from the new cabinet in Bonn met with little responsiveness from a GDR still dominated by Walter Ulbricht, but Moscow proved more receptive. Concerned about an increasingly defiant and assertive Chinese People's Republic along its eastern frontier and drawn by the prospect of expanded trade with the economically robust and technologically advanced Federal Republic, the Soviet Union soon entered into serious negotiations with Bonn about ways to improve relations.

Willy Brandt (left), chancellor of the Federal Republic, 1969–74, meeting with Willi Stoph, chairman of the Council of Ministers of the German Democratic Republic, in the East German city of Erfurt in March 1970

Ulbricht, who still clung to his dream of full diplomatic recognition of the GDR by the Federal Republic, held back. He did, however, permit a meeting between Brandt and the head of the GDR's Council of Ministers, Willi Stoph, at the East German city of Erfurt in March 1970. Stoph presented a stiff set of demands, including reparations payments from Bonn for the talent lost by the GDR through the flight of refugees prior to the erection of the Berlin Wall. Those demands, plus the allergic reaction of the Eastern authorities to the spontaneous demonstrations of welcome that greeted Brandt in the streets of Erfurt, did not augur well for a relaxation of tensions.

By prearrangement, Stoph returned Brandt's visit in May 1970 by meeting with the chancellor in the West German city of Kassel, an occasion marked by unruly street protests against the East German leader's presence in the Federal Republic. At Kassel Brandt presented a twenty-point program that included recognition by Bonn of the authority of the East Berlin regime. Stoph countered by demanding that the Federal Republic immediately extend full diplomatic recognition to the GDR. With the two sides far apart, no substantive progress was made. Still, the glacier-like ice of the Cold War had at least been cracked, and high government officials of the two Germanies had for the first time sat down together to talk.

Meanwhile, negotiations with the Soviet Union progressed rapidly and yielded a non-aggression pact, the Treaty of Moscow, signed in August 1970. Both governments renounced the use of force and stated that they had no claim upon each other's territory or that of any other state. They pledged to respect as "inviolable" all existing frontiers, including those between the GDR and the Federal Republic and between the GDR and Poland (the so-called Oder-Neisse line established in 1945). That amounted to recognition by Bonn of the territorial changes made after the war. The Federal Republic succeeded, however, in excluding from the treaty any mention of the GDR's status or of the Soviet Union's long-standing demand that Bonn grant East Berlin full diplomatic recognition.

For their part, the Soviets insisted that no mention of German reunification appear in the Moscow Treaty, but they did agree to receive a letter in which Bonn stated its position on that issue. In its letter, the Federal Republic expressed the view that the treaty did not rule out an eventual reunification through the exercise, by the German people, of the right of self-determination. That statement obviously had no immediate significance, but it did enable the social-liberal coalition to defend the treaty with the Soviet Union by pointing out that the Russians had raised no objections to the right of Germans to reunite their nation in a peaceful fashion at some time in the future. In addition to the supplemental letter on reunification, Bonn gave the USSR to understand that the Federal Republic would move to ratify the Moscow Treaty only after the Russians had joined with the three other victorious powers to draw up a new four-power agreement regulating the status of Berlin.

The Brandt cabinet's new Eastern policy also called for a

normalization of relations with Poland. A prerequisite for that step lay in final abandonment of the Hallstein doctrine, which had ruled out diplomatic relations with countries (except for the USSR) which recognized the GDR. A second prerequisite to an understanding with Poland was Bonn's readiness to affirm the Oder-Neisse line, since the refusal of previous West German governments to accept Poland's postwar western frontier as valid had kept alive Polish fears of eventual German vengeance. Working within this new framework, Bonn and the Communist regime in Warsaw signed, after lengthy negotiations, the Treaty of Warsaw in December 1970.

In the agreement with Poland, as in the Treaty of Moscow, the Federal Republic pledged to regard the Oder-Neisse line as "inviolable." In return, the Poles accepted wording compatible with the West German position that final determination of postwar boundaries must await a general peace settlement. The Polish government made a further concession to Bonn by agreeing to allow persons of German nationality still resident in Poland to move to either of the two German states if they complied with Polish emigration regulations and procedures. Chancellor Brandt personally journeyed to Warsaw to sign the treaty. He turned his visit—the first by a high official of the Federal Republic to Poland—into a gesture of reconciliation that received worldwide recognition when he dropped to his knees and bowed his head before a memorial to the victims of the Nazi liquidation of the Warsaw ghetto.

The social-liberal cabinet's Eastern initiatives won for it widespread acclaim at home and abroad but also resulted in a loss of parliamentary support. In October 1970 three FDP deputies, including former party chairman Erich Mende, defected to the CDU in protest against the concessions made in the treaties of Moscow and Warsaw, which in their eyes betrayed the cause of German reunification. This left the social-liberal cabinet with a majority of only three in the Bundestag. In view of continuing dissension in the ranks of the FDP, this amounted to a very precarious margin. Since ratification of the treaties with the

Chancellor Willy Brandt kneeling at the memorial for victims of the Nazi liquidation of the Warsaw ghetto during his visit to Warsaw to sign the Polish-West German treaty in December 1970

USSR and Poland had been postponed until the four former occupation powers reached agreement on Berlin, the fate of the new Eastern policy remained highly uncertain.

That uncertainty was heightened by the fact that the CDU/CSU, which vehemently denounced the treaties with the USSR and Poland as unconstitutional violations of the Basic Law's commitment to reunification, controlled a majority in the second federal chamber, the Bundesrat. In order to override a defeat of the Eastern treaties in the Bundesrat the social-liberal cabinet would therefore have to muster an absolute majority of the full Bundestag rather than a simple majority of those present and voting. As the government proceeded with negotiations aimed at expanding its new Eastern policy during the winter of 1970–71, political tension mounted dramatically in the Federal Republic.

During 1971 further progress was achieved with the new Eastern policy. In May of that year the deposition of Walter Ulbricht removed a formidable obstacle to achievement of what the new leaders in Bonn envisaged as the capstone of their new policy: an agreement with the GDR. But another hurdle had to be cleared in order to make that step possible. Recognizing that it would be difficult, if not impossible, to resolve the Berlin problem with the GDR, Bonn had decided that it could not enter into formal negotiations with the Communist regime in East Berlin until the status of the former German capital had been regulated by means of a four-power agreement among the erstwhile allies of World War II. The Western allies were therefore prodded accordingly.

In early September 1971, after protracted and difficult negotiations, the Americans, British, French, and Russians arrived at an accord on Berlin. Because of long-standing differences between the Western powers and the Soviet Union, that agreement avoided defining what was meant by Berlin, referring instead to "the area in question." Rather than solving problems, the accord regulated them. The Western powers affirmed that West Berlin did not constitute a part of the Federal Republic and ruled out meetings there of the Federal Assembly, the body which elected the West German president, as well as plenary sessions of the Bundesrat and Bundestag (though not committee meetings). Sovereign rights in West Berlin would continue to reside with the three Western powers under the wartime and postwar agreements. Since the Russians refused to consider the status of East Berlin, it was not dealt with. In communications to the USSR appended to the accord, however, the Western powers restated their claim to quadripartite occupation rights throughout all of Berlin.

In return for restrictions on West Berlin's ties to the Federal Republic, the Soviets abandoned their oft-repeated claim that West Berlin lay within the territory of the GDR and so fell under its authority. Instead, the USSR now agreed that the Federal Republic could represent West Berlin internationally and extend diplomatic and consular protection to its citizens. The accord also granted access rights to the GDR to West Berliners, who had been forbidden to visit East Berlin or East Germany since construction of the Berlin Wall in 1961, except for a few holiday periods when passes had been granted for family visits. The accord sanctioned, in addition, the presence in West Berlin of numerous agencies of the West German government, which employed more civil servants there than in Bonn. The Russians further promised to facilitate the movement of traffic through the GDR between West Germany and West Berlin, to expand telephone service between West Berlin and the GDR, and to eliminate some local friction points on the periphery of West Berlin by means of minor border adjustments that did not alter the status of the inhabitants.

The four powers agreed to turn over the details of these and other practical arrangements regarding Berlin to the German authorities in East and West and to make implementation of the four-power accord contingent upon their coming to terms with each other on those matters. The Berlin accord thus bestowed upon the GDR the same degree of recognition given the Federal Republic, thereby satisfying one of the Soviet aims. Finally, by the terms of the accord's preamble, the four signatories agreed to renounce the use of force and to seek resolution of all future problems regarding Berlin by means of negotiations. The accord thus held out the prospect of permanently eliminating Berlin as a potential flash point imperiling world peace.

Conclusion of the four-power accord on Berlin removed the last obstacle to negotiations between the Federal Republic and the GDR. Since implementation of the practical measures prescribed by way of regularizing and improving the situation in Berlin had been assigned to the German authorities in East and West, opponents of negotiations in both Bonn and East Berlin stood disarmed. Soviet leader Leonid Brezhnev exerted pressure on the SED regime by inviting Chancellor Brandt to the Soviet

Union and paying a visit of his own to East Berlin, where he emphasized the desirability of lowering international tensions by means of negotiations.

By the end of 1971 the governments of West Berlin and the Federal Republic had achieved agreement with their counterparts in the East on arrangements designed to implement the major provisions of the four-power accord on Berlin. Negotiations, often difficult, proceeded on the remainder, and prospects seemed bright for full implementation of the accord, which in turn would clear the way for action by the Bundestag on ratification of the treaties of Moscow and Warsaw. As 1971 drew to a close, Chancellor Willy Brandt received the Nobel Peace Prize for his part in reducing the international tension in Central Europe that had for so long threatened to plunge the world into war again.

During the first months of 1972 the social-liberal coalition's parliamentary situation deteriorated, threatening to undo the new Eastern policy. Defections to the opposition by coalition deputies in the Bundestag, mainly from the FDP, because of objections to that policy pared down the government's majority to the vanishing point. This emboldened the CDU/CSU to attempt to fell the Brandt cabinet. In the expectation that still more FDP deputies would desert the coalition if put to the test, CDU parliamentary leader Rainer Barzel challenged the government by placing a constructive vote of no-confidence before the Bundestag in mid-April, the first ever attempted in the Federal Republic. If an absolute majority could be won for the motion, Brandt would be deposed and Barzel would become chancellor.

In the often impassioned debate prior to the Bundestag balloting on the constructive vote of no-confidence, the spokesmen of the CDU/CSU portrayed the government's Eastern policy as an unconstitutional desertion of the Federal Republic's obligation to free the East Germans from the yoke of Communism and reunite the nation. They pledged that if the no-confidence motion carried they would form a new government. They would then seek to renegotiate the treaties with the Soviet Union and

Poland so as to bring about reconciliation with those countries on terms that did not bind the Federal Republic to accept the frontiers drawn in 1945 or endanger its sovereignty and ties with the Western alliance (which the opposition contended might be the effect of the Moscow Treaty). When the balloting took place on April 27, 1972, however, the no-confidence motion fell two votes short of the requisite absolute majority of the full Bundestag. Not enough FDP deputies had defected, and from all indications at least two, possibly three, CDU/CSU deputies had made use of the secret ballot to indicate disapproval of their party's motion.

Buoyed by this dramatic victory and by conclusion of the East German–West German negotiations on measures to implement the four-power Berlin accord, the Brandt cabinet pressed ahead toward a parliamentary showdown on its Eastern policy by scheduling the ratification vote on the Moscow and Warsaw treaties for May 1972. By that time, defections by coalition deputies had eliminated the social-liberal majority and produced, numerically at least, a parliamentary stalemate between government and opposition in the Bundestag. The problems of the cabinet were made even more acute by the CDU/CSU majority in the Bundesrat. By the terms of the Basic Law, if the Bundesrat rejected the treaties, ratification could only be effected by an absolute majority of the Bundestag.

By the time the final Bundestag vote on the two Eastern treaties took place in mid-May 1972, such deep divisions had developed in the ranks of the CDU/CSU that efforts to block ratification collapsed. Some of the opposition's deputies had become inclined to acceptance, either because they had come to approve of the new Eastern policy, or because they had grown skeptical about the feasibility of renegotiating the treaties, or because they had come to doubt the political wisdom of blocking what had become a very popular diplomatic initiative. Others in the opposition, particularly in the ranks of the Bavarian CSU, led by its chairman Franz Josef Strauss, remained adamantly opposed and demanded an all-out effort to block ratification. Barzel sought to clear the way for near-unanimous ratification by negotiating a joint government-opposition statement that clarified certain aspects of the treaties and asserted that they did not bind the Federal Republic to permanent recognition of postwar frontiers. Barzel's effort failed, however, to quell opposition within his party.

In order to avoid an open split in the ranks of the CDU/CSU that would leave it in disarray at the time of a new Bundestag election, which was expected soon in view of the parliamentary stalemate, the opposition leadership instructed CDU/CSU deputies to abstain in the votes on the Eastern treaties. Although a few nevertheless cast negative ballots, both treaties passed by wide margins, but not by absolute majorities. This left the CDU/CSU with the option of using its majority in the Bundesrat to block ratification, which would have thrown the matter back to the Bundestag and made an absolute majority there necessary for ratification. Recognizing that in such a situation those CDU/CSU deputies who had come to favor the treaties would probably break ranks and vote with the government parties, the opposition leadership instructed its Bundesrat delegates to abstain also, thus permitting final ratification of the Warsaw and Moscow treaties in May 1972.

Upon final approval of the four-power accord on Berlin by the wartime allies in early June 1972, following a series of East German–West German agreements on its practical implementation, the treaties of Moscow and Warsaw went into effect. The social-liberal government's new Eastern policy had finally begun to show results after nearly three years of sustained effort. By a remarkable series of delicate and interconnected negotiations, Bonn had for the first time assumed a leadership role in the diplomatic sphere. Its initiatives had yielded, as observers both at home and abroad recognized, noticeable improvements in the lot of Germans in both East and West as well as a significant diminution of the peril of a new war arising over unresolved issues left over from the aftermath of World War II.

In the autumn of 1972, the Brandt cabinet decided that the time had come to resolve the parliamentary deadlock brought about by defections from the coalition parties' Bundestag deputations. With the government lacking the votes needed in the chamber for approval of its budget, the situation had reached the breaking point. In order to control the course of events, the chancellor requested a vote of confidence in the chamber in late September and then ensured its failure by having the cabinet members abstain. The opposition desisted from an attempt to find a positive majority for an alternative cabinet. President Heinemann thereupon dissolved the Bundestag and scheduled new elections for November. For the first time in twenty-three years a cabinet had fallen because it lacked a parliamentary majority.

In the election campaign of 1972 the government parties emphasized the progress registered by the new Eastern policy and promised, if returned with a majority, to cap that policy with an agreement normalizing relations with the GDR. Just two weeks before the balloting, Chancellor Brandt and Foreign Minister Scheel were able to unveil the draft of an agreement arrived at in negotiations with East Berlin which soon became known as the Basic Treaty. They could also point out that preparations were under way for admission of both German governments to the United Nations as full members and that all four erstwhile occupying powers stood ready to support that step.

The CDU/CSU opposition, while continuing to voice objections to the government's now-successful Eastern policy, found itself on the defensive. Its candidate for the chancellorship, Barzel, announced that he would, if victorious, not sign the Basic Treaty with the GDR until its government ordered an end to the shooting of refugees seeking to flee to the West. Otherwise, the CDU/CSU leaders sought to shift voter attention away from foreign policy to the economy, where inflation proceeded for the first time at the rate of more than 5 percent a year and threatened to top 6 percent. But with the fate of the Basic Treaty with the GDR dependent upon the outcome of the balloting, the election became largely a plebiscite on the government's Eastern policy.

The public displayed intense interest in the campaign, and a record-breaking 91.1 percent of the electorate participated in the balloting of November 1972. When the votes were counted, the social-liberal coalition stood vindicated at the polls. For the first time, the SPD received more ballots in a Bundestag election than the CDU/CSU and became the strongest party in the Bundestag with 230 seats, a gain of 6. The Social Democrats' partner in the government, the FDP, whose chairman, Foreign Minister Scheel, had played a prominent role in the diplomatic negotiations of the previous three years, made a strong showing that increased its seats by 11, to 41. The losses suffered by the CDU/CSU dropped its representation in the parliament to 225, a decline of 17. After years of struggling to survive, first with minute majorities, then with none, the social-liberal coalition government now controlled the Bonn parliament by a healthy margin.

After the new Bundestag had reinstalled Brandt as chancellor and approved Scheel as foreign minister once more, the government signed the Basic Treaty with the GDR in December 1972. According to its terms, the two German states renounced the use of force in their relations and agreed to regard the frontier between them as inviolable. Each recognized and agreed to respect the other's authority and independence. Each forswore any title to represent the other internationally, which meant for the Federal Republic abandonment of its long-standing claim to be the sole legitimate spokesman of the German people.

For its part, the GDR agreed to join with the Federal Republic in respecting the human rights set forth in the charter of the United Nations. In more specific terms, the GDR agreed to permit brief visits by its citizens to the West in instances of pressing family need. At the insistence of the Federal Republic, the degree of mutual acceptance established by the Basic Treaty stopped short of full diplomatic recognition. Reflecting this limitation, the treaty provided for the exchange not of embassies but rather of "permanent missions" in Bonn and East Berlin. The treaty provided no solution to the "national question," that is, the future of Germany as a whole, mentioning in the preamble only that the signatories held differing views on it.

According to the official West German interpretation of the Basic Treaty, the Federal Republic had recognized the GDR as another sovereign state within the German nation, not as a foreign country. Precedents for this formula abounded in Germany's past, since prior to unification of the country in 1871 it had consisted of numerous states, each claiming to be sovereign without being foreign. Bonn's eventual goal, government spokesmen explained, remained national unity, but in the meantime the Federal Republic had to accept realities, one of which was the incontestable existence of another German polity. Denying realities would not bring reunification closer, they argued. The policy of non-recognition and non-negotiation followed for nearly a quarter century had, they pointed out, achieved no progress toward dismantling the barriers that separated the Germans in the East from those in the West. Indeed, that policy had only enabled the regime in East Berlin to justify its harsh methods of rule by contending that a hostile, predatory Federal Republic threatened the very existence of the GDR and the "socialist achievements" of its citizenry.

Under the circumstances that would in all likelihood prevail for the foreseeable future, spokesmen of the social-liberal government argued, the only hope of furthering the cause of eventual reunification lay in encouraging change in the other part of Germany. That could best be achieved, they held, through a policy of recognition and cooperation with the regime in the GDR on practical matters and by increasing contacts between people in the two parts of the country. In the short run, only that policy held out the prospect of improving conditions for the millions of Germans who had to live behind the barbed wire, mined landstrips, and masonry walls that the SED regime had constructed around the GDR to keep them from fleeing.

During 1973 the second Brandt cabinet applied the finishing touches to the edifice of the social-liberal coalition's Eastern policy. In May the government used its expanded majority in the Bundestag to secure ratification of the Basic Treaty with the GDR. The CDU/CSU again desisted from invoking its majority in the Bundesrat to block the government's foreign policy rather than bring about a showdown that would expose the split in the opposition's ranks. In line with an agreement made with the GDR earlier, both German governments petitioned for admission to the United Nations, which added them to its membership in September 1973. In December Bonn reached agreement with the Czechoslovak Communist regime on a treaty in which each agreed to recognize the inviolability of the other's borders and to renounce the use of force in their relations. That same month the Federal Republic exchanged ambassadors with Bulgaria and Hungary, a step that marked the establishment of diplomatic relations with all the countries of Eastern Europe except maverick Albania. The treaty structure of the new Eastern policy stood completed after four years of busy diplomatic activity which had seen the Federal Republic repeatedly seize the initiative.

Domestic Reform Efforts and Problems of the 1970s

As the Brandt cabinet neared completion of its foreign policy initiatives, its attention shifted increasingly to domestic reform projects. These proved almost as arduous as the new Eastern policy, since profound differences in outlook still separated the coalition partners. The Social Democrats wished to push ahead vigorously toward more social justice by expanding the welfare state and by enacting laws granting a greater role in economic decision-making to those without wealth and property. The Free Democrats, by contrast, sought to defend the freedoms of the citizen against what they saw as governmental encroachment and to protect individual initiative in the economic sphere against what they perceived as the stifling effects of bureaucratization.

Under these circumstances, legislative initiatives in the socioeconomic sphere involved protracted and sometimes acrimonious negotiations between the coalition partners as well as collisions with the CDU/CSU, which continued to hold a majority in the Bundesrat. Nevertheless, the cabinet managed to expand the welfare state by significantly increasing pensions for retired and disabled citizens. It also secured passage in 1972 of a law that broadened the role of works councils in the determination of working conditions and the allocation of employee benefits. Resolution of differences between the SPD and FDP on expansion of industrial codetermination proved more difficult. Although the coalition partners managed in early 1974 to agree on the basic outlines of a bill to expand employee participation in management, it was not to be enacted during the Brandt cabinet. The social-liberal coalition did, however, make progress in revising criminal and civil law codes inherited from past regimes, in some cases as far back as imperial times.

Efforts by the SPD to expand the welfare-state commitments of the Federal Republic encountered new obstacles as a result of the international oil crisis of 1973, which interrupted the economic expansion that had prevailed since the early 1950s. For the first time in nearly twenty years, sustained unemployment set in. By 1974 more than half a million West Germans were out of jobs. The drop in employment and the consequent decline in consumer demand produced a further slackening of business activity and diminished tax revenues sharply. Since the welfare system obligated the government to heavy expenditures despite falling revenues, the inflation rate shot up in 1973 and 1974 to the highest level since the currency reform of 1948: 7 percent. This made it increasingly difficult for the SPD to convince the FDP to go along with plans for additional social programs that would obligate the government to still further expenditures.

The rise in unemployment focused attention on the large number of foreign workers in the Federal Republic. Starting in the 1950s, Italians, Spaniards, Yugoslavs, Greeks, and Turks had streamed into West Germany in response to the labor shortage generated by the economic miracle. Many brought their wives and children with them, giving rise to a resident foreign population of over 4 million by 1975. Some 2.5 million were gainfully employed, which amounted to nearly 11 percent of the total West German workforce. They enjoyed the full benefits of the Federal Republic's welfare state, to which they contributed through taxes and paycheck deductions, like other workers. Their presence was, however, resented by some West Germans. And whereas most of the foreign workers were hard-working and law-abiding, a few among them—or among their children—found adjustment to a new language and a new culture difficult, thus occasioning social problems. The onset of joblessness among Germans led to cries for restrictions on the number of foreign workers in order to increase employment opportunities for Germans. But the Brandt cabinet resisted that pressure, declining to expel people who had, only a few years earlier, been encouraged to come to Germany to work at a time when the country desperately needed labor. Instead, the government sought to halt further recruitment of workers from abroad.

The compromises the Social Democrats had to strike with the Free Democrats in order to move ahead with domestic reforms left the SPD's leadership vulnerable to criticism from within its own ranks. Particularly vehement attacks came from the Social Democratic youth organization, the Young Socialists. Its leaders viewed the SPD's concessions to the Free Democrats and their laissez-faire outlook on economic policy as a betrayal of their party's traditions. The Young Socialists raised increasingly loud demands for a renewed commitment to socialization of at least large-scale, basic industries, to development of a thoroughgoing welfare state, and to democratization of all social institutions, including factories, the bureaucracy, hospitals, and schools. All those who worked within such institutions should, the dissenters within the SPD argued, have a voice in decision-making. The leadership of the SPD successfully resisted the efforts of youth group spokesmen to impose their views on the party, but at the cost of disaffection among some of the SPD's younger adherents, particularly those who had advanced to the upper reaches of the educational system. For them, Social Democracy stood discredited, and they swung to the far left politically, forming a wide variety of quarreling sects, most of which cultivated some variant of Marxist ideology.

The increasing popularity of extreme leftist organizations had by the early 1970s turned many West German universities into ideological battlefields where violence sometimes escalated from the verbal to the physical and spilled over into the streets. In an effort to deal with the very real problems of mass universities still operated by administrative structures designed for the small, elite educational institutions of an earlier age, the governments of the federal states—under whose jurisdiction the educational system fell—enacted new university statutes. In some states, particularly those where the Social Democrats dominated the governments, those laws divided authority in the internal affairs of universities more or less evenly among the faculty, the students, and support personnel. This "tripartite parity" politicized the universities and sometimes led to acrimonious stalemates that hampered their educational operations. After years of dispute, the Constitutional Court in 1973 restored the faculties to preeminence within the universities, at least on matters of research and teaching.

Meanwhile, other developments were reducing tensions among students. The states had at last begun to address legitimate grievances arising from overcrowding and understaffing by founding new universities which were in part financed with funds from Bonn. Whereas in 1964 West German universities and polytechnical academies numbered twenty-six, students could ten years later pursue higher education at forty-nine institutions. The number of faculty members was more than doubled, and appropriations for operations swelled. Nevertheless, a steady increase in the number of students continued to create problems. In order to keep manageable the number of those studying in such sought-after fields as medicine, the states began to restrict admission to the most highly qualified applicants, breaking with the venerable German tradition of free choice for all university students.

A disaffected minority of students active in Marxist sects

posed a dilemma for the state governments of West Germany, which recruited their civil servants and schoolteachers from the universities. The oppositional CDU/CSU, along with some FDP politicians and the conservative press, charged that Communists were infiltrating the bureaucracy and educational institutions for purposes of subversion. In response, the Brandt cabinet joined in January 1972 with the state governments in agreeing to implement loyalty checks that would result in the dismissal of a civil servant or teacher who belonged to an organization found to be hostile to the democratic constitutional order of the Federal Republic.

These loyalty checks occasioned widespread criticism on the grounds that they curtailed the civil liberties of government employees and could give rise to injustices. Much of the SPD viewed the loyalty checks with grave misgivings, but it soon became apparent that sentiment within the FDP made their retention a necessity for preservation of the social-liberal coalition. The government refrained, on the other hand, from banning the German Communist Party, which had been revived in 1968. It polled less than 0.5 percent in the 1972 elections, and the government had no desire to outlaw it, as its poor showing conveniently demonstrated its lack of support among the electorate.

The Chancellorship of Helmut Schmidt

In early May 1974, after four and a half eventful years as chancellor of the Federal Republic, Willy Brandt abruptly resigned. A few days earlier, one of his trusted aides, Günter Guillaume, had been unmasked as a spy for the GDR. Sent to the West in the guise of a refugee more than twenty years earlier, Giullaume had joined the SPD and patiently worked his way up in its ranks until he gained the confidence of Chairman Brandt, who included him in his staff when he became chancellor. Since Guillaume had in that capacity enjoyed access to confidential documents, including some from the NATO alliance, his espionage activity for East Berlin amounted to a major security breach. This rendered Brandt's position untenable, and he withhdrew from the chancellorship but retained the chairmanship of the SPD.

Brandt's successor, Social Democrat Helmut Schmidt, was a very different sort of man. Middle-class in background, he had joined the SPD after serving in the military during the war. An accomplished pianist and able yachtsman, he brought a polished style to a party long known for sensible practicality but lacking in cosmopolitan flair. Energetic and intelligent, Schmidt had risen rapidly within the SPD despite an acerbic tongue that offended some. After distinguishing himself as a minister in the government of the city state of Hamburg, he moved to Bonn as a Bundestag deputy in 1965 and became the floor leader of the SPD in 1967. Two years later he took over as defense minister in the social-liberal cabinet. In 1972 he became the Brandt cabinet's "crisis minister" when he moved to the head of the finance ministry and, briefly, the economics ministry as well. Like Brandt, Schmidt spoke fluent English and enjoyed international recognition.

Schmidt managed to keep the Guillaume affair from disrupting the social-liberal coalition. The only significant change in the cabinet occurred when he named Hans-Dietrich Genscher, chairman of the FDP, as foreign minister. Genscher replaced former foreign minister and fellow Free Democrat Walter Scheel, who was elected federal president in May 1974, succeeding the retiring Social Democratic incumbent, Gustav Heinemann.

Schmidt entered office at an unpropitious moment, just as the full effects of what was to be West Germany's deepest economic recession became manifest. From his experience as finance minister, the chancellor realized that this would impose severe constraints on his options. He therefore proclaimed "continuity and concentration" as the watchwords of his cabinet. In practice this involved preserving the stability of the currency by limiting the growth of the welfare state in line with the reduced tax revenues received by the government. That proved a difficult role for a Social Democrat, since the SPD had long made expansion of the welfare state a high domestic priority. As a result, Schmidt's chancellorship was to be troubled by rebelliousness within the ranks of his own party. A pragmatic man of strong will, the chancellor repeatedly managed, however, to subdue his Social Democratic critics and assert his paramountcy in party and in government.

Under the Schmidt cabinet, expansion of the welfare state slowed. In part, this was a result of the recession. But other factors lay in mounting resistance from the FDP within the coalition and from the oppositional CDU/CSU, whose majority in the Bundesrat enabled it to continue to obstruct welfare-state legislation. The cabinet's major accomplishment in that sphere came with enactment in 1976 of the codetermination bill agreed upon by the Brandt cabinet two years earlier. It provided for equal representation of owners and employees in the supervisory boards of all corporations with more than two thousand employees. Since the law assigned one employee seat to managerial personnel, it failed to satisfy the unions. But it moved the Federal Republic to the forefront of the movement for participation in management by labor.

In the sphere of foreign policy, the Schmidt cabinet held to the social-liberal coalition's commitment to maintain the Federal Republic's strong ties with its Western allies while seeking to improve relations with its neighbors to the East. In continuation of that policy Schmidt visited a number of East European capitals and worked toward solutions to a variety of problems so as to remove long-standing irritants. Toward the GDR Schmidt followed what became known as a "policy of small steps" designed to ameliorate the lot of Germans living in the East and to normalize relations between the two German states. Without fanfare, indeed secretly at the outset, the Federal Republic began to secure the release of a steady flow of political prisoners from the GDR by paying ransom to the SED regime in Western marks, which East Germany needed for purchases abroad. The Schmidt cabinet also arranged for extension of increasing amounts of interest-free credit to the GDR in order to promote trade, an arrangement that was advantageous for the Federal Republic at a time when a general economic slump curtailed markets for West German goods among trading partners in the non-Communist world.

Within the Western alliance, the Federal Republic attained new prominence under Schmidt's leadership. The cordial personal ties he established with French president Valéry Giscard d'Estaing brought West Germany into closer cooperation with its largest Western neighbor than at any time since the days of Adenauer and de Gaulle. At the Helsinki Conference on Security and Cooperation in Europe, the first general meeting of the states of both East and West since the Second World War, the Federal Republic played an active role and joined in signing the set of final principles endorsed by the participants in 1975.

The size and dynamism of the West German economy, together with Schmidt's expertise in that sphere, gave him an increasingly influential voice in the deliberations of Western heads of states as they wrestled with the vexing problems of recession and inflation. This became evident in 1978 when the leaders of the major Western powers met and conferred about common economic problems in Bonn at the first such high-level gathering in the West German capital. A year later the American, British, and French leaders invited Schmidt to join them at a select four-power economic summit in Guadaloupe. Despite friction with the administration of American president Jimmy Carter, whom Schmidt found irresolute and uncommunicative, the Federal Republic carried greater weight within the Western alliance than ever before.

At home the Schmidt cabinet recorded notable successes but also experienced new difficulties. After striking bottom in 1975, the first year since the currency reform when overall production declined, the economy rallied strongly. By 1978 the inflation rate had declined to only 3 percent, the lowest level among major

West European countries. West German exports expanded once more, attaining unprecedented levels by the end of the 1970s. Unemployment, which had left more than a million idle in 1975, began to decline, but only slowly. Joblessness, particularly among young people, proved a stubborn problem, as it did in other Western countries. During 1977, long after general recovery had set in, the unemployed still averaged more than a million annually. By 1979 the figure had sunk, but only to 876,000, and during 1980 it rose again to 888,900.

The Bundestag election of October 1976 registered mounting dissatisfaction with the performance of the social-liberal coalition. Schmidt stood as the chancellorship candidate of the SPD, while the CDU/CSU put forward its chairman, Helmut Kohl. With 90.7 percent of the electorate voting, the SPD saw its seats decline from the high-water mark of 230 attained four years earlier to 214. The FDP also suffered losses, falling from 41 to 39 seats. The coalition emerged with only 10 more seats than the CDU/CSU opposition, which once again became, with 243 deputies—a gain of 19—the strongest single bloc in the chamber. The vulnerability of the chancellor became evident when abstentions by coalition deputies reduced the margin of his reelection in the Bundestag to only one vote. The cabinet then suffered an embarrassment when it reneged shortly after the election on a campaign pledge to raise the government pensions of retired persons by 10 percent, an increase which the opposition had denounced as financially unviable.

The Schmidt cabinet managed to recover some of its prestige through its handling of the problem of leftist terrorism. Since the late 1960s dissident groups of young people had sporadically engaged in terrorist acts, but in 1977 a wave of abductions, assassinations, and bombings culminated in the murders of two prominent businessmen and a public prosecutor. The authorities managed to locate and arrest some of the leading members of the self-styled Red Army Faction that carried out these crimes. In the autumn, however, a group of their confederates hijacked a plane carrying several hundred passengers that belonged to the

West German state airline, Lufthansa, and forced it to land in Somalia on the east coast of Africa. The hijackers demanded release of their jailed accomplices in return for sparing the passengers on the plane. Rather than submit to extortion, the Schmidt cabinet authorized a rescue attempt by crack troops of the West German border police. When that airborne mission dramatically succeeded in liberating the hostages in October 1977, the popularity of the chancellor soared.

The problems caused by the energy crisis of the 1970s proved less tractible than did terrorism. In an effort to cope with the increased price and uncertain supply of oil, a major energy source for which the Federal Republic was 96 percent dependent on imports, the government pushed ahead rapidly with the development of nuclear power. By the end of the 1970s fourteen nuclear power plants had gone into operation and another dozen were under construction. Only after massive investments in these plants did the public become aware of the potential perils of nuclear energy production and the problem of how to dispose of radioactive nuclear wastes that would remain injurious to human health for thousands of years. The result was the rapid growth of an anti-nuclear protest movement. When the Schmidt cabinet nevertheless held to its commitment to expanded use of nuclear energy, that movement began to direct its hostility toward the government. Eventually, the cabinet abandoned its plan to activate a major new nuclear energy plant on which the protesters had concentrated their efforts. But in the meantime, the nuclear issue cost the social-liberal coalition some of its former supporters.

One by-product of the nuclear protest movement was a new political party. During the period of the economic miracle West German industry had expanded rapidly and without much consideration for its effects on the natural environment. As a consequence, the countryside had been left scarred and the atmosphere and rivers had become polluted with industrial discharges. The Schmidt cabinet responded to the consequent hazards to human health with legislation designed to curb such abuses, but because of the need to strike compromises between the parties the resultant laws were often considerably watered down when they reached final form. Dissatisfied with the pace of governmental action, various groups organized "citizens' initiatives" to press for action on environmental problems. Initially, these groups lacked coordination or even communication with each other. But the issue of nuclear power brought many of them together in regional political efforts that gradually coalesced into a loose network throughout the country. By the early 1980s these so-called Green parties had garnered sufficient votes in state elections to gain parliamentary representation at that level and emerge as a political factor throughout the country.

At the turn of the decade, the political situation was marked by puzzling crosscurrents. Thanks to its renewed strength in the Bundestag and gains in the parliaments of the states, the CDU/CSU dominated the Federal Assembly convened in May 1979 to choose a successor to retiring president Walter Scheel. Karl Carstens, a veteran CDU/CSU parliamentarian, became the fifth federal president. Yet in the Bundestag election of October 1980 the CDU/CSU, which had chosen as its candidate for chancellor the controversial minister-president of Bavaria, Franz Josef Strauss, suffered a setback. It salvaged only 226 of the 243 seats it had held in the previous chamber. The coalition parties both increased their tallies. The SPD deputation grew from 214 seats to 218. The FDP, making its strongest showing since 1961, went from 39 to 53 seats. With a comfortable margin of 45 seats over the oppositional CDU/CSU, the social-liberal coalition appeared securely ensconced in office for another four years.

In the wake of the "second oil shock," however, another severe economic recession burdened the Schmidt cabinet. The rate of economic growth fell off sharply in the latter part of 1980 and dipped ever deeper in 1981 and 1982. Unemployment again soared over the million mark in 1981 and by the end of 1982 approached an all-time high of two million. The level of joblessness remained lower than that of most other Western European countries, which also experienced a recession, but that provided scant consolation to West Germans who could find no work. In state elections the partners in the social-liberal coalition began to experience setbacks in 1981, with Chancellor Schmidt's SPD suffering even greater losses than the FDP.

Schmidt also came under increasing fire because of his foreign policy. In 1977 the Soviet Union began stationing in the USSR and Eastern Europe numerous medium-range, nuclear-armed missiles obviously aimed at targets in West European countries, including the Federal Republic. The installation of the new missiles seemed to signal an attempt both to intimidate West European governments and to drive a wedge between the United States and its European allies by holding out the prospect of a Soviet nuclear strike against Western Europe that would not directly involve the United States. This new Soviet strategy raised concern in Western Europe about the United States' willingness to risk nuclear destruction of American cities in order to retaliate for a Soviet attack on its European allies. That in turn seemed to open the possibility of nuclear extortion against the Western European democracies by the USSR.

Taking the lead in devising NATO's response to the Soviet move, Chancellor Schmidt convinced the other allies, including the United States, to adopt a so-called two-track resolution in 1979. It committed the European members of NATO to installation on their territories of American medium-range, nuclear-armed missiles aimed at targets in the Soviet bloc. Simultaneously, however, the resolution committed the allies to cancel those plans if the Soviet Union agreed to dismantle its new middle-range missiles. Since the Federal Republic already contained the largest concentration of nuclear weapons per square mile anywhere in the world—all under the control of foreigners—this plan called forth strong criticism from West German opponents of nuclear weaponry. Since many of those opponents were Social Democrats, dissension spread within the chancellor's own party.

The Schmidt cabinet finally fell in the early autumn of 1982. With the economy in the doldrums and unemployment soaring, the government faced a mounting deficit. As a result, the chancellor found himself caught in a crossfire between the Free Democrats and his own party. The leadership of the FDP wanted to curtail government expenditures for welfare-state measures in order to hold down taxes and encourage economic growth through new investment. By contrast, the SPD and its trade unionist allies demanded that the government fully meet what they saw as its social obligations to disadvantaged groups such as the unemployed even if that meant larger deficits and tax increases for those who were better off. Because of this disagreement and growing concern about the political cost of remaining linked to an SPD that was losing favor among voters, the leaders of the FDP began to position their party for a change by indicating a readiness to enter into coalitions with the CDU at the level of state government.

Although Schmidt largely shared the Free Democrats' outlook on economic policy and chafed under the growing rebelliousness within his own party, he decided to resolve what was rapidly becoming an untenable situation in a way that would rally the SPD behind him. In September 1982 he therefore rejected the demands of the Free Democrats regarding economic policy. This brought about the resignation of the FDP ministers and enabled the chancellor to blame their party for the breakup of the coalition. The chancellor thus ended his government on terms of his own choosing. The chairman of the FDP, Foreign Minister Hans-Dietrich Genscher, responded, as Schmidt expected, by entering into a coalition with the CDU/CSU despite opposition from Free Democrats who preferred cooperation with the SPD. In early October the first successful constructive vote of no-confidence in the history of the Federal Republic toppled Chancellor Schmidt with the votes of CDU/CSU and FDP deputies and installed Christian Democrat Helmut Kohl as chancellor. He promptly named a new cabinet drawn from his own party and the FDP. After thirteen years, the social-liberal era had come to an end.

The Chancellorship of
Helmut Kohl

The first chancellor of the Federal Republic to reach maturity in the postwar era, the fifty-two-year-old Helmut Kohl had been active in Christian Democratic politics since age sixteen. An ambitious young politician with strong backing from Catholic circles in his home state of Rhineland-Palatinate, he gained election to the state parliament at twenty-nine. Within ten years he rose to become minister-president there, a post to which he was twice reelected. In 1973 he was chosen as chairman of the CDU and stood as its unsuccessful chancellorship candidate in 1976. When in 1980 the chancellorship nomination went to the leader of the Bavarian CSU, Franz Josef Strauss, rather than to Kohl, many political observers concluded that his political rise was at an end. But the losses suffered by the CDU/CSU under Strauss in the 1980 Bundestag election revived Kohl's fortunes. As head of his party's Bundestag deputation he played a key role in arranging for the FDP to switch sides in late 1982. That made him the obvious choice for the chancellorship when the Christian-liberal coalition of CDU/CSU and FDP took over.

Upon assuming office, Kohl at once promised that a Bundestag election would be held in March 1983. There was widespread agreement on the need for a new round of balloting to clear the political air. The decision of FDP leader Hans-Dietrich Genscher—who retained the position of foreign minister he had held under Schmidt—to shift his party's parliamentary support from the left to the right had aroused such strong objections within the FDP that disssent within its ranks reduced Kohl's margin of election in the Bundestag to only seven votes. Prominent figures in the FDP denounced Genscher for what they regarded as a breach of their party's pledge at the time of the previous election to continue working with the SPD. Since many West Germans viewed the composition of the Bundestag chosen in 1980 as the product of what amounted to an affirma-

Chancellor Helmut Kohl (right) with Foreign Minister Hans-Dietrich Genscher in the Bundestag, Bonn

tive plebiscite on the social-liberal coalition, the chancellor-elect recognized that his cabinet needed a new mandate from the electorate. Also, from the point of view of the CDU/CSU the timing seemed propitious. After years of Social Democratic leadership, unemployment was approaching the two million level, the budget was badly out of balance, and the SPD was wracked by internal dissension over Helmut Schmidt's support for the stationing of new American middle-range nuclear missiles in the Federal Republic if the USSR refused to dismantle those it had aimed at Western Europe.

There remained the problem of how to obtain a new election, since the Basic Law contained no provision for a dissolution of the Bundestag simply because a chancellor wanted one. In order to clear the way for an election, Kohl arranged for the fall of his own cabinet. This he achieved by calling for a vote of confidence. When most of the CDU/CSU-FDP coalition deputies abstained by prearrangement, while those of the SPD cast negative ballots, the confidence measure failed. Seeing no prospect of finding a majority for an alternative chancellor, President Carstens approved the dissolution of the Bundestag so as to make way for the new election called for by all the parties.

The election was set for March 6, 1983, a year and a half earlier than would have normally been the case. The new coalition of CDU/CSU and FDP campaigned on the program of the Kohl cabinet, which called for "less state, more market; fewer collective burdens, more personal performance; fewer encrusted structures, more mobility, self-initiative, and competition." The chancellor proclaimed that his installation marked a "turning" (Wende) of West Germany away from the path followed by the social-liberal cabinets, thereby coining a slogan that would be used to designate his cabinet. The SPD, led by its chancellorship candidate Hans-Jochen Vogel, former mayor of Munich and West Berlin, defended the record of the social-liberal cabinets but distanced itself from Schmidt's policy on middle-range American nuclear weapons, which the CDU/CSU and FDP now championed. The SPD also found itself with a credibility problem, as Vogel ruled out a coalition or any other form of parliamentary cooperation with the new Green Party, which made a strenuous effort to gain its first representation in the Bundestag. Since only such a coalition held out the prospect of a return to power for the SPD, many observers dismissed Vogel's disclaimer as an effort to discredit the Greens, who threatened to woo voters away from the SPD.

With 89.1 percent of the voters casting ballots, the 1983 election brought a conclusive victory for Chancellor Kohl and his supporters. The CDU/CSU emerged with 244 seats, 18 more than in 1980, thus recording its best showing at the polls since its absolute majority in 1957 at the high point of Adenauer's chancellorship. In part because of resentment on the left wing of the FDP at party leader Genscher's abandonment of the social-liberal coalition, the junior partner in the cabinet lost a third of its 1980 votes and emerged with only 34 deputies, 19 fewer than four years earlier. The SPD made its worst showing in more than twenty years, losing 25 seats and seeing its deputation dwindle to 193. The Green Party succeeded in surmounting the 5-percent barrier handily, captured 27 seats, and became the first minor party to gain representation in the West German parliament since 1957.

Strengthened by the election, the outcome of which weakened the position of Genscher's critics within the FDP, the Kohl cabinet began addressing the problems inherited from its predecessor. On the domestic front the new government adopted a conservative approach toward the economic recession and the mounting joblessness that had led so many voters to switch allegiance. Rather than attempting to stimulate the economy by means of deficit spending, the cabinet embarked upon an austerity program designed to promote recovery by holding down taxes and government expenditures in order to encourage private expenditures and investment. The economy gradually responded, if sluggishly, achieving modest growth rates in 1983 and 1984. The joblessness rate continued to rise, however, remaining above 9 percent during the years 1983–85, when an average of nearly 2.25 million persons lacked work. An especially high level of unemployment among those who had recently completed their educations raised troubling questions about the economy's ability to integrate the younger generation.

The Kohl cabinet found no speedy remedy to the unemployment problem which, as increasingly became apparent, was at least in part the product of structural difficulties in the economy resulting from a tardy adjustment by West German industry to the new breakthroughs in microelectronic technology. The cabinet considered but rejected proposals to increase the number of job openings by forbidding overtime work by employed workers or by lowering the retirement age. Instead, it offered generous cash settlements to foreign workers if they would agree to return permanently to their homelands. The response to that offer proved disappointing, however, and the Federal Republic had to continue paying unemployment compensation and providing other social benefits to some of the foreigners it had so eagerly recruited during the years of rapid economic growth.

Despite the unemployment problem, the Federal Republic had by the 1980s become, in per capita terms, one of the richest countries in the world. Its highly successful industrial products were eagerly sought after all around the world and placed it in the top rank of exporting countries, ahead of Japan and, in some years, even of the much larger United States. Consistently exporting more than it imported, the Federal Republic accumulated one of the world's largest foreign currency reserves.

At home, an elaborate welfare state cared for those in need, although sustained large-scale unemployment began during the 1980s to strain that system to the point where poverty again became a problem for the first time in decades. The FDP, increasingly dominated by advocates of laissez-faire economics and minimal governmental intervention, pressed for curtailment of the welfare state, but the labor wing of the CDU/CSU blocked any significant retrenchment. Advocates of generous welfare-state measures faced a daunting prospect, however. During the 1970s the birth rate began declining markedly, as young West Germans opted for more consumer goods and travel rather than having children. With deaths exceeding births by substantial margins each year into the 1980s, demographic projections foresaw a large older generation dependent in the future on welfare-state entitlements that would have to be paid for by a much smaller workforce.

In numerous respects, West German society came to resemble other advanced industrialized countries closely. The number of blue-collar workers declined steadily, while those in white-collar positions increased. Pay differentials between blue- and white-collar workers diminished, blurring class lines. A mass-consumption-oriented economy enabled an increasing number of wage-earners to acquire such amenities as labor-saving household appliances, cameras, television sets, stereophonic equipment, and automobiles. Six weeks of paid vacation a year had become the rule for organized labor. By the early 1970s the 40-hour week was standard for 90 percent of West German wage-earners, and during the latter part of the decade the trade unions began demanding a reduction to 35 hours. In the mid-1980s the first labor contracts requiring less than 40 hours were signed.

Along with the growth of affluence and leisure came shifts in patterns of life. Workers now joined the millions of other West Germans who spent their vacations abroad. West Germans with higher incomes, like their counterparts elsewhere, moved out of cities into suburbs that stretched into the countryside, so that a new breed of commuters emerged. The increased distances between home and workplace ruled out the large, formal midday meal that had traditionally brought German families together each day. The number of farmers shrank to below 5 percent of the workforce. Agricultural productivity nevertheless reached new heights. Indeed, scientific and technological advances made overproduction of foodstuffs a chronic problem because of strong political pressures, in West Germany as well as in the European Common Market at large, to subsidize farm prices at the expense of urban consumers. The presence of 4.5 million foreign workers and their dependents, on the other hand, ceased to be regarded as a pressing problem. Whether those who had long lived and worked in West Germany and become culturally assimilated should become German citizens remained unresolved, however.

In governing this dynamic society, the Christian-liberal coalition of CDU/CSU and FDP led a precarious existence during its early years despite its solid majority in the Bundestag elected in 1983. The leader of the Bavarian CSU, Franz Josef Strauss, left no doubt about his resentment at being excluded from the Kohl cabinet and subjected government policies to barrages of criticism that sometimes verged on public ridicule. Strauss made FDP foreign minister Genscher a particular target of his attacks and seemed bent upon breaking up the coalition, the survival of which depended upon support from the deputies of the CSU. Within the FDP, left-wing liberals remained unforgiving of Genscher for his abandonment of the alliance with the Social Democrats. Their preference for a social-liberal alignment posed yet another threat to the new coalition, especially when severe election losses in the wake of the FDP's turnabout swept that party entirely out of five state parliaments and reduced its strength elsewhere. Despite all these difficulties, however, the Kohl cabinet weathered its troubled early years and stabilized its hold on power, at least in part because no real alternative seemed at hand.

Aside from the antagonisms between the SPD and FDP that ruled out a return to the social-liberal coalition in the aftermath of the Free Democrats' turnabout, the absence of an alternative to the Christian-liberal coalition of Chancellor Kohl was attributable to the entry of the Green Party into parliament. That new organization amounted more to a loose confederation of citizens' action groups than a traditional political party. Held together only by a mutual commitment to environmental protectionism, the Green Bundestag deputies numbered among their ranks ecologists, feminists, leftists, and opponents of nuclear weapons. In the sphere of foreign policy, most Greens inclined toward neutralism, calling for a withdrawal of both superpowers from Germany in a fashion that seemed for some observers to represent a new form of nationalism. From the outset, they made clear their unwillingness to assume governmental responsibility.

Seeing their role as that of gadflies and educators, the Greens had only scorn for the professional politicians who dominated the Bundestag and the government. At parliamentary sessions they gave expression to their iconoclasm by appearing in casual attire and by displaying irreverence for the pomposity of some veteran deputies and the often labyrinthine procedures of the chamber. To protect their movement from what they saw as the corrupting effects of political careerism, the Green deputies elected in 1983 pledged to surrender their seats to other mem-

Green Party deputies introducing a bit of the natural environment into the sessions of the Bundestag upon their entry into the parliament in 1983

bers of their party after serving half of their parliamentary terms. And despite charges of unconstitutionality from within the other parties, most went through with this "rotation" in 1985, surrendering their seats to other Greens whose names had appeared on the party's successful lists of candidates. Only a few of their deputies refused to comply and remained in the Bundestag for the full terms to which they had been elected.

In state elections the Greens profited from increasing public concern about nuclear issues, both those involving armaments and those arising from nuclear power plants, as well as about the government's neglect of the environment. Mainly at the expense of the SPD and the FDP, the Greens rolled up mounting tallies, making a particularly strong showing among young voters. Although their tallies fell short of 10 percent, they gained sufficient seats in some states to make impossible a parliamentary majority without their support. As a result, they came under pressure to abandon the pledge not to assume governmental responsibility. After long resisting that pressure, the Greens in the state of Hesse opened a new chapter in their party's history by agreeing in October 1985 to join in a coalition cabinet there with the SPD. In the rest of the Federal Republic, however, the Greens became increasingly divided between fundamentalists who believed that the assumption of responsibility would corrupt their party and realists who argued that the Greens could influence policy decisively only by entering into government.

The rise of the Greens gained added impetus from a scandal that dogged the three major parties throughout the first half of the 1980s. In late 1981 *Der Spiegel* began publishing documents which suggested that the Flick concern, a large industrial corporation, had clandestinely made sizable financial contributions to politicians in the CDU/CSU, SPD, and FDP. Those documents further suggested that the politicians involved had not publicly reported those contributions, as required by law. Not long thereafter, a public prosecutor issued indictments of Flick executives and a number of prominent political figures, charging that the recipients of the illegal Flick contributions had helped the firm to evade federal taxes during the time of the social-liberal coalition. Whereas the Schmidt cabinet sought to play down the Flick affair, the Kohl cabinet made a clumsy effort to sweep it away with a special amnesty bill that immediately encountered widespread public indignation and had to be hastily withdrawn. In 1984, one of the most prominent figures in the FDP, Economics Minister Count Otto von Lambsdorff, resigned from the cabinet in order to face charges of implication in the scandal. The complex judicial proceedings finally ended inconclusively in 1987 with partial convictions and suspended sentences. In the meantime, the integrity of the whole political establishment in Bonn had been badly shaken.

The moral stature of the federal government received a lift from the election in May 1984 of Richard von Weizsäcker as federal president. A Christian Democrat who had gained promi-

Richard von Weizsäcker, sixth president of the Federal Republic, taking the oath of office in 1984

nence in Protestant church circles as well as in his party, Weiz-säcker had been called to the head of the West Berlin government in 1981 after a distinguished career in the Bundestag. He arrived in Berlin at a time when the authority of the city government had, under an entrenched SPD leadership, suffered severe erosion. Charges of corruption on the part of long-time city officials had undermined public confidence. So had the city government's heavy-handed response when young people protesting a shortage of low-rent housing took over derelict apartment buildings which the owners had cleared of tenants in order to renovate and lease at higher rents. By attempting forcible eviction, the SPD government had provoked violent resistance and enabled the squatter movement to win the support of many others in West Berlin. As a result, the city had been wracked by repeated clashes between the police on the one hand and squatters and their sympathizers on the other. When the SPD suffered a setback in a city election in 1981, Weizsäcker took over as mayor at the head of a minority cabinet initially backed only by the CDU which, however, gained the support of a majority two years later, when the FDP agreed to join in a coalition. By combining firmness with impressive diplomatic skill and tact, he managed to work out solutions acceptable to most of those involved in the housing dispute and soon restored confidence in the West Berlin government.

As president, Weizsäcker used that office as a pulpit from which to remind the citizens of the Federal Republic of their civic responsibilities and of the moral issues in politics. In May 1985 he won worldwide acclaim with a major address before the Bundestag marking the fortieth anniversary of the German surrender at the end of World War II. In that address, Weizsäcker urged his countrymen to accept the ambiguity of a defeat which had brought with it liberation of the German people from the tyranny of Nazism. His talk amounted to the most forthright declaration by a West German leader since formation of the Federal Republic about the heavy moral burden which the German past unavoidably imposed upon the citizens of the Federal Republic. He closed with an eloquent appeal for Germans to face squarely the dreadful facts of their nation's recent history in order to build a better future of peace and reconciliation with all the many peoples who had suffered so grievously at the hands of the criminal Third Reich.

In foreign affairs the Kohl cabinet held firmly to the Western alliance. Despite much protest and many large-scale demonstrations against stationing new American middle-range nuclear missiles in the Federal Republic, the cabinet upheld the terms of the "two-track" NATO resolution of 1979. Only with those missiles, Kohl argued, would West Germany be protected against nuclear backmail by the Soviets, who had recently installed numerous middle-range missiles aimed at targets throughout Western Europe. Without the American missiles, he maintained, as had Schmidt, Moscow would be in a position to exploit German fears that the United States would not risk destruction of its own cities by retaliating against a Soviet nuclear attack on Europe with missiles based in America. When the Soviet Union failed to respond to NATO's offer to cancel the new weapons if Moscow would dismantle its own middle-range missiles, the American missiles went into place in West Germany in 1984. In the acrimonious debate which preceded that move the SPD, led by Chairman Willy Brandt, turned its back on ex-Chancellor Helmut Schmidt, who continued to uphold the NATO two-track resolution he had so largely designed. Along with the Green Party, the SPD sought in vain to reverse the Federal Republic's adherence to that resolution. As a consequence, some Social Democrats moved increasingly into a posture critical of the Western alliance.

While adhering closely to the NATO alliance during a period of tension between the two superpowers that many saw as a renewal of the Cold War, the Kohl cabinet did not attempt to reverse any of the fundamental components of the social-liberal coalition's Eastern policy. Despite having vehemently opposed the new policy at the time of its inception, the CDU/CSU accepted it as binding on the Federal Republic, just as the SPD had earlier accepted Adenauer's Western policy. Continuity therefore prevailed also with regard to the East, as the new government continued Bonn's pursuit of normalized relations with the GDR and the countries of the Soviet bloc. Somewhat contradictorily, however, Kohl and other members of his cabinet began to emphasize once more the goal of German reunification, which had been soft-pedaled by the social-liberal cabinets. The new cabinet likewise accorded greater emphasis to the Federal Republic's position that the German question and the problem of postwar boundaries could not be permanently resolved until conclusion of a peace treaty ending World War II. Yet despite such verbal reservations, relations between the Federal Republic and the GDR continued to expand and improve at the practical level under the Kohl cabinet.

Certain intangible effects of the policy of growing accommodation with the GDR made themselves felt within West Germany itself. As a consequence of recognizing the East German regime and dealing with it as an equal partner, the Federal Republic had in effect abandoned its claim to be the sole political spokesman of the German people and, with it, some of its sense of purpose and identity. At the outset, everything about the West German state had been provisional, including its constitutional document and its capital city. The assumption had prevailed that the new polity was merely a temporary expedient that would soon give way to a reunited Germany. As that prospect seemed to fade, institutions regarded as provisional took on a more lasting character, especially when housed in increasingly large and formidable buildings in the expanding city of Bonn, which began to assume the aspect of a world capital. Nothing illustrated this more palpably than the government's decision in the mid-1980s to replace the makeshift Bundestag building in Bonn with an elaborate new structure obviously intended for long-term use.

While it was wrestling with the issues raised by its improving relations with the GDR, the Kohl cabinet discovered that there were still limits to the Federal Republic's acceptance by the Western democracies. When in 1984 the chancellor sought inclusion in the commemoration of the Allied landing in Nazi-occupied France forty years earlier, he met with a cool rebuff from the leaders of countries still mourning young men killed by Germans in World War II. In 1985, at the time of the fortieth anniversary of the Third Reich's unconditional surrender, Kohl attempted a symbolic reconciliation by inviting American president Ronald Reagan to join him in visiting a military cemetery in the West German town of Bitburg, where both American and German soldiers killed in the Second World War lay buried. But when it was discovered that the German dead at Bitburg included members of the military wing of the notorious Nazi SS, the ceremony gave rise to indignant protests. The resultant controversy illustrated the limitations that Germany's past set on

the Federal Republic's efforts to find identity among the democracies.

As the Bundestag election of 1987 approached, political activity became increasingly dominated by the parties' efforts to
position themselves for the campaign. A succession of heavy
setbacks for the SPD in state elections and public opinion polls
seemed to portend major losses for the main opposition party.
So did divisions within its ranks which pit centrist, pro-NATO
Social Democrats against a growing neutralist, leftist faction. As
its candidate for the chancellorship, the SPD chose Johannes
Rau, the minister-president of North Rhine-Westphalia, who
was not identified with either of the party's factions. He was
handicapped, however, by unresolved internal differences
which led the SPD to adopt unclear positions on a number of
major issues during the campaign, including nuclear power
plants, which those concerned about deadly accidents wanted
to close down but those concerned about the jobs of workers in
the growing nuclear industry and the overall effect on the economy wanted to keep in operation. As the balloting approached,
all signs pointed to heavy gains by the CDU under incumbent
chancellor Kohl. Despite a number of gauche public statements
about the GDR and the USSR and their leaders, the chancellor
seemed in a commanding position during a time of general
prosperity marred only by chronic high unemployment. However, the CDU's Bavarian sister party, the CSU under its chairman, Franz Josef Strauss, introduced discord into the ruling
coalition by criticizing the chancellor and, even more vehemently, the conduct of the Federal Republic's diplomacy by
Foreign Minister Genscher of the FDP. In response to these
attacks on Genscher, the Free Democrats focused their campaign
on a pledge to prevent Strauss from gaining control over foreign
policy and altering Bonn's policy of accommodation with the
GDR.

The balloting of January 1987, which was marked by the
lowest voter participation since 1949, 84.4 percent, produced a
number of surprises. The CDU/CSU, which had confidently

predicted victory, experienced an embarrassing setback and its heaviest losses in a quarter century. Its portion of the vote dropped to the lowest level since 1949, which left the party with only 223 of the 244 seats it had won in 1983. The SPD also suffered losses, but these were smaller than expected by most observers, so that the SPD retained 186 of the 193 seats it had held in the old chamber. The FDP registered handsome gains, emerging with 12 additional seats and an expanded delegation of 46 deputies. The biggest surprise resulted, however, from the solid advances registered by the Greens, who increased their seats from 27 to 42 despite continuing friction in their ranks between fundamentalists and realists. Although the outcome of the election left Chancellor Kohl somewhat weakened, the coalition of CDU/CSU and FDP still commanded a majority and continued in office, but with the FDP and Foreign Minister Genscher in a stronger position.

6
The Collapse of the GDR and the Reunification of Germany

Erich Honecker's GDR

During the 1970s, when the Federal Republic's Eastern foreign policy initiatives and a relaxation of tensions between the United States and the Soviet Union captured the headlines, a new leader emerged in East Germany: Erich Honecker. Born the son of a coal miner in the Saarland near Germany's western border in 1912, Honecker joined the Communist Party's youth organization at age ten. At seventeen he entered the party and in 1931, at nineteen, became an official of its youth organization. In 1935, after two years of underground work for the party in the Third Reich, Honecker was arrested and began ten years of imprisonment during the Nazi regime. Upon his release in 1945 he reported to Walter Ulbricht, who charged him with development of the Free German Youth, the Communist young people's organization. After a decade in that post, Honecker moved on to other prominent assignments. In 1950 he became a candidate member of the Politburo and in 1958 a full member. In 1961 he was assigned the difficult task of erecting the Berlin Wall, and that achievement greatly enhanced his stature within the SED regime. During the 1960s he came to be generally regarded as Ulbricht's obvious heir. It thus came as no surprise when in May 1971 the departing leader proposed Erich Honecker as his successor at the head of the party. As a model *apparatchik*, a loyal servant of the SED leadership, Honecker seemed a logical replacement for Walter Ulbricht.

Honecker quickly established himself as the preeminent figure in the regime. In June 1971 he was elected by the People's Chamber to succeed Ulbricht as chairman of the National Defense Council. Ulbricht nominally remained at the head of the Council of State, but that body lost much of its former significance as Honecker reversed the tendency toward assigning authority to government agencies at the expense of the party. Ulbricht quickly passed into obscurity; his formerly ubiquitous photograph vanished from public places, his name from the press.

After Ulbricht's death in 1973, Willi Stoph, longtime head of the Council of Ministers, was chosen to head the Council of State. Horst Sindermann, a close associate of Honecker's, succeeded Stoph as head of the government apparatus. But in 1976 Honecker himself took over chairmanship of the Council of State, Stoph returned to his old position, and Sindermann was relegated to a lesser post. Within only five years Honecker, as chief of the party secretariat and chairman of both the National Defense Council and the Council of State, had thus come to hold the same triad of party and state offices that had formed the basis of Ulbricht's dominance. By 1976 his party title had become general secretary, reflecting his unchallenged sway over the actual locus of power, the Politburo of the SED. Virtually from the beginning of his reign, his official photograph graced thousands of walls, and his words were reverentially quoted in publications of the regime. The characteristic Communist "cult of personality" suffered no interruption in the GDR.

Once he consolidated his position, Honecker broke with the

innovative aspects of Ulbricht's interpretation of Marxist-Leninist doctrine and swung the GDR onto a course of economic development parallel to that of the Soviet Union. Most experiments with economic decentralization were abandoned, and far-reaching centralized planning and control by SED-dominated organs reinstituted. In part under the impact of the Gomulka regime's collapse in the face of popular unrest in neighboring Poland in December 1970, a general return to orthodoxy took place. The absolute authority of the SED was incessantly stressed. Ideology was again accorded unchallengeable primacy over technical-economic considerations, and key positions in the government apparatus again went to reliable party wheelhorses rather than to reform-minded experts. In June 1971, just a month after Honecker took over the SED secretariat, a party congress discarded Ulbricht's position that socialism represented a distinct historical phase.

In the course of 1972 the regime gave tangible expression to this revision of doctrine by converting most remaining private businesses into state enterprises and eliminating private participants from most firms in which they had previously shared ownership with the state. In 1971 the output of wholly state-owned enterprises amounted to some 82 percent of total industrial production; by the middle of 1972 it exceeded 99 percent. With rare exceptions, private and mixed-ownership business survived only in the retail and service branches, and even there the number dwindled under the regime's pressure for socialization. In agriculture a similar pattern unfolded as the regime converted to full state ownership most of those collective farms in which elements of private enterprise had survived. The number of collective farms steadily diminished through consolidation into huge units on the Soviet model. Whereas previously the regime had explained its measures in terms of the exigencies of "building socialism," it began in 1973 to boast of having achieved "real, existing socialism."

Throughout this period of hard-line retrenchment, the GDR was feeling the first effects of West Germany's new Eastern pol-

Helmut Schmidt (right), chancellor of the Federal Republic, 1974–82, chatting with Erich Honecker (left), head of the East German regime since 1971, at the Helsinki conference in 1975

icy. The most welcome of these was the diplomatic recognition outside the Soviet bloc which had long been one of the regime's most sought-after goals. Prior to agreement with Bonn on the Basic Treaty in 1972, only nineteen countries—those of the Soviet bloc plus some in Africa and Asia—had accorded the GDR diplomatic recognition. But once it became clear that the Federal Republic would abandon its Hallstein doctrine and establish formal relations with the East German regime, the barrier fell for other non-Communist governments. By the end of 1973, sixty-eight countries had established full diplomatic relations with East Berlin. Dozens of others soon followed, including the United States in 1974. In 1973 the GDR became, along with the Federal Republic, a member of the United Nations. By 1975 it had been recognized by 115 countries and become a full participant in world diplomacy. The prestige of the SED regime reached new heights that year when Honecker and West German chancellor Helmut Schmidt sat in adjacent chairs as the Conference on Security and Cooperation in Europe convened for its first meeting in Helsinki, Finland.

The respectability which the regime garnered from its acceptance in international circles was to some extent offset in the eyes of the SED's leadership by the greatly increased contact between East Germans and West Germans made possible by the new agreements with Bonn. Thanks to the liberalization of access, some 7.5 million visits from the West took place in 1972, more than twice as many as in the previous year. Telephonic communication also increased dramatically as a result of an agreement to institute direct dialing. While in 1969 some half million calls were made by West Germans to East Germans (no figures are available on those from East to West), by 1978 the number had risen to well over 17 million annually. These increased contacts with the West brought the regime in the GDR certain advantages, as visitors spent valuable West German marks there and trade increased through improved communications. But such contacts also gave rise to unsettling problems for the SED regime as more and more East Germans learned at first hand, often from trusted persons, about the higher standard of material life and greater personal freedom in the West. In addition, as a result of the SED regime's acceptance in 1972 of an accord that enabled Western journalists to operate in the East and vice versa, the people of the GDR began receiving more information about their own society than ever before. Despite numerous restrictions imposed by Eastern authorities on the activities of journalists from the West, their eyewitness reports from within the GDR and interviews with internal critics of the SED regime now reached East Germans through Western radio and television broadcasts.

The regime's response to the problem of increased exposure to the West came to be known as *Abgrenzung*, or "delimitation." At the propaganda level it took the form of a campaign to emphasize the differences between the GDR and the Federal Republic. The two were irreconcilable, East Germans heard, not merely because of differences in their economic and political systems but, more basically, because they belonged to entirely different phases of history in the Marxist scheme of analysis. The GDR belonged to the progressive, proletarian future, whereas West Germany was rooted in a decaying bourgeois order condemned to death by inexorable historical forces. By way of illustrating the gulf that purportedly separated the two parts of Germany, prominent attention was accorded in the press and electronic media to unemployment, crime, inflation, and other social problems in West Germany.

The regime also instituted a number of more direct measures to reduce contact between East Germans and visitors from the West. In November 1973 it increased the amount of its non-convertible currency that visitors were required to purchase with Western money for each day spent in the GDR. As a consequence, extended visits from the Federal Republic declined sharply during 1974. But the following year the number of West German visitors began increasing again, reaching levels of between 7 and 8 million a year until in 1980 another increase in the requirement for currency purchase once more reduced the flow of travelers from the West. Nevertheless, with over 5 million Western visitors in the GDR annually—nearly one for every three East Germans—exposure to the West remained high in subsequent years. Although this gave rise to concern on the part of the regime, the SED authorities showed reluctance to diminish travel from the West still further, in part because of the predictably adverse reaction of its own citizenry but also because visitors from the Federal Republic left behind millions of coveted Western D-marks desperately needed for purchase of materials essential to the GDR's economy. The regime sought at least to insulate its own personnel from subversive influences by forbidding personal contact with Western visitors on the part of some 2 million persons in the GDR whom it now classified as "bearers of secrets," including draftees and reservists of the People's Army, members of the People's Police, and most SED officials.

The policy of delimitation necessitated a drastic revision of the regime's position with regard to German nationhood. At the time of the GDR's formation its founders had pledged to seek reunification at the earliest possible time. Throughout the Ulbricht era the regime continued to recognize the ongoing existence of national cultural ties linking all Germans, even in a time of political division. In the course of pursuing delimitation, however, the SED sought systematically to deemphasize those links. The GDR was now described not merely as a separate state but also as a separate "socialist nation" quite distinct from the "bourgeois nation" of the Federal Republic. References to shared aspects of the national heritage disappeared from the media and from publications in the GDR. The once ritualistic pledges to pursue reunification ceased to be heard.

This denial of an overarching German nationhood found its most striking expression in a set of constitutional revisions enacted in 1974. Institutionally, these changes reshuffled responsibilities between the Council of State and the Council of Ministers, again designating the latter as the nominal focus of governmental authority but without abridging the SED's control over the state. The most notable change involved, however, the virtual elimination from the constitution of the word "German" (*Deutsch*) except in the combination German Democratic Republic. The 1968 constitution had declared the GDR to be "a socialist state of the German nation." By the revision of 1974 it became "a socialist state of workers and farmers." References to the "German people" were systematically eliminated, as was the old constitution's pledge to seek reunification. By contrast, an inseparable link with the Soviet Union was now asserted, as the revised constitution proclaimed the GDR to be "forever and irrevocably allied with" the USSR. A new treaty of friendship and mutual support between the GDR and the USSR, which received enormous publicity when it was signed in 1975, served to underline the distance that separated East Germany from West Germany according to the official SED viewpoint.

This ideological shift in the interest of delimitation coincided with a resort to harsh measures against intellectual dissent. Upon assuming leadership of the GDR, Honecker had denounced intellectual taboos and called for a broader and richer spectrum of cultural creativity within the framework of socialism. In the first phase of his leadership, the regime abandoned attempts to suppress such youthful manifestations of symbolic defiance as rock music, long hairstyles for men, and blue jeans for both sexes. Indeed, domestically produced jeans and rock music were promoted. Some venturesome fiction and poetry appeared, along with plays and films that occasionally reflected the real attitudes of GDR citizens, including their misgivings about the system within which they lived. By 1976, however, it became evident that there were still limits to the SED's tolerance for cultural deviancy. In that year the authorities in East Berlin revoked the citizenship of the balladeer Wolf Biermann, an idealistic Communist who had left West Germany in 1953 to live in the GDR, where he satirized the shortcomings of the regime in his popular songs. Biermann learned of his expatriation while on a concert tour of the West, from which he was not permitted to return. The following year Rudolf Bahro, a low-level Communist functionary who, in a book on the East German economy published in the West, had portrayed the regime as a stifling dictatorial bureaucracy, was arrested and convicted of betraying "state secrets." Sentenced to an eight-year prison term, Bahro was released and expelled to the Federal Republic in 1979, after two years behind bars, under an amnesty marking the thirtieth year of the GDR's founding.

Another dissenter who fell afoul of the renewed tightening of ideological controls was the respected scientist Robert Havemann, a longtime Communist who had been incarcerated with Honecker in the same Nazi prison. Havemann had begun to speak out during the 1960s under Ulbricht about what he saw as a growing discrepancy between the regime's practices and the ideals of Communism. Even after the authorities stripped him of his teaching post and membership in the Academy of Sciences, Havemann continued to voice his dissenting views, often in West German publications. In 1968 he publicly denounced the

GDR's participation in the Warsaw Pact invasion of Czechoslovakia. When Havemann persisted under Honecker in his criticism of the regime he was placed under house arrest, denied access to print, and fined for alleged currency violations in connection with his publications in the West. His voice nevertheless continued to be heard in the GDR until his death in 1982, as some of his writings were smuggled to the West, where his views were cited in radio and television broadcasts that could be received in the East.

The electronic media reached almost all parts of the GDR from transmitters in West Germany and West Berlin despite Eastern efforts at jamming, thus making it impossible to isolate the population altogether. Increasingly, the regime dealt with prominent persons who took up deviant ideas or voiced criticism by stripping them of citizenship and expelling them to the West. After the GDR signed the 1975 accord on human rights reached in Helsinki by the Conference on Security and Cooperation in Europe, which included a guarantee of the right to emigration, tens of thousands applied for permission to leave. But only a few thousand were allowed to go each year. For most East Germans the only hope of escape involved risking the bullets of border guards under orders to shoot to kill or the shrapnel from deadly explosive devices primed to go off automatically when anyone approached East Germany's heavily fortified borders without official authorization.

Under Honecker a combination of accommodation and tension continued to mark relations between the regime and the Christian churches. Protestant leaders had already made a major concession when they complied under Ulbricht with the SED's demand that they separate organizationally from the church in the Federal Republic. In 1971 a conciliatory Protestant bishop, Albrecht Schönherr of Berlin, held out an olive branch to the regime by proclaiming the clergy's readiness to serve as a "church within socialism." The Roman Catholic church, which comprised only about 7 percent of religiously active East Germans, proved less willing to alter its organizational structure, in part because of its supranational character. Although the Catholic church also effected some administrative adjustments in the mid-1970s that had the effect of loosening ties between church authorities in East and West, it refused to exclude West Berlin from the diocese that encompassed the northern part of the GDR. Grudgingly, the SED authorities granted permission to the bishop of Berlin, whose see was located in East Berlin, to spend thirty days each quarter-year in the Western part of the city.

The regime's militant propagation of atheism in the schools remained a source of friction with both churches. And while relations between the religious leaders and the regime improved somewhat during the 1970s, clergymen at the grass-roots level continued to encounter a host of state-imposed obstacles in their efforts to serve the religious needs of parishioners. This was made manifest in the latter part of the 1970s by the suicides of two Protestant clergymen who publicly set themselves on fire to protest against the regime's policies. But despite all their difficulties, the churches remained the only institutions in the GDR that escaped government control over their internal affairs and provided places where people could assemble without having to request permission from the government. The churches were thus able to preserve small islands of free expression in a society subjected to enormous pressures for conformity to a rigid official ideology.

In most matters of public policy, the churches refrained from challenging governmental measures, but where moral questions became involved, the clergy, backed by church members, protested. One such matter was abortion. When a bill supported by the regime in 1972 called for legalization of abortion as late as three months after conception, the Catholic clergy denounced it. As a consequence, the first negative votes ever registered in the People's Chamber were cast by fourteen deputies of the East German CDU. Another eight absented themselves from the balloting, which resulted in the SED bill's passage by a wide margin.

When the regime announced plans during the late 1970s to introduce military training into the school curriculum, both

Catholic and Protestant clergymen protested. The churches and their members remained powerless, however, to prevent the addition of small-arms and other military instruction as a compulsory part of the standard schooling of East German teenage boys and girls in 1978. Despite the pressing need in some parts of the GDR for new church buildings or the replacement of old ones, the regime responded only slowly and grudgingly to requests from the religious authorities for permission to undertake construction or make repairs with funds in large part provided by West German coreligionists.

In contrast to the churches, the non-Marxist political parties of the GDR caused the regime no problems. Their leaders, who served at the pleasure of the SED, ritualistically proclaimed its paramountcy and docilely endorsed its policies. Their candidates unfailingly accepted without complaint the minority allotments of places on the unity lists of the National Front that ensured their powerlessness in the People's Chamber and regional parliamentary bodies. On the rare occasions when the People's Chamber convened—seldom for more than three or four days a year—the deputies of the CDU, the LDP, NDPD, and DBD voted unanimously for government bills, with the sole exception of the dissent by some CDU deputies on the abortion bill of 1972. In 1978 the CDU claimed 115,000 members, the LDP 75,000, the NDPD 80,000, and the DBD 92,000, whereas the SED numbered over 2 million.

For the two non-Marxist parties which had originally been autonomous organizations, as opposed to creations of the regime, the CDU and the LDP, these figures revealed declines since 1949 of 50 percent and 62 percent, respectively. Still, those parties, like the NDPD and DBD, continued to function with the aid of the regime, which found them useful in reaching those parts of the population that remained unresponsive to the Marxist-Leninist doctrines and proletarian rhetoric of the SED. Those who joined the GDR's non-Marxist parties found membership useful in obtaining advancement at their places of work, or, in the case of professionals and other independent persons, official favors such as enhanced access to scarce items. To remain "un-political," on the other hand, was to risk the suspicion of those in power, who preferred to have even non-Communists neatly organized in formal, identifiable categories. During the 1980s all the parties of the GDR claimed increases in membership, but a conspicuous slackening of public interest cast doubt upon the degree of commitment on the part of their members, many of whom had joined merely in pursuit of personal advancement.

Soviet-style elections for the People's Chamber continued to be held ritualistically under Honecker. Unfailingly the SED regime announced afterward an overwhelming endorsement by the electorate of the National Front unity lists of candidates by near-unanimous margins. In 1971 a law increased the interval for elections of the People's Chamber from four to five years. A 1979 law provided for the first time for direct participation of East Berliners in those elections. Previously, deputies from East Berlin had been chosen by its city government—as continued to be the case with the Bundestag deputies from West Berlin—in deference to the four-power occupation status of the old capital.

By the end of the 1970s the economy of the GDR had begun to falter. Under the impact of the worldwide oil crisis of that decade, the cost of that vital fuel rose much more rapidly than the prices of the exports which provided the GDR with the foreign exchange needed to pay for the oil it had to import from abroad in order to operate its industry. For a time, the USSR supplied oil at prices somewhat below the world-market level, but Soviet prices also spiraled upward during the decade. As a result, the GDR began to incur chronic trade deficits. In order to purchase in the West the many materials necessary for its industries, the regime had to borrow extensively in Western credit markets at the high interest rates then prevailing. Whereas the GDR had owed Western creditors about a billion dollars in 1970, knowledgeable estimates placed its Western debts at between 10 and 11 billion dollars by 1981.

As a result of the oil crisis and growing indebtedness, a greatly increased portion of the goods produced in the GDR had to be exported to pay for essential imports. The resulting disruptions hampered the overall performance of the economy, which fell far short of the targets set by the five-year plan for 1976–80. The growth that did take place tended to expand old lines of production rather than open up new, advanced ones. The centralized, bureaucratized economy of the GDR proved resistant to the kinds of innovations, such as those in the field of microelectronics, which were producing something approaching a new industrial revolution in the West. Rather than run the risks that accompany experimentation and innovation, the entrenched managerial personnel of East German industry generally preferred to go on turning out familiar products by proven methods. This resistance to change, along with the tight rationing of investment capital, contributed to a failure to replace antiquated industrial machines with more up-to-date models. The overall efficiency of the economy also suffered because of the regime's guarantee of jobs to all citizens of working age, regardless of their competence or diligence, and its practice of granting vocational advancement on the basis of political loyalty rather than accomplishment on the job. As a consequence of these and other handicaps, the economic gap that separated the GDR from the Federal Republic widened during the 1970s.

During the early 1980s the regime struggled to cope with its increasing economic difficulties. Austerity measures at home, coupled with a drive to increase exports and reduce imports, succeeded in halting the growth of indebtedness to the West and reduced it to about 8.5 billion dollars by 1984. But this could be achieved only at the cost of diminishing the availability in the GDR of consumer goods and such imported items as chocolate, tobacco, and tropical fruits. Resistance on the part of East German industries to innovation made it increasingly difficult, however, for them to compete in Western markets. As a consequence, the GDR's industrial exports outside of the Soviet bloc now went predominantly to countries in Africa, Asia, and the Middle East that did not demand the most advanced products. Its exports to industrialized Western countries became more and more restricted to long-established, less sophisticated products and semifinished materials. The low prices which such goods brought in the highly competitive world market forced the regime to devote an increasing share of industrial output to export items in order to satisfy its need for foreign currency. That, in turn, placed limits on the production of consumer goods for the GDR. So did a belated drive to invest in microelectronic technology, to which the authorities devoted increasing resources in the 1980s. By the latter part of the decade, foreign indebtedness was again on the rise.

For East German consumers, these developments brought a slowdown in the improvement of their living standard. An analysis carried out on behalf of the Federal Republic in 1986 concluded that whereas the average income of a wage-earning household in the GDR had in 1970 amounted to 64 percent of such a household in West Germany, it had dropped to 46 percent by 1983. Shortages of the familiar kind and long waiting periods for major purchases continued to vex consumers. The spread of durable goods of the sort that were in the West approaching a saturation level similar to that of the United States nevertheless continued. Whereas in 1969 only 14 of every 100 East German households owned an automobile, 46 had acquired one by 1985. The corresponding percentages for television sets were 66 and 93, for refrigerators 48 and 99, for washing machines 48 and 89. Increasingly, however, those figures reflected an accumulation of older, outmoded equipment that masked a failure to replace, as in the West, worn and obsolescent items with more advanced models at prices affordable for consumers. Color television sets, for example, amounted to 38 percent of the total in the East by 1985, or less than half the level in the West, where almost all washing machines were by that time fully automatic, as opposed to only one in ten in the GDR. Qualitatively, the gap between consumer goods in the East and those in West became ever wider in the 1980s. Other differentials also increased, such as access to telephones, with which only 13 percent of households in the GDR were equipped in 1983, as compared to 88 percent in West Germany.

The most conspicuous discrepancy in consumer goods lay between the quality of automobiles available in the GDR and of those produced by car manufacturers in the Federal Republic, which stood at the forefront of automotive styling and design. West German drivers graduated from one generation of sophisticated cars to the next, which by the 1980s were equipped with catalytic converters to reduce exhaust emissions into the atmosphere. Those East Germans who had the patience to endure long waiting periods required for the purchase of new cars had to settle for shoddily made vehicles built to designs that were decades old. The smaller and by far the most numerous of the two models made in the GDR was the Trabant, whose name, which means "satellite," had been bestowed in honor of the Soviet Union's pioneering achievements in outer space in the 1950s. The diminutive Trabant had a plastic body and a noisy two-cylinder, two-stroke motor that required as fuel a mixture of gasoline and oil that produced clouds of air-polluting exhaust. For increasing numbers of East Germans, the "Trabi," as it was called both affectionately and disparagingly, came to symbolize the distressing shortcomings of the GDR's consumer goods industries.

In an effort to cope with the housing shortage that had kept much of the population in cramped, substandard quarters since the war, the regime allocated an increasing amount of manpower and resources to construction of dwellings. In the course of the 1970s the annual outlay for new housing more than tripled, accounting for 10 percent of national income by 1980. As a consequence, millions of East Germans moved into fresh new structures with what seemed to them very modern conveniences. That those structures were monotonously rectangular in design, ruthlessly standardized in appointments, and far less spacious on the average than those in the West did not, under the circumstances, seem important to most of their new occupants. An augmented supply of furniture and decorative items enabled consumers to indulge long-thwarted personal tastes. Despite this progress, a housing shortage persisted into the latter half of the 1980s, and the regime held out the prospect of a resolution no sooner than 1990. Meanwhile, those millions of East Germans who occupied older housing watched the rapid physical deterioration of the buildings they lived in, as the regime channeled resources to new mass-produced apartment houses at the expense of older dwellings, especially single-family houses, which were viewed as out of keeping with socialism. Dilapidated older buildings in some sections of East German cities were abandoned or became slums, a development that led sardonic wags to suggest that the motto of the GDR should be *Ruinen schaffen ohne Waffen* (Make ruins without weapons).

The regime sought as well to improve the conditions of work and retirement. Throughout the 1970s wages gradually moved upward. In 1975 vacations were lengthened. In 1976 both the minimum wage and the level of pensions were raised. Both nevertheless lagged far behind those in the West. In 1977 the hours of work were shortened. In plants with three shifts a day, the normal workweek became 40 hours, in those with two shifts daily 42 hours. Not only was the average workweek longer than in the West, but workers in the East had to put in far more hours than their Western counterparts to cover the cost of virtually all goods. In 1983, for example, the typical worker in the GDR had to labor 846 hours to earn enough to pay for a color television set, while a similar wage-earner in the Federal Republic could cover the cost of such a set in 15 hours. The comparable figures for a refrigerator were 293 and 40, for a standard woman's dress 40 and 5, for a pair of children's shoes 7 and 2.

The regime's efforts at economic improvement were hampered by demographic developments that produced a chronic labor shortage and imposed heavy burdens on the economy. The birthrate declined as a consequence of the flight by hundreds of thousands of young East Germans to the West before the erection of the Berlin Wall and because the housing shortage made it difficult for the young couples who remained to find dwellings of their own. The result was a contraction in the population. Whereas a census in 1949 registered 18.7 million inhabitants (including East Berlin), that of 1981 yielded a figure of 16.7 million. In an effort to raise the birthrate, the regime offered generous maternity leaves and special economic benefits for parents. The ratio of births to deaths nevertheless remained unfavorable through most of the 1970s, although in contrast to West Germany, where deaths continued to exceed births into the 1980s, a mild reversal of that trend had set in by 1979.

One reason for the sluggish birthrate was a weakened family structure. By the mid-1980s the GDR had a divorce rate nearly half again as high as in the West, and one out of three children was born to unmarried parents, as compared to a rate of about 9 percent in the Federal Republic. Because of the decline in the birthrate and the flight of young people to the West, as well as improved medical care of the elderly, the population increasingly contained a disproportionate number of older people. The GDR thus found itself, even more so than did the Federal Republic, with a growing part of the population ineligible for work because of age but dependent upon the government for pensions and medical care that had to be paid for by the labor of a shrinking workforce.

To cope with this labor shortage, the regime increased its efforts to mobilize women for the workforce. By 1960, 67 percent of women of working age were employed outside the home, but by 1983 more than 86 percent held jobs, although in many cases only on a part-time basis. In the West the comparable figure was by the latter year about 50 percent. Even with this addition to the labor force of the GDR, its economy still suffered from a chronic lack of workers. In an effort to fill the widening gap in the workforce, the regime brought in laborers from the Communist-ruled countries of Eastern Europe, Mozambique, and Vietnam. The number of foreign workers in the GDR remained, however, minuscule compared to that in West Germany.

Under the trying economic circumstances of the 1970s the readiness of the Federal Republic to extend generous terms of trade proved attractive to the regime in the GDR. Particularly enticing at a time of high interest rates and rapidly growing foreign indebtedness was the interest-free "swing" credit extended by Bonn for East German purchases in West Germany. Increasingly valuable at a time of greatly heightened international competition was duty-free access for East German goods to the Federal Republic, which refused, in line with its insistence that there was still one German nation, to treat those goods as foreign. Once in the Federal Republic, East German products could then be sold throughout the West European Common Market, so that the GDR enjoyed in effect a shadow membership in that trading community. In part because of these advantages provided by West Germany, East Germany's trade with Western countries increased during the 1970s. Whereas in 1965 exchanges of goods with non-Communist countries had amounted to 26 percent of the GDR's overall foreign trade, by 1976 the figure had grown to 33 percent. East Germany's economic dependence on the other Communist-ruled countries thus lessened at least somewhat.

In line with its new Eastern policy, Bonn accommodated the economically troubled GDR in a number of other ways. To encourage road traffic to West Berlin, the Federal Republic began making large annual lump-sum payments to East Berlin in "hard" Western D-marks so as to relieve travelers from paying the transit fees demanded by the GDR. The regime in the East could then use the readily convertible Western currency for purchase of needed items anywhere in the non-Communist world. Still more West German marks flowed to the East by virtue of new agreements on repair of the highway and railway links between the Federal Republic and West Berlin, all of which were also used for travel and transport of goods within the GDR.

The increasing numbers of West Germans who visited the East

under the liberalized access arrangements resulting from the new Eastern policy brought with them sought-after hard currency. Some of these D-marks went directly to the regime in the form of visa charges and mandatory purchases of East German currency by visitors from the West, the level of which was reduced by a third in late 1974 after being doubled the previous year. Eased financial regulations enabled West Germans with families in the East to help them materially by sending them D-marks. Their relatives in the GDR could then use those marks to purchase otherwise unavailable consumer goods in special stores run by the regime which accepted only Western currency. Additional D-marks were sent into the GDR by church organizations in the Federal Republic to finance the repair of church buildings and the construction of new ones as well as to extend other forms of assistance to coreligionists.

This aid from the Federal Republic solved problems for those officials of the GDR charged with its troubled economy, but it caused problems for those concerned primarily with political issues. The latter remained determined—in line with the policy of delimitation—to continue emphasizing the differences between the two parts of Germany and minimizing contact between them. This again became evident during 1980, as the Polish Solidarity labor reform movement shook the regime in that neighboring Communist-ruled country. In an obvious effort to reduce the number of West Germans visiting the GDR, bringing with them subversive ideas and news of the outside world, the SED regime again drastically increased in October 1980 the amount of its non-convertible currency that visitors had to purchase with D-marks for each day spent in the GDR. As a result, the stream of Western visitors once more fell off sharply, as those who could not afford the new, higher expenditure had to forgo visits with their families in the East.

Also in October 1980 Honecker cooled down relations with the Federal Republic. Raising anew issues the GDR had pressed for in vain during the negotiations that produced the Basic Treaty of 1972, he demanded that Bonn exchange ambassadors, rather than emissaries, with East Berlin. He insisted as well that the Federal Republic accord East German citizenship the same recognition as that of a foreign country, which would mean that refugees from GDR could no longer immediately become citizens in the West without lengthy immigration procedures. The Federal Republic, he announced, must also close down the institute it maintained to keep records of human rights violations in the GDR and those responsible for such violations. Finally, Honecker demanded that the Federal Republic and the GDR divide a disputed portion of the Elbe River along their border which the West had hitherto controlled.

Since Bonn had long since left no doubt about its unwillingness to give in on these points (with the possible exception of the Elbe dispute), Honecker's demands amounted to a transparent move to reduce official East-West interaction. It seemed no coincidence that this move came at a time of instability in the Soviet bloc, to which the GDR was tied in countless ways. Another expression of this increasingly cool attitude was the postponement in the fall of 1980, at East Berlin's request, of a long-planned visit to the GDR by West German chancellor Helmut Schmidt.

When the citizenry of the GDR proved immune to the unrest that had produced the protracted and grave Polish crisis, the SED regime's relations with the Federal Republic began to thaw again. In December 1981 Chancellor Schmidt finally made his long-postponed trip to East Germany, conferring with Honecker at Werbellinsee, outside of Berlin, thus keeping the meeting below the protocol level of a state visit to the GDR's capital. The meeting took place in an atmosphere of conspicuous mutual cordiality despite Honecker's renewed insistence that Bonn accord foreign status to East German citizenship. Ignoring that demand, Schmidt affirmed, to the evident satisfaction of his host, the "sovereignty and statehood" of the GDR.

The amicable tone of the Werbellinsee meeting gained special significance in view of its having taken place at a time of deteriorating relations between the United States and the Soviet Union that interrupted nearly a decade of superpower détente. The Russians' installation, beginning in 1977, of new medium-range nuclear missiles aimed at Western Europe, along with their invasion of Afghanistan in 1979, had put an end to the efforts of the Carter administration to reduce tensions. The new American administration that took office in January 1981 under President Ronald Reagan adopted a hard line toward the Soviet Union. When, at the time of the Werbellinsee meeting of Schmidt and Honecker, the Communist regime in Poland imposed martial law and suppressed the Solidarity movement, the Reagan administration responded by imposing trade sanctions against Poland and the USSR. Yet, although Bonn had long functioned as one of the closest allies of the United States, the Schmidt cabinet conspicuously refrained from joining in the American sanctions.

The handshakes and smiles with which Schmidt and Honecker parted at Werbellinsee in December 1981 suggested to many observers a new closeness in the relations between the two Germanies. At least for the time being, the leaders of both had clearly concluded, after a brief hiatus occasioned by the Polish crisis, that their interests were best served by a continuation of détente between Bonn and East Berlin. They were unwilling to interrupt the mutual accommodation between their two governments because of the freeze in relations between the two superpowers to which they were respectively linked.

Once it became clear that the political shift to the right that brought Helmut Kohl to the chancellorship of the Federal Republic at the end of 1982 would not result in Bonn's abandonment of détente, the SED regime displayed a growing willingness to make concessions to the West in return for economic help. Some of that help arrived under the unlikely auspices of CSU chairman Franz Josef Strauss, previously one of the most outspoken critics of the new Eastern policy and a proponent of non-recognition of the GDR. After a visit to East Berlin in the summer of 1983, Strauss sponsored a guarantee by the Federal Republic of a West German bank loan of a billion D-marks to a

GDR desperate for hard currency. Afterward, the SED regime quietly and unofficially let it be known that removal had begun of the deadly automatic explosive devices installed along the GDR's western frontiers since 1971 to discourage escape attempts by its citizens. The shoot-to-kill order to its border guards, however, remained in effect.

Mutual accommodation proceeded in a variety of ways. In the summer of 1984 the Federal Republic guaranteed another major West German bank loan to the GDR, this time for 950 million marks. Shortly thereafter, the SED regime lowered the barriers it had erected to limit West German travel to East Germany by reducing the amount of its non-convertible currency that retirees visiting the GDR were required to purchase upon crossing the border. Organized visits to the GDR by schoolchildren from the West became possible, and by 1987 some 77,000 young West Germans had met with their counterparts in the East. Beginning in 1986, cities in East and West entered into sister-city agreements, exchanging delegations and disseminating information about each other among their residents. By the end of 1988, more than forty such agreements had come into being. The once highly secretive arrangement whereby the Federal Republic had been ransoming political prisoners from the GDR since the mid-1960s began to assume routine, business-like form; in 1985 some 2,500 imprisoned East Germans reached the West and freedom in return for payments to the GDR in D-marks.

Economic activity between the two Germanies quickened significantly during the 1980s. Trade increased rapidly and by 1985 stood at more than double the level of a decade earlier, thanks largely to credits advanced by West Germany to the GDR, which ran a chronic trade deficit with the Federal Republic. In order to obtain Western marks to offset this imbalance, the SED regime had during the 1970s established some 250 special government shops at which luxury items from the West could be purchased with D-marks of the Federal Republic. Those East Germans fortunate enough to have generous relatives in the West could acquire there coveted items not otherwise available in the GDR. The flow of hard currency sent them by their relatives passed into the hands of the regime, which could apply it to its debts in the West.

In other respects, economic relations between the two Germanies became increasingly business-like. In 1984, at the time of the Leipzig trade fair, the GDR for the first time permitted commercial airline flights between a city in the East and one in the West, Frankfurt am Main. That same year the Volkswagen Corporation announced an agreement to install in the GDR sophisticated machinery that would make possible the production of advanced automobile engines there. Eastern officials contracted to buy Volkswagen cars produced in the West, while Volkswagen agreed to purchase various automotive products in the East, including motors to be manufactured with the new equipment it would export to the East. Municipalities in the Federal Republic, hard-pressed for ways to dispose of garbage and other waste, contracted with Eastern officials for the use of dumping sites in the GDR. These and many other transactions indicated by the latter part of the 1980s that the trend toward economic separation of the two parts of Germany had been reversed, even though the effects of four decades of division still predominated.

In the 1980s the SED regime began quietly relaxing travel restrictions on its citizens in hopes of defusing the widespread resentment arising from those restrictions. Previously, visits to West Germany had been permitted only for those who had reached retirement age and therefore no longer belonged to the workforce or those who could demonstrate "urgent family matters," such as funerals or weddings of near relatives. Now, for the first time, large numbers of East Germans were accorded permission to visit the West for specified periods of time, but only one family member at a time and with a meager supply of Western currency. In 1986 over half a million East Germans visited the West, and by 1987 the number of such trips reached 1.2 million. As Honecker proudly pointed out to visiting West German politicians, virtually all returned home.

Less successful were the regime's experiments with officially approved emigration to West Germany. In response to pressure from the West, the East Berlin authorities began to process the backlog of applications submitted by East Germans who wanted to leave permanently for the Federal Republic. Whereas in 1983 only 7,729, mainly retired, persons had been permitted to emigrate, about 30,000, mostly younger, applicants were allowed to leave during the first half of 1984. When GDR officials became alarmed at the size of this exodus of working-age citizens they slowed their procedures drastically. This produced something of a panic among those desperate to leave for the West. In hopes of forcing the Federal Republic to take them under its protection, hundreds of men, women, and children entered the West German diplomatic mission in East Berlin and demanded asylum, refusing to leave until they were permitted to emigrate. When the mission in East Berlin became so crowded with would-be refugees that Bonn had to lock the doors, other East Germans traveled to Prague and encamped in the West German embassy there, likewise demanding to go westward.

Rather than sacrifice the progress made toward rapprochement with the GDR, Bonn went to great lengths to resolve the problem of the desperate would-be refugees by quiet, behind-the-scenes diplomacy. It secured assurances from the SED regime that no charges would be pressed against the East Germans who had sought the diplomatic protection of the Federal Republic if they left the buildings where they had taken refuge. The GDR authorities promised, moreover, to process their emigration applications without prejudice. The would-be refugees eventually gave in when it became apparent that Bonn did not intend to attempt to move them directly westward from its diplomatic buildings in the East. During the second half of 1984 the GDR permitted an additional 5,000 East Germans to emigrate to the Federal Republic. Authorized emigration dropped to below 19,000 in 1985, rose to nearly 20,000 in 1986, declined again in 1987 to under 12,000, and then increased to 29,000 in 1988.

In the sphere of foreign policy, Honecker displayed increasing independence from Moscow. This became conspicuous when he ostentatiously traveled to Rumania in August 1984 to take part in that country's observance of the fortieth anniversary of its liberation from German occupation. This verged on an open affront to the USSR, which, along with the rest of the Soviet bloc, boycotted the occasion because of Rumanian Communist dictator Nicolae Ceauşescu's refusal to conform with the foreign policies of the bloc. In other respects, too, East Berlin demonstrated an assertiveness in the international sphere that contrasted sharply with its previous servility to the USSR.

During the mid-1980s relations between the GDR and the Federal Republic continued to improve, and in the fall of 1987 Erich Honecker reached the pinnacle of his political career when he paid an official visit to the Federal Republic. As chairman of the State Council of the GDR, and thus head of state, he was received in Bonn by Chancellor Kohl with full military ceremonial honors. The GDR's flag flew next to that of the Federal Republic, and its national anthem was played along with the Western anthem. On what amounted to a triumphant tour of West Germany, Honecker was cordially greeted by politicians of all parties. West German officials repeatedly insisted that the welcome accorded the leader of the GDR in no way diminished the Federal Republic's commitment to reunification. But the cordial reception of Honecker seemed to belie their statements. To many observers it appeared that the German Democratic Republic had at last achieved the kind of acceptance by Bonn that would ensure its durability. Yet even as Honecker struck triumphant poses in the West, his regime's foundations were eroding at home.

Infirmities of the Communist Regime

In addition to the mounting difficulties the SED regime encountered in the 1980s as it attempted to meet the material desires of the East German people

The leaders of East and West Germany, Erich Honecker and Helmut Kohl, on
the occasion of Honecker's official visit to Bonn in 1987

and cope with their restiveness at being denied freedom to
travel westward, it suffered increasingly from a host of less
tangible infirmities.

Once the GDR had achieved recognition by the Federal Republic and other Western countries and entered into normalized
relations with them, the problems of identity and legitimacy
that had plagued it from the outset became acute. Unlike the
other Communist-ruled countries in the Soviet bloc, East Germany could not plausibly lay claim to a national identity, since
its very existence conspicuously divided the German nation.
During its early years the SED regime sought identity and legitimacy by portraying East Germany as part of a dynamic revolu-
tionary phalanx led by the Soviet Union that would inevitably
displace a decaying and doomed capitalism throughout the

world. Once that process had been completed, Germany would be reunited under the banner of a triumphant world communism.

By the 1980s, with relations between the Soviet bloc—including the GDR—and capitalist countries increasingly normalized, the promised world revolution came to seem ever more remote and implausible. As time passed, the democracies of the West showed no signs of the collapse predicted by Communist ideologists. Instead, their citizens enjoyed ever greater prosperity. By contrast, the Soviet bloc fell ever further behind in terms of material goods supplied to working people. The Federal Republic, which was ruled throughout the 1970s by a left-of-center government, particularly failed to conform to the SED regime's propaganda. Whereas the Communist authorities portrayed West Germany as an aggressive, imperialistic polity dominated by exploitative capitalists and neofascists, West Germans enjoyed unprecedented freedom and a rapidly improving standard of living. After adoption of the new Eastern policy, Bonn entered into agreement after agreement with the GDR, even under the right-of-center government of Chancellor Kohl. The SED regime, meanwhile, continued to rule with a heavy hand and exhort its citizens to accept material sacrifices in order to "build socialism," a goal that perennially receded into a future that seemed increasingly theoretical.

In an effort to deal with these problems, the SED regime resorted to a variety of expedients aimed at buttressing the identity of the GDR among the citizenry and legitimizing its own domination. Prominent among these was lavish support of accomplishment in international athletic competition. The regime had begun in the 1950s to promote sports in a concerted fashion and provide handsome incentives for athletic prowess. Children judged to have promise in sports were identified at an early age and given intensified training. Those who continued to improve were placed in special schools emphasizing sports and were provided with elaborate facilities. A college-level athletic academy completed the training of the most adept. Upon reaching adulthood, the products of this system frequently pursued full-time careers as athletes under the aegis of sporting clubs attached to the factories where they were nominally employed. Those who met with success in international competition received privileges of the sort ordinarily accorded only to the most lofty circles of the Communist elite in the GDR, such as spacious dwellings, foreign luxury items, and permission to travel abroad.

This system of regime-promoted training in sports paid off handsomely when athletes from the GDR began to win a growing share of prizes in international competition. In 1968, when a separate East German team was admitted to Olympic competition for the first time, its members equaled the number of medals won by West German athletes. Four years later, the team from the GDR far outstripped the Federal Republic's, and in 1976 East Germany won more gold Olympic medals than did the American team, finishing second in aggregate points to the USSR, which similarly cultivated "amateur" sports. The next two Olympic games were incompletely attended because of political boycotts, but in 1988 the East German team again finished second to the Soviets, well ahead of the Americans, garnering over two and a half times as many medals as West Germany, which had a population more than three times that of the GDR.

In its quest to establish the identity and legitimacy of the GDR, the SED regime sought to find roots for that polity in the German past. The traditions of Prussia, which included austerity and self-sacrifice on the part of the individual for the well-being of the whole, took on new appeal after decades during which the Prussian past had been pilloried as the embodiment of reaction and militarism. This positive reevaluation of the Prussian tradition found conspicuous symbolic expression in 1980, when an equestrian statue of Frederick the Great, the eighteenth-century soldier-king whose wars of conquest made Prussia a major power, was restored to the prominent location in East Berlin from which it had been removed for preservation during the war.

In 1983 the GDR embraced still another part of the German

past it had previously scorned when it sponsored a year-long commemoration of the five-hundredth anniversary of Martin Luther's birth in Saxony, now part of East Germany. Long portrayed by the atheistic SED regime as an obscurantist religious fanatic as well as an enemy of the common man because of his denunciation of peasant uprisings at the time of the Reformation, Luther was now viewed in positive terms as a champion of progress. Equally surprising was the appearance in 1985 of a lengthy scholarly book about Bismarck which for the first time gave East German readers a balanced view, rather than the usual negative caricature, of the first imperial chancellor. The problematic aspect of upgrading Bismarck, the unifier of nineteenth-century Germany, escaped few observers in the light of statements by Honecker and other spokesmen of the SED regime to the effect that a unification of socialist East Germany and capitalist West Germany was no more possible than a merger of fire and water.

Even aside from the blatant contradiction between the SED regime's continuing rhetorical denunciations of the Federal Republic and its simultaneous pursuit of closer economic ties, the policy of mutual accommodation with West Germany confronted Honecker and his associates with a troublesome dilemma. On the one hand, the economic gains made possible by increasing material aid from the West seemed to strengthen the SED regime. On the other hand, the concessions in the sphere of human rights which the East Berlin authorities were forced to make in return had the effect of relaxing their tight grip on the population. The loosening of restrictions on travel to the West by GDR citizens potentially ran an especially grave risk. By exposing large numbers of East Germans personally to Western freedom and affluence for the first time since the erection of the Berlin Wall, that policy seemed likely to heighten discontent with conditions in the GDR. Yet the popularity among East Germans of that and other human-rights concessions to the Federal Republic, as well as the economic benefits of cooperation, made it difficult for the regime to consider backing away from the course of ever-greater mutual accommodation. There were grounds, however, to be concerned about whether that course could ever fully satisfy the millions of Germans in the GDR without political changes so great as to undermine the authority of the SED regime.

The proliferating contradictions between reality and theory in the GDR had the effect of eroding the regime's ideological underpinnings. Marxist-Leninist doctrine, although still a required component of education at all levels, rapidly lost its plausibility. The classless society and the withering away of the state predicted by that doctrine seemed no closer to realization than ever as the Communist regime approached the fortieth anniversary of its founding. The regime's ritualistic calls for material sacrifices in order to make possible a plentiful future for generations to come sounded shopworn after decades of repetition, especially to young East Germans. Marxist-Leninist ideology, once the object of respectful awe as the purported key to scientific construction of a bountiful and just society free of classes, became the butt of ridicule for many. According to a quip that circulated clandestinely, the GDR must surely have already achieved the regime's goal of a classless society, since only three categories of people were left: the upper classless, the middle classless, and the lower classless.

Cynicism of this sort was nourished by the behavior of the entrenched Communist rulers. Headed by a small, aging group of veteran functionaries around Honecker who had wielded power ever since formation of the regime, the inner circles of the SED had become isolated from the realities of life in the GDR. Taking their exalted positions for granted, they availed themselves of ever-greater privileges. The top leaders of the party, including Honecker, took up residence in comfortable, modern single-family houses located in a heavily guarded compound north of Berlin that was off limits to the citizenry. There they purchased Western goods and other luxuries in special shops maintained by the government solely for their convenience. Whereas most East Germans fortunate enough to acquire automobiles had to content themselves with outmoded vehicles built in the GDR, the rulers sped to their offices in East Berlin in a fleet of late-model, Swedish-manufactured, chauffeur-driven limousines. Large hunting preserves, vacation resorts, and luxury hotels were reserved for party officials, who paid little or nothing for their use.

Despite the tight censorship imposed by the SED regime, its policies continued to give rise to internal dissent in the 1980s. Some criticism came from idealistic Communists who, like Biermann, Bahro, and Havemann earlier, accused the GDR's rulers of betraying the ideals of Marx and Lenin. Since the SED claimed sole authority to interpret Marxist-Leninist doctrine, it denounced such critics as schismatic heretics. In response to their appeals for reforms that would bring about true socialism, the authorities maintained that the GDR had already achieved "real, existing socialism" and that there could therefore be no other. Those who persisted in arguing to the contrary were branded as traitors of the working class, which the SED claimed it alone represented. Those who were party members were expelled. They and other such dissidents lost their jobs and were denied access to the media and other public forums. Those who remained defiant were either imprisoned or stripped of their GDR citizenship and expelled to West Germany.

A far more difficult challenge to the Communist regime came from the independent peace movement of East Germany. An official Peace Council created and dominated by the SED had, from the very formation of the GDR, claimed a monopoly on antiwar activity. In line with Communist propaganda, the Peace Council attributed belligerence solely to the capitalist countries of the NATO alliance, which it held responsible for the Cold War and the danger of a nuclear holocaust. The Soviet Union and its Warsaw Pact satellites were portrayed, by contrast, as the guardians of peace. In the judgment of many thoughtful East Germans this amounted to manipulation of the widespread fear of war by the SED regime for its own political advantage. These dissidents espoused what they saw as a true form of pacifism and called for disarmament of both the Warsaw Pact and NATO. They also called for an end to SED propaganda that depicted the Federal Republic as a bellicose state bent on armed aggression against the GDR. Under the auspices of Protestant clergymen, these independent advocates of peace began during the early 1980s to sponsor meetings at churches to which like-minded East Germans were invited. Unwilling to incur the opprobrium of persecuting advocates of peace, the regime permitted these gatherings to take place, even though the existence of a popular movement beyond its control caused it mounting concern.

Additional dissent came from a nascent environmental movement. In its pursuit of economic productivity, the SED regime had ruthlessly exploited the natural resources of East Germany with little or no regard for the effects on the environment. The result was some of the worst pollution of air, soil, and water in the industrial world. When the authorities proved impervious to pleas for a halt to even the most egregious forms of pollution, citizens' groups began to meet, usually also in churches, to exchange information and consider lines of action to rescue the threatened environment. By the mid-1980s groups of this sort were clandestinely circulating literature about pollution in the GDR. The SED regime felt less compunction about suppressing such activities than was the case with the independent peace movement, and in the autumn of 1987 the police raided a church in East Berlin, seizing an environmental library recently assembled there and arresting members of the movement on charges of subversive activities. The movement continued to grow, however, since the regime turned a deaf ear to warnings about the damage being done to the environment by the industries of the GDR.

Dissidents in the GDR derived encouragement from developments in other Communist-ruled countries. During the first half of the 1980s the growth of the antiregime Solidarity movement in neighboring Poland revealed that Communist rule was not invulnerable to challenge. In the second half of the decade a very different and far more potent threat to Communist orthodoxy of the sort practiced by the SED burst forth from a totally unexpected source: the Soviet Union. Following the installation of Mikhail Gorbachev as head of the Communist Party of the USSR in 1985 the authorities in East Berlin became increasingly appalled at the new Soviet leader's policies of glasnost, which called for freedom of expression, and perestroika, which entailed a radical restructuring of government in the direction of democracy.

Initially, the aging, entrenched leadership of the SED sought to ignore Gorbachev's departures from previously sacrosanct Soviet orthodoxy. His iconoclastic speeches were reported in the official GDR news media in abridged versions that omitted his most pointed criticisms of long-standing Communist practices. By 1987, however, with Gorbachev's demands for reform becoming ever more radical, spokesmen of the regime began openly to voice scorn for his program. In April of that year SED ideologist Kurt Hager, like Honecker a seventy-five-year-old veteran Communist functionary, responded to a question about whether Soviet-style perestroika would be applied to the GDR with the dismissive answer, "If your neighbor put up new wallpaper would you feel obliged to have your wallpaper changed, too?" Other SED officials suggested that the GDR had outstripped the Soviet Union in the realization of socialism and therefore needed no such reforms. On the surface, relations with Moscow remained cordial despite these mounting tensions. But when the SED regime began during 1987 and 1988 to suppress the circulation of Soviet publications in the GDR because of fear that their contents were dangerously subversive, it became apparent that a wide gulf had opened between the East German state and the USSR that had created it and sustained it throughout its existence.

Encouraged by Gorbachev's policies in the Soviet Union, dissidents in the GDR became bolder in their criticism of the SED regime. In January 1988, on the occasion of the SED's annual march in East Berlin to commemorate the murders in 1919 of Communist leaders Karl Liebknecht and Rosa Luxemburg, a band of protesters disrupted the usually routine ceremonies. Defying the authorities, they unfurled banners containing quotations from the martyred pair in favor of freedom of expression and in opposition to authoritarian rule. The regime responded by arresting the leaders of this unauthorized demonstration and charging them with treasonable relations with foreigners. A wave of popular indignation swept across the GDR, as outraged East Germans gathered, usually in churches, to protest these repressive measures. Nevertheless, a number of those who had taken part in the demonstration received jail sentences while others, confronted with a choice between lengthy imprisonment or emigration, reluctantly abandoned their quest for reform in the GDR and left for West Germany.

Dissident elements again asserted themselves publicly at the time of local elections in the GDR in May 1989. Availing themselves of a right guaranteed by law, critics of the regime watched over the ballot counts at local polling places in a number of cities and then pooled the results of their counts. Since the official tally grossly understated the number of votes cast against the so-called unity list of candidates so as to assure the usual near-unanimity of affirmation, the organizers of the action charged the authorities with election fraud. When demonstrators took to the streets to protest, some 120 were arrested. Others sought to file suits against the authorities for violation of their rights as voters.

Further popular indignation against the SED regime resulted from its response to the bloody suppression by Chinese Communist authorities of the popular movement for reform at Peking's Tiananmin Square in June 1989. In the aftermath of that massacre, which most East Germans could witness via Western television, Honecker's heir apparent, Egon Krenz, endorsed the measures adopted by his Chinese comrades as necessary to "restore order." Striking a defiant pose, the regime in effect warned dissidents against actions such as those that had led the Chinese freedom demonstrators to violent deaths. Earlier, in January 1989, Honecker had sought to dash any hope that the

SED regime would abandon its policy of restricting travel by citizens of the GDR to the West by proclaiming that the Berlin Wall would stand for another century. As events were soon to demonstrate, Honecker had miscalculated by ninety-nine years.

The Bloodless Revolution
of 1989

The GDR's denial to its citizens of the right to travel abroad freely, which for nearly two decades appeared to have strengthened the SED regime, ultimately led to its swift and total downfall. During the latter part of the 1980s requests for officially approved emigration to the West mounted, but the regime continued to deal in dilatory fashion with the huge backlog of applications to leave. Despairing of ever securing official permission, twenty would-be emigrants entered the West German mission in East Berlin at the beginning of January 1989, vowing not to budge until the Federal Republic arranged transit for them to the West. When Bonn indicated its inability to comply with their wishes, they returned home later in the month, taking with them assurances from the Eastern authorities that they would not be punished and indications that their emigration applications would be processed with dispatch. In the next six months the SED regime permitted more than 46,000 GDR citizens to emigrate to West Germany. Although this represented close to a doubling of the rate during the previous year, the backlog of emigration applications remained enormous, and frustration continued to grow. Those who contemplated an unauthorized crossing of the border to the West received a forceful warning in February 1989, when a twenty-year-old East German was shot dead by GDR guards while attempting to scale the Berlin Wall.

By early August 1989 more than a hundred more would-be emigrants had encamped in the West German mission in East Berlin. To halt the influx, which dangerously overtaxed the limited facilities of the building, Bonn was forced to suspend access to the mission. When it again became apparent that the Federal Republic could not arrange for transit to the West, the thwarted would-be emigrants left the mission and returned home during August and early September. In contrast to the earlier episode, however, the GDR authorities held out to them only the prospect of immunity from prosecution, not accelerated emigration procedures.

With hopes of reaching West Germany directly through official channels dashed, East Germans bent upon leaving the GDR turned their attention to Hungary. There a reform-minded Communist regime, as part of its liberalization policy, had begun in May to dismantle the barbed-wire entanglement that had previously prevented unauthorized border crossings to Austria. With Hungarians now permitted free access to the West, many East Germans saw a new opportunity for escape. Since Hungary had long been a vacation goal for some million and a half GDR citizens annually, tens of thousands had obtained in advance the necessary travel documents for trips during the summer of 1989. Once in Hungary, many sought to cross over that country's newly opened border to Austria. Although Hungarian guards turned back East Germans at railway and highway crossing points to Austria, the absence of barriers in the countryside offered numerous opportunities for clandestine departures. By mid-August some 1,600 East Germans had reached West Germany via Austria. On one day later that month an additional 661 took advantage of a celebration of the open border to flee westward.

As news spread of this aperture in the barriers behind which East Germans had been closed off from the West since the erection of the Berlin Wall nearly three decades earlier, a hasty migration to Hungary began. Frightened by rumors that the SED regime would cut off travel to that country, thousands of East Germans headed there. The boldest sought to cross the border from Hungary into Austria clandestinely, which sometimes resulted in altercations with Hungarian border guards and in one case led to the fatal shooting of an East German. More cautious would-be emigrants sought refuge in the West German embassy in Budapest and requested help from the Federal Republic. When the embassy building became dangerously overcrowded, Hungarian officials made additional shelters available. By early September more than 3,500 citizens of the GDR waited in Hungary, demanding to be allowed to leave for the West.

With no end in sight to an accelerating migration that threatened to overwhelm local facilities, the Hungarian government unexpectedly announced on September 10 a crucial policy reversal: henceforth East Germans who wished to cross into Austria would be allowed to do so freely. This step enraged the GDR authorities, who had not been consulted by Budapest. The SED regime denounced the Hungarian government for violating a long-standing agreement among East bloc countries not to allow each other's citizens to exit to the West. Additional denunciations were directed at the Federal Republic, which the official East German press accused of engaging in "commerce in human beings" by enticing citizens of the GDR with spurious promises of material betterment in the West. East Germans were warned that behind the flight to the West via Hungary lay a plot by revenge-seeking, reactionary elements which controlled the Federal Republic and were bent upon reestablishing the German Reich in its prewar boundaries and undoing the accomplishments of forty years of socialism in the GDR.

Despite this propaganda campaign by the SED, news that the Hungarian border to Austria now lay open produced a new surge of unauthorized emigration. Within three days some 15,000 East Germans reached West Germany via Hungary and Austria. In an effort to halt the flow, authorities in the GDR began to employ bureaucratic pretexts to thwart East Germans attempting to travel to Hungary. Communist-ruled Czechoslovakia cooperated by unofficially closing its borders with Hungary to would-be emigrants from the GDR. Some of those who arrived to find the crossing points to Hungary blocked desperately sought to reach its territory by swimming across the Danube, which formed the border with Czechoslovakia, and some drownings in front of horrified onlookers resulted.

These obstacles to travel to Hungary merely deflected the flow of East Germans to Czechoslovakia and, to a lesser extent, Poland, the only two countries to which they could still travel freely. While hundreds of would-be emigrants went to Warsaw and demanded that the West German embassy there arrange for them to leave for the Federal Republic, Prague became the focal point of the mounting drama of mass escape from the GDR as thousands sought refuge in the West German embassy there during September. Whole families arrived, having abandoned everything except the few possessions they could carry. When the Czech police intervened to turn East Germans away from the entrance to the overcrowded embassy, many scaled the iron fencing around the grounds. Western television cameras recorded scenes of infants and elderly persons being handed over the fence to helping hands inside the grounds. After all the space in the embassy building had been occupied, a makeshift encampment began to fill the surrounding grounds. In all, some 3,000 men, women, and children of all ages had crowded into the embassy and its grounds by late September. With food in short supply, sanitary facilities hopelessly inadequate, and chill autumn rains soaking those camped outside, the situation soon became untenable.

With the international news media daily exposing the plight of the would-be emigrants in Prague to the world, including East German viewers of Western television, the SED regime gave way at the end of September. It agreed to permit those encamped at the embassies in Prague and Warsaw to travel to the Federal Republic on condition that they left through East Germany, an arrangement that would permit the SED regime to claim that it was expelling them. West German foreign minister Hans-Dietrich Genscher, himself a refugee from the GDR, flew to Prague on the last day of September to inform the East Germans at the embassy that they would soon be free. During the first days of October nearly 15,000 rode in special trains from Prague and Warsaw through the GDR to West Germany. One of the departures from Prague was delayed while East German police fought off a crowd of 3,000 who besieged the Dresden railway station in hopes of boarding the refugee train when it passed through that city.

In an effort to stanch the human hemorrhage from the GDR the SED regime acted in early October to obstruct travel to Poland and end visa-free travel to Czechoslovakia. East Germans could no longer travel to any other country without permission from the authorities. While these measures did not completely halt the flow of would-be emigrants to Prague and Warsaw, they greatly slowed it. But, more importantly, sealing all the borders of the GDR to its own citizens had the effect of containing within the country the mounting unrest among East Germans. What had begun as a flight from the GDR became a struggle to alter it from within.

During the summer East German dissidents had become more assertive than ever before. Protest meetings at churches began to spill into the streets, where they became non-violent demonstrations against the SED regime's policies. Despite large-scale arrests, often accompanied by gratuitous violence on the part of the police, these demonstrations grew and spread during the early autumn. Emboldened by the increasing mood of defiance, groups of intellectuals and professional people began during September to announce publicly the formation of independent civic organizations. The earliest of these called itself New Forum and was soon followed by others named Democracy Now and Democratic Awakening. By early October these had been joined by a Social Democratic Party, which used the initials SDP to distinguish itself from the SPD of West Germany. The SED regime angrily denounced these organizations as "hostile to the state" and refused to accord them official recognition. They nevertheless grew and gave public expression to the views of their members.

With the shift in the focus of unrest inward, an important change in the thrust of the mounting upheaval occurred. Whereas the would-be migrants who had set the mounting crisis in motion rejected the GDR and socialism, those who came to the fore at the head of the new civic organizations wanted to pre-serve the East German state and pursue what they envisioned as a truer socialism by means of reform. Although these organiza-tions differed somewhat on aims, they agreed on the need, as first steps, for free elections and an end to restrictions on travel.

In the midst of the supercharged political atmosphere of early October 1989 the SED regime carried through a long-scheduled five-day celebration of the GDR's fortieth anniversary. The usual procession of military units, factory delegations, women's leagues, youth groups, and other Communist organizations filed past festively decked reviewing stands in East Berlin, accom-panied by martial music. The aging oligarchs of the SED, led by Honecker, delivered the customary addresses extolling the "so-cialist accomplishments" of the GDR. The pretense of normality was marred, however, by brutal police attacks on peaceful pro-testers, many of whom were arrested and mishandled while behind bars.

The most striking aspect of the anniversary celebration was the behavior of the guest of honor and leader of the patron state of the GDR, Mikhail Gorbachev, president of the USSR. In his official speech Gorbachev made clear that the days of the mono-lithic Soviet bloc were over and that each country must work out its own policies. In informal utterances to the press and to crowds in the streets he indicated sympathy for those demand-ing reforms. In return, the crowds appealed to him to support reform of the GDR and accorded him spontaneous cheers denied to Honecker and the other SED leaders. Gorbachev's visit left East German dissidents bolstered by the belief that they need not fear a repetition of the Soviet repression of June 1953.

After the anniversary commemoration, the city of Leipzig became the focal point of the upheaval. Prayer meetings for peace which had been held for years on Monday nights in a Protestant church there began in late September to be followed by orderly marches through the streets of the city, despite ha-rassment by the police and many arrests. When the size of these weekly demonstrations swelled to 15,000 at the beginning of

October, the authorities ostentatiously made preparations for forcible repression. As the evening of Monday, October 9, approached, downtown Leipzig was heavily patrolled by People's Police as well as by army units and armed factory militias loyal to the regime. But despite this show of force, 70,000 persons took part in that evening's march.

The march of October 9 in Leipzig proved a turning point in the upheaval. To the amazement and relief of the participants, the SED regime made no use of the forces at its disposal to halt the march, which remained peaceful and orderly. Various explanations would later be offered for the absence of repression, but regardless of who was responsible, a watershed was passed that evening. Never again would the authorities attempt to crush dissent with force. Opponents of the regime who had hitherto hesitated to take the risks involved in demonstrating their dissent publicly now joined in. The next Monday night march in Leipzig numbered more than 100,000, and that of October 23 swelled to over 300,000. In the streets of other East German cities similar peaceful demonstrations multiplied and grew in size.

As demands for reform rapidly mounted, the leadership of the SED sought to appease its critics by deposing the unyielding Erich Honecker, who had refused to admit that the regime was imperiled. On October 17 a majority of the Politburo removed him as general secretary of the party and replaced him with the man long regarded as the most likely successor, Egon Krenz. The following week the People's Chamber elected Krenz to succeed Honecker as chairman of the State Council, that is, as head of state. A member of the second generation of Communist functionaries in the GDR, the fifty-two-year-old Krenz had acquired the reputation of a hard-liner while holding a variety of party and state positions. Upon taking office, he called for dialogue between the regime and its critics but proposed no specific reforms other than a vaguely worded commitment to a new law on travel. But no significant changes were made. Since Krenz's role in dismissing accusations of vote fraud during the May local elections and justifying the massacre at Tiananmin Square in June was well known, he became a target of the protesters. So did many local SED officials, some of whom resigned in the face of massive public rejection.

When the new leadership sought to assuage public resentment by reopening the GDR's border to Czechoslovakia at the beginning of November, the result was another human hemorrhage. A flood of East Germans descended upon Prague, once again filling the West German embassy and its grounds to overflowing. Faced with a repetition of the embarrassing scenes of the previous month, the SED regime hastily agreed to an arrangement it described as temporary whereby Czechoslovak authorities would allow East Germans to leave via Austria, beginning November 3. Within a week an additional 48,000 had arrived by that route in West Germany, where they joined the more than 170,000 who had fled earlier.

With the resumption of mass unapproved migration, the upheaval within the GDR once more underwent a transformation. The SED regime now found its claim to legitimacy challenged doubly, by departing citizens voting against it with their feet and by angry demonstrators vowing to stay at home and bring about sweeping reforms. Whereas the secret police, or Stasi, counted twenty-four unauthorized protest demonstrations involving an estimated 140,000 persons in the period October 16–22, the corresponding numbers for October 30–November 5 were 210 and 1.35 million. On November 4 the ferment in the GDR found expression in the largest protest to date, as over half a million demonstrators gathered in East Berlin. Seeking to mollify the swelling ranks of its opponents, the regime granted permission for this rally and sent the party boss of East Berlin, Günter Schabowski. His conciliatory words were, however, largely drowned out by jeers from the crowd. The intellectuals and leaders of young civic organizations who served as spokesmen of the rally denounced the repressive policies of the past and demanded freedom and democracy. But their goal continued to be preservation of the GDR and realization of a purified form of socialism.

In an effort to halt the swelling westward flow of emigrants through Czechoslovakia, the regime published with great fanfare on November 6 the draft of a new law designed to regulate travel and emigration to the West. The draft departed from existing statutes in explicitly recognizing the right of all GDR citizens to have a passport and to travel abroad for up to thirty days a year. But it did nothing to alter the requirement of official permission for both emigration and visits to the West. Nor did it meet the widespread demand for the right to purchase West German currency for use while visiting in the Federal Republic.

The draft travel law, a classic example of too little, too late, backfired massively. Officially proclaimed as the subject of a public discussion that would extend until the end of the month, it appeared at a moment when some three hundred East Germans were fleeing to the West via Czechoslovakia every hour. When others who were considering that step saw that the draft law would not improve the prospects for unfettered migration to the West, additional thousands joined the flight to the Federal Republic through Czechoslovakia. Similar disappointment among those resolved to stay in the GDR and work for reform gave rise on the evening of November 6 to some of the largest and angriest street demonstrations to date. In Leipzig alone half a million braved a cold, drenching rain to demand an end to all restrictions on travel.

Having inadvertently spurred both the exodus to the West and the demand for reform, the SED regime sought to appease the increasingly unruly citizenry of the GDR. On November 7 the members of the Council of Ministers, or government cabinet, resigned, including longtime minister-president Willi Stoph. The next day the elderly members of the decisive body, the SED's Politburo, submitted their resignations to the Central Committee of the party. They were replaced with a smaller, younger group of Communist functionaries nominated by General Secretary Krenz. The Central Committee also extended belated recognition to the earliest of the now civic organizations, New Forum. Outside the hall where the Central Committee was meeting in East

Berlin, thousands of SED members demonstrated to demand a new leadership that would be more responsive to the people.

On November 9 the SED regime suffered a self-inflicted wound from which it never recovered. At the end of that day's sessions of the Politburo and Central Committee, East Berlin party boss Schabowski briefed the press on the decisions reached. At the end of a long recitation he mentioned a new law on travel abroad. That measure was designed to halt the embarrassing exodus of emigrants via Czechoslovakia by making it possible to apply for official permission to go directly to West Germany, either to visit or to emigrate, under a new set of relaxed rules and expedited procedures. But in replying to questions about the new regulations, Schabowski left the impression that anyone who wished to go to the West could, from then on, immediately obtain an exit visa at the border. Led by radio reports and televised excerpts from Schabowski's interview to believe that the wall was open, thousands of East Berliners headed for the checkpoints leading to the Western part of the city, eager to visit what had for twenty-eight years been a forbidden region for most. The astonished guards, confronted by jubilant crowds demanding to pass and citing Schabowski's announcement, opened the gates. Some who passed through had their identification papers duly stamped by the guards, but the crowds grew so large that others simply walked across the border without official certification. Through ineptitude on the part of the SED the Berlin Wall had been inadvertently breached.

The breach proved permanent. When news spread that the wall was open, tens of thousands of additional East Berliners surged into the Western part of the city, where an impromptu all-night street party took place. Before television cameras of the international media, crowds of Berliners from East and West joyfully celebrated the opening of the barrier that had separated them for nearly three decades. Afterward, virtually all the East Germans who had crossed to the West returned home in the expectation that they could now move freely back and forth. For its part, the SED regime elected to claim credit for opening the

West Germans greeting East Germans as they drive through the Berlin Wall on the night of November 9, 1989, when it was opened after twenty-eight years of dividing the former capital city

wall rather than attempt to reimpose bureaucratic travel controls on an increasingly rebellious population. Thenceforth East Germans could obtain official permission to go westward simply by presenting their identification papers to the GDR guards at border crossing points to either West Berlin or the Federal Republic. Those crossing points were soon increased in number, as additional openings were made in the wall and the fortifications on the border to West Germany. Soon thereafter dismantlement of the wall began. A large part of the citizenry of the GDR quickly made use of its new freedom. During the first four days after the wall was opened, 4.3 million people, more than a quarter of the entire population, visited the West. Most returned home, often laden with goods purchased with the hundred D-marks the

East German troops standing atop the Berlin Wall watch the beginnings of its demolition in November 1989

Federal Republic had long bestowed on each visitor from the East to compensate for their lack of convertible currency.

With its position badly shaken, the SED sought to regain control of the situation by seizing the initiative. On the day after the wall was breached, Egon Krenz announced an "action program" to a rally of 150,000 Communists in East Berlin. It contained a lengthy list of proposed reforms, including a voting law that would for the first time permit free elections. But as critics of the regime pointed out, the program's pledges to put an end to unconstitutional practices amounted to a damning indictment of the SED regime's past record. Moreover, the program left unchallenged the party's claim to be the decisive political force in the GDR. On November 13 the People's Chamber, or parliament, elected a new Council of Ministers headed by Hans Modrow, a Communist functionary who had gained a reputation for modesty and integrity as SED chief of Dresden. But despite Modrow's

The Brandenburg Gate, before and after the breaching of the Berlin Wall on
November 9, 1989

good reputation, demonstrations continued in the streets of East German cities as protesters demanded an end to the SED's self-proclaimed leadership role and early free elections.

During November it became clear that the mounting rebelliousness in the GDR extended well into the ranks of the SED itself. Party underlings who had long taken orders from an imperious, self-perpetuating leadership that showed little or no respect for their views now began to vent their frustration and resentment. This came out in denunciations of the old leadership from the floor of the People's Chamber and in creation of a commission to investigate charges of official corruption aired by newly emboldened East German press media. At the demand of the SED delegation in the Chamber, former minister-president Stoph and other old-line Communists were removed from the Council of State. They and others closely linked to the old leadership were deprived of their parliamentary seats. Procedures aimed at expelling Honecker and many of his associates from the party were set in motion. At the grass roots, the rank and file of the SED deposed entrenched local party bosses and other lower officials. Under insistent pressure from increasingly assertive East German authors and journalists, censorship was abolished at the end of November. On December 1 the Communist-dominated People's Chamber voted unanimously to remove from the constitution the wording that had designated the SED as the leading political force in the GDR.

These measures failed to pacify the lower ranks of the SED. Anger among rank-and-file Communists was fed by ever more startling disclosures in the now liberated East German press about the privileges of the party elite as well as allegations of official crimes and corruption, including secret armament sales to African and Middle Eastern countries by a regime that had ceaselessly proclaimed its devotion to the cause of peace. When SED members took to the streets of East Berlin early in December to denounce the new leadership, Egon Krenz relinquished his government posts after only forty-four days. The once all-powerful Politburo and the Central Committee were dissolved, never to be reconstituted.

The SED itself was dismantled at a special party congress that met in December. Angry delegates repudiated the dictatorial leadership of the past and demanded that the party's authoritarian structure be democratized. Honecker and many members of his inner circle were expelled from the party and criminal proceedings were initiated against them. Rather than perpetuate the powerful position of general secretary, which Ulbricht and Honecker had used to control the party, the congress created a new post of chairman and filled it with an outsider, a young Communist lawyer named Gregor Gysi. He pledged to give the GDR a new, democratic form of socialism. The name of the party was changed to Socialist Unity Party–Party of Democratic Socialism. Soon the old name disappeared altogether and the party went by the initials PDS. The new leadership and the change of name did little, however, to revive the plummeting prestige of the party, which by the end of the year had lost 800,000 of its 2.3 million members.

With the fall of Egon Krenz, the dissolution of the Politburo, and the rebellion of the Communist rank and file, the SED regime, as constituted since its formation in 1949, ceased to exist. A popular, peaceful revolution wholly lacking in central leadership had, in a rapid succession of stages, undermined the authoritarian structure that had ruled East Germany with an iron hand for forty years.

Reunification

In the wake of the peaceful revolution, the state structure of the GDR began during December 1989 to function for the first time as something other than an instrument of the SED. The State Council and the National Defense Council, the two organs that Ulbricht and Honecker had used to control the governmental apparatus, rapidly lost influence and the latter was soon dissolved altogether. The subservient leader of the Liberal Democratic Party, Manfred Gerlach, succeeded Krenz as provisional chairman of the State Council; but although nominally head of state, he wielded no real power. Executive authority shifted, as provided by the constitution, to the cabinet—the Council of Ministers—headed by Minister-President Hans Modrow. With no Politburo to issue orders as in the past, the cabinet was for the first time in a position to make policy on its own. But since Modrow and his ministers had been installed by votes of the SED and its satellite parties in a parliament—the People's Chamber—which was itself the product of now-discredited fixed elections, the new cabinet had a dubious claim to legitimacy.

Into this political vacuum moved an informal group known as the Round Table which had been convened in East Berlin early in December under the auspices of church authorities. Dedicated to the preservation and democratization of the GDR, it was composed of representatives of the new oppositional civic groups on the one hand and the parties of the old regime on the other, including a delegation of the PDS led by Gregor Gysi. At the Round Table's meetings, which soon became weekly, each of these two sides commanded an equal number of votes. The Round Table quickly proclaimed its intention to subject the actions of the Modrow cabinet to surveillance until free elections could be held for a new People's Chamber. The Round Table also established a committee to draft a new GDR constitution for submission to the voters in a plebiscite.

The Modrow cabinet at first held aloof from the Round Table. But since the Communist-dominated People's Chamber increasingly became the target of popular hostility, the cabinet soon began to accede to resolutions adopted by the Round Table in order to buttress its own claim to legitimacy. The cabinet thus accepted the Round Table's proposal that the quadrennial parliamentary election scheduled for the latter part of 1990 be moved forward to the spring. A test of strength took place early in January when it became known that the cabinet planned to reconstitute the internal security system of the GDR, despite demands by the Round Table for its dissolution. Since the despised secret political police, or Stasi, had been the most important component of that system, news of the government's plans set off a wave of public indignation. On January 15 an irate crowd stormed the Stasi headquarters in Berlin, occupied the building, and destroyed some of the secret surveillance records before Round Table representatives intervened to preserve those records. The oppositional groups thereupon threatened to withdraw from the Round Table unless the cabinet abandoned its plans and dissolved the Stasi completely. Faced with the prospect of being left with the backing only of the old, discredited parties of the GDR, Modrow gave in to this ultimatum. The Round Table had in effect established a significant degree of veto power over the cabinet's policies.

In mid-January Modrow attended a meeting of the Round Table and requested its guidance in the drafting of reforms. The People's Chamber, which continued to go through the motions of a parliament, rubber-stamped reform measures agreed upon by the cabinet and the Round Table. These included amendments to the GDR's constitution of 1974 designed to eliminate that document's institutionalization of Communist domination. In early February Modrow sought to strengthen his cabinet by including eight Round Table representatives of oppositional groups in what was called a "cabinet of national responsibility." The first free election of a People's Chamber was scheduled for March 18, two months earlier than originally planned.

The need for early free elections and a broadened cabinet that would inspire greater public confidence gained special urgency because of the continuing flood of emigrants to West Germany. With the opening of the GDR's western border in November thousands of East Germans a day began emigrating. By the end of 1989 the total of those who had turned their backs on the GDR that year reached 344,000, more than a third of whom—at a rate of over two thousand a day—had left since November 9. This same staggering daily rate persisted during the first months of

1990. By the time of the March election nearly 150,000 more had given up on the GDR and sought new lives in the West. Since most of those who departed were young workers and professional people, their loss to the workforce was a major factor in the profound economic slump that gripped the GDR. The exodus also contributed to an atmosphere of demoralization that became contagious as East Germans arrived each morning at their places of work to discover the absence of ever more co-workers. The effects were particularly damaging to medical services, as thousands of physicians, dentists, and nurses left to take jobs in the West that paid many times more than those in the GDR. To keep hospitals functioning, the Modrow cabinet had to assign army draftees to their staffs.

An even more dire problem for the Modrow cabinet was rising sentiment among East Germans in favor of unification with West Germany. Whereas rejection of the SED regime had produced a broad united front, that regime's collapse now raised questions about the future that divided the opposition. This was evident from a shift in slogans. During October demands for a voice in the government of the GDR had given rise to the street chant "We are the people!" But by late November that chant was increasingly challenged by another—"We are one people!"—which expressed a growing desire for unification of the two parts of Germany. With the border to the West open, millions of East Germans had been able to compare for themselves conditions there with those in the GDR. Most liked what they saw and returned highly skeptical about pledges on the part of the Modrow cabinet and the Round Table to construct a new and better form of socialism in an independent, democratic GDR. Compared to that uncertain prospect, unification with the prosperous western part of Germany seemed a far more attractive alternative to a growing number of East Germans. Buttressing this tendency was a rebirth of the national sentiment so long repressed under the SED regime, which now found expression in the street chant "Germany, united fatherland."

West Germany had initially reacted with cautious optimism to the upheaval in the GDR. Contrary to allegations by the SED, the popular protest movement in the East took shape and successfully challenged the regime there without guidance or material support from the West. Indeed, apprehensive Western political leaders, fearing bloody confrontations with the police, repeatedly admonished demonstrators in the East to exercise restraint. At first, the West hoped at best for a reformed and democratized East Germany that would at last respect the human rights of its citizens, including the right to travel freely and emigrate. But as more and more East Germans demonstrated for reunification, political leaders in the West began to realize there might be a possibility of realizing what had been a paramount goal of the Federal Republic since its inception. The Modrow cabinet, seeking to dampen sentiment that threatened the very existence of the GDR, held out the prospect of a "treaty community" that would lower barriers between the two Germanies but preserve their existence as separate and independent states.

Virtually everyone in the West who gave thought to reunification initially assumed that it would involve an arduous and lengthy process. In late November 1989 Chancellor Kohl took what was regarded by some in West Germany as the recklessly bold step of setting forth a program for bringing together a democratized GDR and the Federal Republic. But his plan, which provided for a series of gradual stages—beginning with joint commissions to deal with shared problems, then moving to a confederation, and eventually to a federation of the two Germanies—would have taken many years to implement. That seemed to be the most likely course when Kohl and Minister-President Modrow met in Dresden in mid-December and announced their intention to form a "treaty community."

The thought that reunification might be possible much sooner than expected began to gain acceptance early in 1990 when growing street demonstrations for unity in the East were accompanied by mounting doubts about the GDR's economic viability. Modrow, facing staggering foreign currency debts, a plummeting credit rating in international money markets, and a stagnating economy, found himself forced into the role of a supplicant entreating the Federal Republic for financial aid. In an effort to win Western assistance and also slow the massive exodus of East Germans, Modrow moved closer to Kohl's position on reunification at the beginning of February by proposing a similar set of stages leading eventually to a federation. His stipulation that such a unified Germany must be neutral in international affairs was, however, rejected by Kohl, a determined advocate of NATO, who insisted that a German state must have the same right as others to enter into defensive treaty arrangements.

During the campaign for the March election of the first freely chosen People's Chamber the political landscape of the GDR underwent a major transformation. The civic organizations that had emerged during the previous autumn grouped themselves into several new parties. The Social Democratic Party formed in the East in October under the initials SDP merged with the Western SPD. The Eastern CDU deposed the leaders who had so long followed the SED subserviently and linked itself with the Western CDU. Breakaway elements of the satellite LPD formed into three liberal parties that presented a united list of candidates, called the League of Free Democrats, which formed ties with the Western FDP. A German Social Union (DSU) with close links to the Bavarian CSU emerged. The remnants of the once all-powerful SED campaigned under the new name Party of Democratic Socialism (PDS). Since the election was on the basis of strict proportional representation, with no minimal threshold as in the Federal Republic, a score of other parties offered candidates, including the Democratic Farmers' Party and the National Democratic Party, formerly satellites of the SED. In all, twenty-four parties presented lists of candidates.

In the election campaign, the parties with Western links came to dominate the political stage alongside the PDS, which still commanded the considerable resources of the once all-powerful SED. The biggest crowds were drawn by Western politicians such as Chancellor Kohl, Foreign Minister Hans-Dietrich Genscher, and former chancellor Willy Brandt. They were far more familiar to most East Germans via Western television than were the new local leaders who had emerged during the peaceful revolution. The campaign efforts of the Western SPD, which had been banned in the GDR since the forced merger with the KPD in 1946, were limited in comparison to those of the CDU and FDP, which could make use of the organizational structures of the Eastern CDU and the LPD.

As the March election approached, the future of East Germany quickly became the dominant issue. So strong was the tide in favor of unification that even the Communist PDS, which had initially advocated maintaining the separate existence of a democratized GDR, ended by endorsing a gradual linking of the two Germanies, but in such a way as to preserve much of the economic and social system of the GDR. The parties formed by the new civic organizations also endorsed eventual merger of the two German states but attached various provisos designed to protect the environment and the socially disadvantaged. The SPD favored union with the West, but by means of the time-consuming process of adoption of a new constitution for all of Germany by the parliaments of the GDR and the Federal Republic. The League of Free Democrats advocated swift replacement of socialism with market economics and early reunification. The shortest path to unity, however, was proposed by the CDU and two smaller parties, the civic organization Democratic Awakening and the CSU-supported DSU, which had formed an Alliance for Germany. The Alliance platform called for rapid and complete unification through absorption of the GDR into the Federal Republic. Only in that way could economic conditions in the East be swiftly improved by comprehensive introduction of market economics, Chancellor Kohl argued, promising that no one would be worse off materially after unification.

Although most informed observers as well as most opinion polls had predicted a strong showing for the left, especially by the SPD, the election of March 18 for a new People's Chamber, in which over 93 percent of the eligible voters took part, brought the CDU a sweeping victory. By itself it tallied nearly 41 percent of the vote; together with its partners in the Alliance for Germany it came close to an absolute majority with more than 48 percent, which brought control over 192 of the 400 seats in the new People's Chamber. The SPD captured less than 22 percent of the votes and gained 88 seats. The Communist PDS emerged from its first test in a free election with only 16 percent and 66 seats. The League of Free Democrats won slightly over 5 percent and 21 seats. The biggest losers were the parties formed by the civic organizations that had played a leading role in the peaceful revolution and in the Round Table. Together, they tallied less than 4 percent of the vote and won fewer than 20 seats. In their first free general election the people of East Germany had voted decisively against preservation of a reformed German Democratic Republic, against a gradual amalgamation of the two German states, and for the earliest possible union with the Federal Republic.

On April 12, after lengthy negotiations among the parties, a new cabinet for the GDR won the support of a majority in the People's Chamber elected in March. The new minister-president was Lothar de Maizière, an attorney in East Berlin and longtime member of the Eastern CDU who had played a leading role in replacing the leaders of that party long subservient to the SED. His cabinet was supported by a broad coalition composed of the three parties of the Alliance for Germany—the CDU, DSU, and Democratic Awakening—as well as by the SPD and the liberals of the League of Free Democrats. The coalition's command of the two-thirds majority required by the GDR's constitution for amendments placed the new government in a position to revise the constitution or vote it out of existence altogether in favor of unification with the Federal Republic.

The de Maizière cabinet proclaimed the election outcome a mandate for rapid movement toward reunification. As the means of achieving that goal the cabinet proposed use of Article 23 of the Basic Law, which provided for the admission of additional states to the Federal Republic and had been used to incorporate the Saarland in 1957. Rapidly deteriorating economic conditions added to the sense of urgency. Although the exodus of East Germans slowed somewhat after the election, it continued at the rate of about four thousand a week through April. Domestic industries sagged as consumers held back in anticipation of soon having access to higher-quality Western goods. And as change swept through the former Soviet bloc, the Comecon trading system that had absorbed most of East Germany's exports began to falter. Trade with the West also fell off as purchasers there became reluctant to place orders with state enterprises with dim prospects for longevity. As a result, large-scale unemployment began to afflict the GDR for the first time.

In an effort to arrest the deterioration of economic conditions in the GDR and slow, if not halt, the flow of East Germans to the West, the Kohl government announced two days after the East German election a bold plan to effect an economic union of the two Germanies by July 1. Once that goal had been achieved, temporary housing and financial aid would no longer be provided for those moving westward. The de Maizière government responded favorably, and intense negotiations between Bonn and East Berlin began. Plans for thorough reform of the GDR were abandoned. The draft constitution for a reformed and democratized GDR drawn up by participants in the Round Table was shunted aside, and a temporary constitutional order was patched together by means of amendments to the 1974 document adopted by two-thirds majorities in the new People's Chamber. A burst of legislative activity replaced statutes of the SED regime with new laws compatible with those of West Germany, particularly in the economic sphere. By the middle of May negotiators for the GDR and the Federal Republic had reached agreement on a state treaty of economic union, which both parliaments quickly ratified. In the GDR a bill effecting the alterations necessary to remove constitutional obstacles passed by a two-thirds majority.

The treaty on economic union, which took effect on July 1, 1990, absorbed the GDR economically into the Federal Republic. The Western D-mark replaced that of the East as legal tender.

Earlier plans had called for an exchange rate of one D-mark for two East marks, which amounted to a considerable overvaluation of the Eastern currency. But in the face of angry protests in the GDR, the Kohl government agreed to a still more generous exchange rate of 1:1 for most Eastern currency held by individuals. Other categories of money were pegged at 2:1. Wages, salaries, rents, and pensions were adjusted by the 1:1 formula. The principal elements of the economic and social legislation of the Federal Republic were extended to the GDR. From July 2 on, Germans crossing the former borders between East and West were no longer checked for documentation, so official figures on the migration from East to West could no longer be compiled. But a variety of evidence indicated that the exodus, which slowed as economic union approached, had greatly diminished.

Since upon implementation of the treaty on economic unity the government of the GDR ceased to exercise authority over many vital spheres of state activity, the need for its continuance became questionable. Some in the GDR, including Minister-President de Maizière, had initially hoped to perpetuate the GDR long enough to clear away the legal and institutional debris of the SED regime and enact a new body of legislation that would prepare in orderly fashion for amalgamation with West Germany. The Bonn government increasingly inclined, however, to a rapid process of political unification that would permit conversion of the quadrennial balloting for the Bundestag scheduled to take place in December into an all-German election.

Minister-President de Maizière, despairing of any improvement in the economic plight of the GDR through its own efforts, also began to press for swift unification. Early in July, soon after the treaty on economic unity took effect, the de Maizière cabinet agreed to an all-German election in December and announced plans for elections in October of parliaments for the five Eastern federal states eliminated by the SED when it centralized the government of the GDR in 1952. There was general agreement that those states would join the Federal Republic. Opinions varied, however, among the parties of the de Maizière coalition

Effective July 1, 1990, East Germany's economy was absorbed into that of the Federal Republic by the Treaty of Monetary, Economic, and Social Union, which was signed by the finance ministers of the two on May 18, 1990. In the background are East German minister-president Lothar de Maizière and West German chancellor Helmut Kohl

government as to whether that should occur before or after the all-German election. Disputes about the timing of unification eventually tore apart the governing coalition during the summer, but Minister-President de Maizière remained at the helm of the government in the absence of any alternative.

As the two German governments laid plans for political reunification, the international ramifications remained to be dealt with. Chancellor Kohl's government, with the strong backing of the United States, had secured the support of Britain and France for early and complete reunification, despite some initial hesitations in London and Paris. The three Western victors of World War II joined with Bonn in calling for NATO membership for a united Germany. In February 1990 the Americans, British, and French had agreed with the Soviets to deal with the issue of reunification within the context of what came to be known as two-plus-four negotiations: the two German states were to lay their joint proposals before the four former occupying powers, which still claimed residual authority over Germany as a whole. For a time the Polish government sought inclusion in this arrangement after becoming alarmed by some equivocal remarks about the future status of the former German territories in the East made by Chancellor Kohl with an eye to cultivating the votes of those expelled from those regions. But when the Bonn government agreed to include in the treaty regulating the international aspects of reunification a strong reaffirmation of the permanence of the Oder-Neisse boundary, the Poles were satisfied. Later in the year a German-Polish treaty confirmed the inviolability of that boundary.

By the early summer of 1990 the only remaining obstacle to reunification was the attitude of the USSR, which, with some 400,000 troops on the territory of the GDR, was in a position to block a union of the two Germanies. In the immediate aftermath of the SED regime's collapse the Soviets had categorically opposed unification and supported the efforts of the Modrow cabinet to shore up a reformed GDR. But by the time Modrow visited Moscow in March 1990, in the midst of the campaign for the East German parliamentary election, he had himself concluded that eventual reunification was inevitable. Accordingly, Soviet president Gorbachev publicly indicated a readiness to accept a union of the two Germanies, provided it came about in a manner acceptable to the rest of Europe, including the USSR. As soon became clear, this meant that the Soviets were prepared to assent to unification only if West Germany first withdrew from the NATO alliance. It appeared that as the price for assenting to German unity the USSR was intent upon bringing about the dissolution of NATO, which could not long survive without German participation.

To the great relief of the Germans, the USSR chose not to

exploit its ability to block their unity. Instead, when President Gorbachev received Chancellor Kohl at a vacation retreat in the Caucasus in mid-July he not only agreed to German reunification but also withdrew Soviet objections to NATO membership on the part of a united Germany. In return, the Federal Republic extended credits in the amount of 5 billion marks to the USSR.

With Soviet objections removed, the two German governments moved swiftly toward reunification lest some new international complication arise to frustrate realization of that goal. They were also spurred on by a continuing deterioration of economic conditions in the GDR, where after the currency and economic union of July demand for East German goods had plummeted among consumers eager for the western products so long denied them. By mid-summer close to 20 percent of the workforce was either jobless or reduced to part-time employment. Strikes and demonstrations added to an atmosphere of growing disorder. Only a large financial subsidy from the Federal Republic enabled the GDR's government to continue functioning, and those funds were rapidly being depleted. Seeing no prospect of checking this decline short of full unification, Minister-President de Maizière pressed for speed. Negotiations accelerated, and by the end of August the two German governments had reached agreement on a treaty providing for the political absorption of the five Eastern states into the Federal Republic on October 3. In the third week of September the parliaments in East and West ratified the treaty by overwhelming majorities.

On September 12, the international aspects of reunification had been resolved by conclusion of the Two Plus Four Treaty. Confirming the permanence of the Oder-Neisse border with Poland, the treaty specified that a united Germany, enjoying full sovereignty over its internal and external affairs, would consist solely of the territories of the Federal Republic, the German Democratic Republic, and the city of Berlin. Germany was to be free to join an alliance of its choice, a provision that in effect affirmed its NATO membership. For its part, Germany reaffirmed the Federal Republic's renunciation of biological, chemical, and nuclear weapons and pledged to limit its army to 370,000 men in the future. The Soviet Union agreed to withdraw all its troops from the area of the GDR by the end of 1994, until which time no German forces under NATO command would be stationed there. The treaty further specified that after 1994 no foreign forces or nuclear weapons would be deployed on the territory of what had been the GDR. The small American, British, and French military contingents in Berlin were authorized to remain there until the Soviet withdrawal was completed. A separate treaty with the USSR established a schedule for removal of Soviet troops and provided for German financial aid of that process in the amount of some 12 billion marks, plus 3 billion in interest-free credits. On October 1, Britain, France, the Soviet Union, and the United States agreed that their residual rights and prerogatives concerning Germany would end with the joining of the two parts of that country.

With international obstacles cleared away, reunification took place on October 3, 1990. A minute after midnight that morning the GDR ceased to exist and the Federal Republic gained full sovereignty over Germany's territory. The previous federal states were joined by the five that had recently been reconstituted in East Germany: Brandenburg, Mecklenburg–Western Pomerania, Saxony, Saxony-Anhalt, and Thuringia. The long-divided city of Berlin, now designated capital of the country, was united into a single federal state, making a total of sixteen. The Basic Law, with minor modifications, now applied to all of Germany, and a decision on whether to replace it with a new constitution after unification, as specified in one of its articles, was deferred. With a few unavoidable exceptions, the statutes of the Federal Republic replaced the laws of the GDR. The former National People's Army was placed under the command of the West German Bundeswehr, and other elements of the GDR's government came under the authority of the Federal Republic. On October 4 the Bundestag, now augmented by 144 deputies representing the parties of the People's Chamber, convened in the former Reichs-

tag building in Berlin and on the following day ratified the Two Plus Four Treaty. At its birth the new united Germany had a population of 79.7 million, of whom over 5 million were non-Germans.

The reunification process was quickly affirmed at the polls. On October 14, 1990, parliamentary elections in the five new eastern federal states registered a further decline in support for the successor to the SED, the PDS, and overwhelming affirmation of the parties that had formed the de Maizière cabinet and charted the dissolution of the GDR. In four of the five state parliaments the CDU emerged as the largest party, but the SPD made a stronger showing than in March, especially in Brandenburg, where it topped the CDU by nearly 10 percent. On December 2 voters throughout the country went to the polls to choose the first freely elected all-German parliament since the downfall of the Weimar Republic. In order not to disadvantage unfairly the new parties recently formed in the former GDR, the threshold requirement of 5 percent of the votes or three direct constituency seats was applied separately in East and West. A relatively low turnout of just under 78 percent produced a victory for the governing coalition of CDU/CSU and FDP, which gained, respectively, 319 and 79 of the 662 seats in the expanded chamber. The SPD, with slightly over a third of the vote, received 239 seats. The PDS continued to decline, garnering only 17 seats with 2.4 percent of the national vote (11.1 percent in the former GDR). The Western Greens, who had opposed swift absorption of the GDR into the Federal Republic, failed to surmount the 5 percent threshold required for representation and departed from the chamber, but a small Green Party from the East, in alliance with other former dissidents there, formed part of a delegation of eight deputies. When the new Bundestag convened, Helmut Kohl was reelected chancellor and promptly renewed the coalition alliance with Foreign Minister Genscher and the FDP.

Two striking features of the long-sought realization of German reunification were the sober manner in which it was carried out and the restrained public response. Aside from an officially staged celebration in front of the Reichstag building, complete with fireworks and an orchestral rendition of the national anthem, little in the way of nationalistic euphoria shone through. Instead, Germans in East and West seemed daunted by the enormity of the task of rehabilitating the part of their country subjected to Communist misrule for forty-five years. Still, everyone except die-hard adherents of the SED regime expressed relief that at last the long, painful chapter of the country's division had come to an end.

7

Fundamental Factors during Four Decades of Division

An account of the kaleido-scopic events of the period 1945–1990 runs the risk of obscuring fundamental factors that channeled the many shifting forces and influences that made themselves felt during the time of division. As the swift and ignominious collapse of the German Democratic Republic abundantly demonstrated, that polity was, from its inception to its demise, an artificial construct of foreign origin, imposed without regard to the will of its citizens. It was called into being by the occupation authorities of the Soviet Union, sustained by that country's military might—overtly at the time of the 1953 uprising and latently thereafter—and abruptly fell when that prop was removed in 1989. The Kremlin allowed the SED regime considerable autonomy in its internal policies, but the GDR remained a Soviet puppet state throughout its existence. Like all authoritarian regimes, that of the SED enjoyed the allegiance of a minority consisting of those who subscribed to its ideology and those who enjoyed privileged positions in return for loyal service. Most East Germans remained indifferent or skeptical toward the regime but came to see no feasible alternative to it in view of the hardened front of the Cold War between the super-powers that ran through the middle of their country and separated them from Germans in the West. Intimidated by a pervasive system of secret police spies, most therefore eventually accommodated themselves, in varying degrees of acceptance and acquiescence, to a regime that was not of their choosing. That regime failed, however, ever to attain in the eyes of the bulk of its citizens the kind of legitimacy the Federal Republic quickly achieved among West Germans. When East Germans were given the opportunity, they massively rejected the SED and the Communist system it had imposed.

Although the two parts of Germany were torn apart politically and economically by division, they were never entirely separated. A persistent consciousness of a common past and a shared culture as well as myriad familial ties continued to link Germans in East and West in countless ways. As a result, neither of the two Germanies could ignore the other, nor could either avoid affecting the other. A reciprocal interaction constantly took place between them, as a common language facilitated a continuous flow of information, particularly through the electronic media but, as travel restrictions lessened in the GDR, increasingly through personal contact. Whatever happened in one part of Germany soon became known in the other, affecting expectations and behavior. Unavoidably, the two Germanies were constantly measured against each other by their citizens.

This interaction influenced the development of the two Germanies in numerous ways. Knowledge of the "occupation socialism" imposed on East Germany unquestionably weakened the appeal in the West of socialization proposals, thus handicapping the still socialistic SPD in the formative phase of the Federal Republic and mustering support for the new, antisocialist CDU/CSU. The course of developments in the Soviet Zone and, later, in the GDR eliminated Communism as a major force in West German politics much earlier than in the comparable cases of France and Italy. Yet without the pressure to respond to the all-encompassing welfare state in the GDR, the conservative forces that dominated the first decades of the Federal Republic would hardly have acquiesced as readily as they did in the enactment of far-reaching and expensive government social programs. Conversely, without the plenty showered upon West Germans by the economic miracle in the Federal Republic, the SED regime would scarcely have moderated its drive to invest in further industrialization to the extent it did in order to provide more consumer goods for the citizens of the GDR. East Germans were also spared thoroughgoing propagandization, for their ready access to Western radio and television broadcasts ruled out the kind of comprehensive media control exercised in other Communist-ruled countries.

The overthrow of the SED regime and the reunification of the country served to vindicate the policies with regard to the German problem followed during four decades by the leaders of the Federal Republic. The events of 1989–90 bore out the prediction of Konrad Adenauer that if the West Germans put aside the question of reunification and established a democratic state linked with the Western democracies it would one day prove an irresistible magnet for the other part of the country. Adenauer's Western policy worked, however, only when augmented by the Eastern policy initiated by the Social-Liberal cabinet of Willy Brandt. By following a strategy of "transformation through rapprochement," the cabinets of Brandt, Helmut Schmidt, and Helmut Kohl not only diminished the isolation of the GDR by multiplying human contacts and economic ties between the two Germanies; they also undermined the SED regime's always precarious claim to legitimacy. Previously, that regime had been able to win a degree of acceptance at home by claiming that the Federal Republic's refusal to acknowledge even the existence of an East German state revealed an intention to destroy it, very likely by force, and rescind its "socialist accomplishments" so as to open the way to capitalist exploitation. That argument lost plausibility, however, when West Germany accorded official recognition to East Germany and began extending it generous aid. Coupled with a widening material gap between the socialistic East and the capitalistic West that cast doubt upon the GDR's accomplishments, this loss of plausibility contributed to the profound estrangement of the East Germans from their government that came to expression in the autumn of 1989. The Western policy of Adenauer, in combination with the Eastern policy of Brandt, had prepared the ground well for the end of the time of two Germanies.

Further Reading

Below is a listing of informative works in English on the topics dealt with in this book. For readers seeking additional titles, including those in German, an extensive listing of publications bearing on cultural as well as political aspects of the two Germanies is available in Gisela Hersch, *A Bibliography of German Studies, 1945–1971* (Bloomington, Ind., 1972). Further coverage may be found in Anna J. Merritt and Richard L. Merritt, *Politics, Economics and Society in the Two Germanies, 1945–1975* (Urbana, Ill., 1978). Up-to-date listings of books and articles on both Germanies appear regularly in *Bibliographie zur Zeitgeschichte*, installments of which appear in the quarterly *Vierteljahrshefte für Zeitgeschichte*. A convenient registry of topically organized titles dealing with the Federal Republic may be found in Dietrich Thränhardt, *Bibliographie Bundesrepublik Deutschland* (Göttingen, 1980). A useful compendium of translated excerpts from basic official documents of the Federal Republic's history is provided by Carl-Christoph Schweitzer et al., eds., *Politics and Government in the Federal Republic of Germany* (Leamington Spa, 1984). A parallel volume for East Germany is J. A. K. Thomaneck and James Mellis, *Politics, Society, and Government in the German Democratic Republic* (Oxford, 1988). Helpful surveys of developments in the two Germanies, as well as further bibliographic information, may be found in Michael Balfour, *West Germany: A Contemporary History* (London, 1982); Dennis L. Bark and David R. Gress, *A History of West Germany* (2 vols., Oxford,

1989); David Childs, *The GDR: Moscow's German Ally* (2nd ed., London, 1988); and Martin McCauley, *The German Democratic Republic since 1945* (London, 1983).

Defeat, Cold War, and Division

W. Philips Davison, *The Berlin Blockade* (Princeton, 1958).

John Lewis Gaddis, *The United States and the Origins of the Cold War, 1941–1947* (New York, 1972).

John Gimbel, *The American Occupation of Germany* (Stanford, 1968).

Henry Krisch, *German Politics under Soviet Occupation* (New York, 1974).

Bruce Kuklick, *American Policy and the Division of Germany* (Ithaca, 1972).

Daniel J. Nelson, *Wartime Origins of the Berlin Dilemma* (University, Ala., 1978).

J. P. Nettl. *The Eastern Zone and Soviet Policy in Germany* (Oxford, 1951).

Tony Sharp, *The Wartime Alliance and the Zonal Division of Germany* (Oxford, 1975).

John N. Snell, *Wartime Origins of the East-West Dilemma over Germany* (New Orleans, 1959).

Ian D. Turner (ed.), *Reconstruction in Post-War Germany: British Occupation Policy and the Western Zones, 1945–55* (Oxford, 1989).

F. Roy Willis, *The French in Germany, 1945–1949* (Stanford, 1962).

The Birth of Two New Governments

Klaus von Beyme, *The Political System of the Federal Republic of Germany* (Guildford, England, 1983).

David Conradt, *The Germany Polity* (New York, 1978).

John Ford Golay, *The Founding of the Federal Republic of Germany* (Chicago, 1958).

Guido Goldman, *The German Political System* (New York, 1974).

Arnold J. Heidenheimer, *The Governments of Germany*, 4th ed. (New York, 1977).

Gerhard Loewenberg, *Parliament in the German Political System* (Ithaca, 1967).

Peter H. Merkl, *The Origin of the West German Republic* (New York, 1963).

The Ulbricht Era in East Germany

Arnulf Baring, *Uprising in East Germany* (Ithaca, 1972).

Thomas A. Baylis, *The Technical Intelligentsia and the East German Elite* (Berkeley, 1974).

Norman Gelb, *The Berlin Wall: Kennedy, Khrushchev, and a Showdown in the Heart of Europe* (New York, 1968).

Heinz Heitzer, *GDR: An Historical Outline* (Dresden, 1981).

Gert Leptin and Manfred Melzer, *Economic Reform in East German Industry* (Oxford, 1978).

Peter C. Ludz, *The Changing Party Elite in East Germany* (Cambridge, Mass., 1972).

Martin McCauley, *Marxism-Leninism in the German Democratic Republic* (London, 1979).

Gregory W. Sandford, *From Hitler to Ulbricht* (Princeton, 1983).

Jack M. Schick, *The Berlin Crisis, 1958–1962* (Philadelphia, 1971).

David Shears, *The Ugly Frontier* (London, 1970).

Robert M. Slusser, *The Berlin Crisis of 1961* (Baltimore, 1973).

Jean Edward Smith, *Germany beyond the Wall* (Boston, 1969).

Kurt Sontheimer and Wilhelm Bleek, *The Government and Politics of East Germany* (New York, 1975).

Carola Stern, *Ulbricht* (New York, 1965).

Two Decades of Christian Democratic Leadership in the Federal Republic

David Childs, *From Schumacher to Brandt: The Story of German Socialism, 1945–1965* (Oxford, 1966).

Karl W. Deutsch and Lewis J. Edinger, *Germany Rejoins the Powers* (Stanford, 1959).

Gordon D. Drummond, *The German Social Democrats in Opposition, 1949–1960: The Case against Rearmament* (Norman, Okla., 1982).

Lewis J. Edinger, *Kurt Schumacher* (Stanford, 1965).

———, *Politics in West Germany* (Boston, 1977).

Alfred Grosser, *Germany in Our Time* (New York, 1971).

Graham Hallett, *The Social Economy of West Germany* (London, 1973).

Wolfram F. Hanrieder, *West German Foreign Policy, 1949–1963* (Stanford, 1967).

Arnold Heidenheimer, *Adenauer and the CDU* (The Hague, 1960).

Catherine M. Kelleher, *Germany and the Politics of Nuclear Weapons* (New York, 1975).

Roger Morgan, *The United States and West Germany, 1945–1973* (London, 1974).

Geoffrey Pridham, *Christian Democracy in Western Germany* (London, 1977).

Terence Prittie, *Konrad Adenauer* (London, 1972).

David Schoenbaum, *The Spiegel Affair* (New York, 1968).

Thomas A. Schwartz, *America's Germany: John J. McCloy and the Federal Republic of Germany* (Cambridge, Mass., 1991).

Gordon Smith, *Democracy in Western Germany* (London, 1979).

Kurt Sontheimer, *The Government and Politics of West Germany* (London, 1972).

H. J. Spiro, *The Politics of German Codetermination* (Cambridge, Mass., 1958).

Henry C. Wallich, *The Mainsprings of the German Revival* (New Haven, 1955).

The Social-Liberal Era and the Return to Conservatism in the Federal Republic

Karl E. Birnbaum, *East and West Germany* (Lexington, Mass., 1973).

Jonathan Carr, *Helmut Schmidt* (New York, 1985).

Honoré M. Catudal, Jr., *The Diplomacy of the Quadripartite Agreement on Berlin* (Berlin, 1978).

———, *A Balance Sheet of the Quadripartite Agreement on Berlin* (Berlin, 1978).

William Griffith, *The Ostpolitik of the Federal Republic of Germany* (Cambridge, Mass., 1978).

Wolfram F. Hanrieder, *Germany, America, Europe: Forty Years of German Foreign Policy* (New Haven, 1989).

Peter H. Merkl, *German Foreign Policies, East and West* (Santa Barbara, 1974).

Peter Merkl, ed., *The Federal Republic at Forty* (New York, 1989).

Terence Prittie, *Willy Brandt* (New York, 1974).

Gordon Smith, William E. Patterson, and Peter Merkl, *Developments in West German Politics* (London, 1989).

Angela Stent, *From Embargo to Ostpolitik* (Cambridge, 1981).

Lawrence L. Whetten, *Germany's Ostpolitik* (London, 1971).

Philip Windsor, *Germany and the Management of Detente* (London, 1971).

The Collapse of the GDR
and the Reunification of Germany

David Childs, ed., *Honecker's Germany* (London, 1985).

Heinz Lippmann, *Honecker and the New Politics of Europe* (New York, 1972).

A. James McAdams, *East Germany and Detente* (Cambridge and New York, 1985).

C. Bradley Scharf, *Politics and Change in East Germany* (Boulder, Colo., 1984).

Lawrence L. Whetten, *Germany East and West: Conflicts, Collaboration, and Confrontation* (New York, 1980).

Roger Woods, *Opposition in the GDR under Honecker* (Basingstoke, Hampshire, 1986).

Index